D1346334

The Celebrated Mrs. Centlivre

MRS. SUSANNA CENTLIVRE

THE
Celebrated
MRS.
CENTLIVRE

By John Wilson Bowyer

GREENWOOD PRESS, PUBLISHERS
NEW YORK   1968

Foreword

*T*HE *Busy Body* and *The Wonder: A Woman Keeps a Secret* survived through the nineteenth century as stockpieces in the English and American theater. Except for Shakespeare, this statement can be made for only four comedies of acknowledged literary merit which were written before 1750—these two by Susanna Centlivre, *A New Way to Pay Old Debts* by Philip Massinger, and *She Would and She Would Not* by Colley Cibber.

Mrs. Centlivre was the most prolific playwright in England from 1700 to 1722, and for her might reasonably be claimed the rank of the most popular woman dramatist in English. The continued popularity of her plays kept her name before the public, not as the author of historical classics, but as a part of the living theater. Most of the great actors and actresses of the eighteenth and nineteenth centuries won reputation in her comedies. The rivalry of David Garrick and Henry Woodward in the role of Marplot has perhaps not been matched. Also Garrick had such extraordinary success as Don Felix, the jealous young lover of *The Wonder*, that he chose this role in which to close his acting career.

Susanna Centlivre was a person of some importance in the literary life of the first quarter of the eighteenth century. She published letters in the popular fashion and wrote an imposing list of complimentary and occasional poems for the great and

near-great. She was the friend of George Farquhar, Nicholas
Rowe, Sir Richard Steele, and others whose names are now
less often remembered. She became the enemy of Alexander
Pope, who blasted her with the title of "The Cook's Wife in
Buckingham Court." She received gifts as well as thanks from
George I and the Prince of Wales, later George II, for her
service to the Whigs and the House of Hanover.

Many of the references to Mrs. Centlivre mention her
early life as an adventuress, particularly her residence with
Anthony Hammond at the University of Cambridge, and
thrust her back into the romantic days of Charles II and Nell
Gwyn. She wrote in the unfettered masculine style of her
age, somewhat softened following the Restoration, but she did
not descend to scandal as Mrs. Behn and Mrs. Manley had
done. In fact, after her early waywardness, she seems to have
settled down to a proper and respected existence as housewife
and author. Other women who came after her found it easier
to adopt writing as a career.

Although a dozen ambitious young German scholars have
prepared dissertations on the sources and analogues of Mrs.
Centlivre's plays, this is the first attempt to make a complete
study of her life, writings, stage history, and literary relations.
It aims to remove her from the realm of impressions and
rumor. The personal nature of her nondramatic writings, which
have been largely overlooked, helps especially to bring her alive
in the London of her day.

For various favors I am indebted to the late George Lyman
Kittredge, to Professors R. P. Bond, Gale Noyes, George Bond,
and to many others. My greatest indebtedness is to the libraries
of Harvard University and the British Museum. No real
understanding of the eighteenth-century stage can be had without access to the great newspaper collections of the English
national library. I desire also to record my obligation to the
late Earl of Crawford and Balcarres for permission to use his
copy of Mrs. Centlivre's verse epistle to Mrs. Wallup and the

library of Yale University for *The Masquerade.* Finally, I must add that publication has been forwarded by a grant from a Carnegie Research Fund, jointly sponsored by the Carnegie Foundation and Southern Methodist University.

J. W. B.

Contents

Illustrations

Strolling Actress:
Youthful Adventuress

R EADERS and students of English drama know Susanna
Centlivre as a playwright whose pieces continued to be
acted after the theater managers had forgotten most of
her contemporaries. Collectors of spicy stories invariably include her among the gay young adventuresses of English letters. A few recognize her as a minor celebrity in early eighteenth-century London literary circles and perhaps the most
eminent woman dramatist in English. Yet "the celebrated Mrs.
Centlivre," as she is known in stage history and popular biography, has never been adequately studied, though perhaps no
author of comparable significance has been the victim of more
misstatements.

In her initial career as a strolling actress, in her appeals for
women writers, in her poems of polite compliment, and in her
adherence to the Protestant succession and the Whig party, Mrs.
Centlivre's life may be regarded as a series of footnotes, often
illuminating, on the literature and history of her age. But in
the main hers is the story of her plays, several of which lived to
provide Garrick with favorite roles, attracted the favorable attention of William Hazlitt and Leigh Hunt, and held the
boards to the end of the nineteenth century.

From 1700, when Susanna's first play was acted and her
first nondramatic works appeared in print, until her death in

* Unless otherwise indicated all books mentioned in the notes were published
in London.

1723 it is possible to trace her career with considerable fulness. Even though exact dates and other specific details seem not to be recoverable for her early life, the contemporary records do give us a general understanding of her derivation.

Since Giles Jacob[1] says that most of the accounts of living authors included in *The Poetical Register* (1719) were written by their own hands, his sketch provides a point of departure for her biography:

> This Gentlewoman, now living, is daughter of one Mr. *Freeman*, late of *Holbeach*, in *Lincolnshire*, who married a daughter of Mr. *Marham*, a Gentleman of a good Estate at *Lynn Regis*, in the County of *Norfolk*. There was formerly an Estate in the Family of her Father; but he being a Dissenter, and a zealous Parliamentarian, was so very much persecuted at the Restoration, that he was necessitated to fly into *Ireland*, and his Estate was confiscated: Nor was the Family of her Mother free from the Severities of those Times, they being likewise Parliamentarians.

Jacob does not name the place of her birth, but the *Flying Post* for June 21-23, 1716, carries a story about "Mrs. Centlivre, who was Born at Holbeach." Since the parish records at Holbeach make no mention of her, however, it is probable that she was born elsewhere, possibly even in Ireland, and that the *Flying Post* merely assumed that she was a native as well as an early resident of the town. Scouting the possibility that pertinent records might be available in her mother's parish—King's Lynn is only about twenty miles from Holbeach—I have had the records at King's Lynn searched, but without effect. Among the wills at Lincoln is one[2] dated March 4, 1673, and proved June 23, 1674, that may be of significance; by this time a political exile might reasonably have returned home. Edward

---

[1] Mrs. Centlivre was at the height of her popularity at the time Jacob was compiling his work; she must have been known to him personally as another of the writers for the printer Edmund Curll.

[2] Miscellaneous Wills, Lincoln, A.68, Probate Registry.

Freeman, yeoman of Holbeach, the deceased, left his wife Susanna executrix of a small estate. The youngest of the six children, also named Susanna, received twenty shillings. This Susanna may very well be our quarry, but the names alone are not sufficiently distinctive to constitute proof.[3]

All the early biographers except Abel Boyer[4] connect Susanna's father with Holbeach, a small market town near the Wash, in the Fen district of Lincolnshire. Boyer gives no hint as to where she came from. A number of Freemans lived in Holbeach during the second half of the seventeenth century. Some of them must have been Susanna's relatives, for we have convincing evidence that she visited Holbeach in 1716 and 1718. The *Flying Post* for June 21-23, 1716, describes a tavern party which she gave in Holbeach on King George's birthday for the widows who received collections from the parish. Also a poem *"writ on King George's Birth-Day, by Mrs.* Centlivre, *and sent to the Ringers while the Bells were ringing at* Holbeach *in* Lincolnshire"[5] was obviously written there in 1716 or possibly even in the preceding year. Finally, in 1718 Mrs. Centlivre's good friend, Nicholas Rowe, was seriously ill, and she sent him a consolatory epistle, "From the COUNTRY, To Mr. *ROWE* in Town. M.DCC.XVIII.":

From a lonesome Old House, near *Holbeach* Washway,
(The Wash, you must know, is an Arm of the Sea,)
A poor Wanderer writes, . . .[6]

---

[3] For example, a Susannah, daughter of Thomas and Susanna Freeman, was baptized at St. Botolph, Bishopsgate, London, on Sept. 16, 1677.—*The Registers of St. Botolph, Bishopsgate, London*, transcribed by A. W. Cornelius Hallen (1895), III, 270.

[4] Boyer included an obituary in *The Political State of Great Britain*, XXVI (Dec., 1723), 670-71. He was a friend and correspondent of hers in 1700, though there is no evidence that they had enjoyed a close friendship during the intervening two decades.

[5] *A Collection of State Songs, Poems, &c. That have been Publish'd since the Rebellion: and Sung in the several Mug-Houses of London and Westminster* (1716).

[6] *A New Miscellany of Original Poems, Translations, and Imitations* (1720).

Susanna must have been born about 1670. If she died, as
W. R. Chetwood[7] says, "in the 56th Year of her Age," she
would have been born in 1667. If she died "when she was
near forty-five Years old," as the editor of her *Works*[8] has it,
she would have been born as late as 1677 or 1678. Her editor
adds also that she wrote her first play when she was twenty, an
exaggerated compliment perhaps, which would place her birth
sometime before 1680.

Jacob reports that Susanna's father died when she was three
and that her mother died before she was twelve. According
to John Mottley,[9] her mother died when she was a child, "and
her Father marrying again, she was so ill-treated by her
Mother-in-Law, when her Father was dead also, that she determined to come to *London*." Chetwood likewise has her
leaving home after the death of her father to escape the "Ill-
usage of her Step-mother."

These statements are consistent on the one assumption that
Susanna's father died when she was three, that her mother remarried but died before Susanna was twelve, and that her step-

---

[7] *The British Theatre. Containing the Lives of the English Dramatic Poets*
(Dublin, 1750). Chetwood appeared first as an author in 1720. He became
prompter at Drury Lane in 1722 or 1723. He probably knew Mrs. Centlivre
personally, and as bookseller, author, prompter, and associate of actors and
actresses, he must have heard most of the stage gossip from Mrs. Centlivre's
lifetime. Yet, since he was in prison at the time he wrote his history of the
stage, he must have depended largely on his memory, and at times gossip
and fact may have become mingled in his report.

[8] The biographical sketch for her *Works* (1761-60) was supposedly written by a woman who had known her. The account is largely a condemnation of the English for not have erected a monument in Westminster Abbey
to the "manes" of the celebrated Mrs. Centlivre.

[9] *A List of All the Dramatic Authors, with some Account of their Lives;
and of all the Dramatic Pieces ever published in the English Language to the
Year 1747,* appended to Thomas Whincop's *Scanderbeg: or, Love and Liberty* (1747). There seems no reasonable doubt that Mottley was chiefly
responsible for the *List*. Inasmuch as the account of Mrs. Centlivre mentions
the dedication of *The Wonder* to "his present Majesty," it was obviously
written before the death of George I in 1727. Mottley is linked with Mrs.
Centlivre by this statement, not recorded elsewhere, regarding *A Bold Stroke
for a Wife:* "In this Play she was assisted by Mr. *Mottley*, who wrote one or
two entire Scenes of it." Mottley's sketch is demonstrably accurate in many
details not included by the other biographers.

father himself remarried shortly afterward. If her father was the Edward Freeman previously mentioned, it would be easy to accept as true the primary condition, that he died when she was three.

All her early biographers think Susanna's education worthy of mention. Jacob says that "Her Education was in the Country" and that "what Improvements she has made, have been merely by her own Industry and Application." Boyer thinks that her education was "mean" but that she "improved her natural Genius, by Reading and good Conversation." Chetwood credits a neighboring French gentleman with teaching her French so that she could read Molière before she was twelve. It is possible that she studied with a Huguenot exile who was eking out an existence by tutoring. If Mottley is right in saying that "From her first coming to *London*, she took care to improve both the Charms of her Person and her Genius; she learnt *French*, and read a great deal of Poetry especially, but studied Men as well as Books," she may have begun the study of French with Boyer in London. The life in her *Works*, with customary effusiveness, says that her "Education was such as the Place of her Nativity afforded; where tho' she had but small Instruction, yet by Application to Books, she soon became Mistress of the *Latin, Italian, Spanish,* and *French* Tongues." It is clear from her use of the French drama in her own plays that Susanna secured a good working knowledge of French, but there is no real reason for thinking that she ever learned Latin, Italian, or Spanish.

Before she was fifteen, Susanna left home, motivated no doubt by ambition as well as by distaste for life with her stepmother. Boyer says that he is drawing a veil over several gay adventures and refers to her first husband as Carroll. But Mottley tells us that the runaway made up her mind to go to London, despite the little money in her purse and her lack of almost every necessity of life. Then he relates a romantic incident of her residence for a time at the University of Cambridge under the private tutelage of Anthony Hammond. His narrative has been woven so completely into the texture of her biography that we cannot omit it.

She had not travelled many Miles, but fatigued with her Journey and filled with a thousand perplexing Thoughts, she sat her down, with Tears in her Eyes, on a Bank by the Side of the Road, bewailing her lamentable Condition, when a young Gentleman from the University of *Cambridge* [*Anthony Hammond* Esq;] afterwards well known in the Polite and Literary World, chancing to come that Way, could not but take Notice of our weeping Damsel, then in the Bloom of Youth and Beauty, not quite fifteen Years of age, her Charms not diminished but rather heightened by her Tears: having enquired into the Cause of her Distress, he was so much moved with her Story, and the simple and affecting Manner in which she related it, and more especially with her lovely Shape and Features, that he found himself so attached to her Person and Interest, that he could not think of parting with her, and of suffering her to pursue her painful Journey in the Condition she was in; he therefore intreated her to put herself under his Protection, which after some modest and faint Reluctance she consented to.

Hammond had her outfitted in a suit of boy's clothes and introduced her privately into the university as his Cousin Jack, who had come to spend a few days with him.

Jack was a smart little rogue, who insisted that he be shaved along with his cousin. He also studied grammar and acquired some of the terms of logic, rhetoric, and ethics. And so the two spent some months very agreeably together. Then one morning the squire told Jack that they were attracting too much attention and that they would have to separate. Susanna resumed the sex she had laid aside and set out for London, her heaviness of heart somewhat alleviated by a handsome present of gold and by "a Letter of Recommendation he gave her to a

Gentlewoman of his Acquaintance, to treat her as the Daughter
of a deceased Gentleman his Friend." Hammond assured her
that as soon as he could he would post after her "with the Wings
of Love." In London Susanna was occupied by the diversions
of the town and as the days passed regretted less and less the
loss of her university friend; "and indeed she saw him not in
many Years after."

This story of the weeping girl and the university student
sounds like a folk anecdote which became attached to historical
figures.[10] But Mottley's testimony, in view of his detailed
knowledge of other incidents in Mrs. Centlivre's career, cannot
be disregarded. It is supported by the allusion to "gay Adventures" in Boyer's account and by the hints in Chetwood's.

So far as chronology goes, the incident may well be factual.
Anthony Hammond was admitted to the College of St. John
the Evangelist on April 2, 1685, aged sixteen, and he may
have graduated in 1689, though there is no record of his having
received the bachelor's degree. He was married on August 14,
1694, was chosen M.P. for Huntingdonshire, his home county,
in October, 1695, and was returned for the University of Cambridge in July, 1698, on this occasion being made Master of
Arts as a member of St. John's.

It seems likely that the story of Hammond's friendship with
Susanna is based on an incident during his residence as an under-
graduate. Mottley's statement that after leaving Cambridge
she did not see Hammond again for many years is reasonable.

[10] It seems to have developed into something akin to a folk tale. In *Notes
and Queries* (4th ser., XII [1873], 128) "A.E." inquires regarding a "Lady
Student at Oxford," of whom a foreign friend has sent him an account. Susan,
the story goes, was overtaken by an Oxford student on the highroad to the university and accepted a ride with the young man. Having been persuaded to don
masculine attire, she entered herself as a student at the university, where she
took to studies as "to the manner born." But in time her lover became
bored and hinted that he was keeping her from making a settlement in life.
"Susan eventually married a rich nobleman, and moreover obtained considerable reputation as a writer of romances." In the next issue of *Notes and
Queries* (XII, 153) H. T. Riley identifies the story with the Hammond-
Centlivre episode.

Toward the end of her life, however, they were members of the same group, perhaps an informal literary club, and in 1720 she contributed poems to his poetic miscellany. The clinching piece of evidence is one of his own poems, addressed to Astraea, Mrs. Centlivre's poetic name. He must have written it more than thirty years before, just following her departure from Cambridge, with its "flowing Stream, cool shades, and cheerful Fields":

TO ASTRAEA

Though Nature here, what most delights us, yields
A flowing Stream, cool shades, and cheerful Fields;
My drooping Mind, indulgent to its Grief,
Neglects th' Amusements that should give Relief.
All views of Power once pursu'd by me,
Friendships and Pleasures center now in Thee;
Thee, Dear *Astraea*, Thee! who art above,
Powers, Friends, Pleasures, Thee, my only Love.
In how great Rapture did I lately burn,
In how great Anguish now your Absence mourn;
Think of those Joys, believe these Pains and then
Forget me, Dear *Astraea*, if you can.
No! thou bless'd Darling of my Eyes and Soul,
    Nothing thy constant Faith can e'er remove;
This Thought does ev'ry anxious Doubt controul,
    And joins our Hearts in mutual Bands of Love.
So may Just Heaven its Blessing deal to me,
As I perform the Vows I've made to Thee.[11]

The poem certainly reached Susanna, who found a means of turning it to her own use. The first four lines she thriftily repeated, slightly edited, in "*An Epistle in Verse. Astraea to Damon* [George Farquhar]," published in Boyer's volume of letters in 1701:

[11] *A New Miscellany of Original Poems, Translations, and Imitations* (1720), p. 64.

Tho Nature here what most delights us yields
A flowing stream, cool shades and chearful Fields,
Yet my sad Soul indulgent to its grief,
Neglects the Pleasures that should give relief.

The least credible part of the Hammond story is the initial tearful scene by the side of the road. It seems unlikely that Susanna would have started out for London without some plan in mind. Both Mottley and Chetwood assert that she became a strolling actress, and it is possible that she was already acting when she met Hammond. Chetwood says that she escaped the ill usage of her stepmother by joining a company of strolling players:

> At the Time she had formed this Resolution [to leave home], a Company of stroling Players came to *Stamford*, where she joined them, with little persuasion, and set out with the part of *Parisatis*, in the Play of *Alexander* the Great: But having a greater inclination to wear the Britches, than the Petticoat, she struck into the Men's Parts. She had a small Wen on her left Eye lid, which gave her a Masculine Air.

Strolling companies were active in the vicinity at this time.[12] Several companies were performing for set periods at Norwich and in the towns between Norwich and Cambridge. Susanna may have acted with John Power, who had apparently taken over the Newmarket company from Robert Parker by 1687. When, as we shall see, she became a member of Power's company, the Duke of Grafton's Servants, in 1706, she was probably returning to a group with whom she had been previously associated.

Stamford is only about twenty-five miles from Holbeach. The company would normally have been performing in the towns of Lincolnshire, Norfolkshire, and thereabouts. Not far from Stamford are Somersham, the home of Anthony Ham-

---

[12] Sybil Rosenfeld, *Strolling Players & Drama in the Provinces, 1660-1765* (Cambridge, 1939), pp. 35-47.

mond, and Cambridge, at both of which Susanna may have acted
and at either of which she may have attracted the young student's fancy. Her skill in male parts may have suggested the
masquerade, or her successful masquerade at Cambridge may
have suggested her suitability for male roles.

According to Mottley the young actress attracted many admirers in the playhouse, but "one Mr. *Fox,* a Nephew of the
late Sir *Stephen Fox,* . . . bore her off in Triumph from a
Cloud of Rivals." "To this Gentleman," he adds, "she was
married, or something like it; in the sixteenth Year of her Age;
but, whether by Death, or whatever Accident it happened, they
lived not together above one Year." Jacob has her married
to Fox's nephew before she was fifteen, but he agrees with
Mottley that they lived together but a year.[13]

After the year with Sir Stephen's nephew and possibly additional years of strolling, Susanna married a Mr. Carroll, an
army officer, who died a year and a half later in a duel. The
biographers refer to this as a regular marriage, and they imply
that Carroll had not been dead long before she turned to writing,
in 1700. But the army lists and court records are of no help
in identifying him more definitely.[14] As we shall see, the license

---

[13] In his will, a long and complicated document befitting a very wealthy
man, Sir Stephen makes generous bequests to various relatives but excepts
Charles Johnson, an "ungrateful nephew." Mrs. Centlivre was afterwards
a friend of Charles Johnson the playwright, but there is nothing to connect
him with the young stroller or with Sir Stephen.

[14] Walter and Clare Jerrold (*Five Queer Women* [1929]) identify him
with a William Carroll mentioned in the *House of Lords Manuscripts: 1706-8,*
N.S., VII (1921), 21. On Jan. 29, 1707, William Carroll, a minor, the son of
William Carroll then deceased, through his guardian, Anthony Carroll, and his
mother, Susanna Carroll, filed a petition and appeal with the House of Lords
to reverse a decree in the Chancery of the Court of Regalities of the county of
Tipperary in Ireland. William Carroll, father of the petitioner and son of
Major Charles Carroll, had claimed certain lands in Ireland as a result of a
deed signed by his grandfather, Thomas O'Meara, and confirmed by O'Meara's
will. The documents went back to 1684. William Carroll had won an arbiter's
decision in 1699, but William O'Meara, his uncle, and Thomas Otway, an interested party, had refused the decision and begun proceedings in Chancery.
Meanwhile William Carroll had died. In October, 1706, the court had decreed
that a jury of the county should decide whether "Thomas O'Meara was
compos mentis when he made the feofment and his will."

STROLLING ACTRESSES DRESSING IN A BARN

for her marriage to Centlivre refers to her as "Susannah Caroll
als Rawkins . . . Widdow." Though probably factual, since
false information in the application for a license might have
invalidated the marriage, this reference to her name and condition in life is cryptic. If the marriage with Carroll was binding,
a natural assumption since she is called a widow, then "Rawkins"
must have been an alias for Carroll. If she was not actually
Carroll's widow, the relict of a binding marriage, the introduction of "Rawkins" constitutes a problem. In that case it may
have been the name of her father, her mother, her stepfather,
a family with whom she lived as a child, or Fox's nephew.
Boyer's obituary by no means solves the problem: "Her Father's
Name, if I mistake not, was *Rawkins,* her first Husband's,
Carol." Boyer was right in associating the name "Rawkins"
with Susanna, but he may have been mistaken after the passage
of years in making the man her father. On the whole, perhaps the most reasonable conclusion would be to accept her
father's name as Freeman and "Rawkins" as an alias for
Carroll.[15]

Despite the uncertainty as to names and dates, the events

The Lords (*Journals of the House of Lords,* XVIII, 220) on the same day
(Jan. 29, 1707) ordered that Thomas Otway have a copy of the appeal and
that he be required to submit his answer on the following February 26. In
the meanwhile proceedings on the decree complained of were ordered stayed.
There is no record of any further action.

It is possible that the Susanna Carroll of the petition is the dramatist, but
there is nothing except the identity of names to connect the two.

[15] Cf. James R. Sutherland, "The Progress of Error: Mrs. Centlivre and
the Biographers," *Review of English Studies,* XVIII (1942), 169: "What is
one to make of Rawkins? . . . Rawkins, therefore, was almost certainly her
maiden name. . . . What, then, was her relationship, if any, with Mr. Freeman of Holbeach? She may possibly have been his illegitimate daughter, and
Rawkins and his wife—people of 'mean parentage'—the couple to whom she
was farmed out in her infancy. Certainly Mr. Freeman, or at any rate, Holbeach, has to be reckoned with."

In Sir Stephen Fox's correspondence in the British Museum there is a
letter, dated Jan. 25, 1686/7, in which Sir Stephen asks a friend and official
in Ireland to help John Rawkins, "an honest but unfortunate man," in any
way possible. But I have not been able to connect John Rawkins with
Susanna.

narrated fit harmoniously into the kaleidoscopic story of a small-town girl without wealth or social position who acquired a meager education, including a good knowledge of French, and was determined to make her way in the world. As a strolling actress she could not expect to achieve dignity or even independence. The next question is whether she could stake out a claim for herself in literature.

Friends, Letters, *And A* Play

JACOB says that Susanna was "inclin'd to Poetry when very Young, having compos'd a Song before she was Seven Years old." The life in her complete works adds that it was set to a "sprightly" tune and became a famous country dance. Be that as it may, her first published work appeared in 1700. According to Mottley she turned to the Muses as a means of diverting her melancholy following the death of her husband "and partly perhaps for a Support." It is possible that she continued to act, but from this year on she spent much of her time in London.

Abel Boyer's collection of letters, to which we have already referred, enables us to trace Mrs. Centlivre's first appearance in print. In a letter from *"Mr. B - - -r to Astraea"*[1] appears this statement: *"Briscoe's* Book is out, and your Letters in it, with Answers to the same, both which are no small Ornament to the Collection. 'Tis a great Reflection on your Vanity, that you should be at so great Expence of Wit and Humour, when you write for the Publick, and only fill your Letters with Business, when you write to your private Acquaintance." This information leads directly to a group of five consecutive letters in

---

[1] *Letters of Wit, Politicks and Morality. Written Originally in Italian, . . .; also, Letters of Gallantry out of the Greek, Spanish, Latin, and French. To which is added a large collection of Original Letters of Love and Friendship by Mr. Granville, Tho. Cheek, Esq; Capt. Ayloffe, Dr. G - - th, Mr. B - - - - -by, Mr. O - - - - - - - -n, Mr. B - - -r, Mr. G - - - - -, Mr. F - - - - - - -r, Mrs. C - - - - -l, Mrs. W - - - - -n, &c.* (1701), pp. 358-60.

Familiar and Courtly Letters, Written by Monsieur Voiture to Persons of the greatest Honour, Wit, and Quality of both Sexes in the Court of France. Made English by Mr. Dryden, Tho. Cheek, Esq; Mr. Dennis . . . To which is added, a Collection of Letters of Friendship, and other Occasional Letters, written by Mr. Dryden, Mr. Wycherley . . ., printed for Sam Briscoe on May 11, 1700.[2]

Early in 1700 Briscoe had fallen upon hard times and been reduced to bankruptcy. Tom Brown undertook to edit this volume for him, and Farquhar,[3] Dryden, Dennis, Cheek, Wycherley, Ned Ward, and others contributed. Five letters from the correspondence of Mrs. Centlivre, then known as Mrs. Carroll, are headed *"To Madam* C----ll," *"Madam* C----ll's *Answer to* -----," *"His Answer to Mrs.* C----ll," *"An Answer,"* and *"To Mrs.* ------- ------- *By another Hand."* Two additional letters, *"To Mr.* B---- *in* Covent-Garden. *An Account of a Journey to* Exon. *&c."* and *"The Answer"* are likewise parts of her correspondence. The last two letters are included in later editions of Tom Brown's works, so that Mr. B---- was obviously Brown himself.

The five love letters are clever but somewhat artificial. The first taunts Susanna for being in love with the sons of the Muses to the exclusion of men with gold, even though "half a Crown damns a *Poet* at any time, and for a Shilling, you may buy what he has puzl'd his Brains about half a Year to Collect." Her correspondent says that he may be reasonably sure that her husband is "a *very Husband*," a fool, since she is so eager for the opposite, a wit. Mrs. Centlivre replies that she scorns to be beholden to any man for money:

> Cou'd I value a Man upon his Fortune, I shou'd condescend to Converse with a *Fool*, . . . my Conversation with the *Sons* of the *Muses*, is purely for my Diversion;

---

[2] The *Post Boy* for Tuesday, May 7–Thursday, May 9, 1700, says that the *Familiar and Courtly Letters* will be published on Saturday.

[3] In the "new" prologue to *The Constant Couple* Farquhar remarks that he had no hand in *"Bankrupt Brisco's Fate."*

. . . You propose a *little Mony,* and a *little Wit;* but I
scorn to be beholding to any Man for the former, and the
latter I have it already, without the Arrogance of *Riches,*
and the ill Manners of *Vanity.*

She adds that her husband (probably a part of the epistolary
fiction) has commanded her to answer the letter and advises
her correspondent to have his valet transcribe his letters in order
to improve the spelling.

Her correspondent thereupon compliments her as a woman
of sense, but he doubts that many women are of her mind: "For
I tell you, *Madam, Gold* is the *Womens God;* and there's
scarce a *Dutchess* in this *Kingdom,* that can't find an use for a
superfluous Sum." Good spelling, he adds, "is beneath a
Gentleman." As for her husband, he would like to be acquainted with him, for that is the best way to carry on an intrigue: "If he is a *Courtier, Flattery makes him my Friend;* if
he's a *Citizen, Custom in his way of Trade;* if he serves the
King, a Bribe may do the Business; if a *Man below these,* a
hard Word, and a *big Look* makes you mine."

In her last letter of the series Mrs. Centlivre asks her correspondent, whom she takes to be a member of Parliament, to
be kind to the Duke of Norfolk, who was trying to get a divorce
bill against his wife through Parliament, though the case had
not been first acted upon in the ecclesiastical courts. The bill
was passed by the two houses and was returned to the House
of Lords with the royal assent on April 11, 1700. Hence these
letters must have been written about March, 1700.

The fifth letter, by another hand, is merely conventional.
The writer admits that Susanna is very handsome, but he insists that he has no intention of dying for her, since as a
woman of sense she must "prefer the *living* Lover to the *dead.*"

The letter to Tom Brown, dated April 8, 1700, tells of a
stagecoach trip to Exeter, a topic suggestive of a piece of prose
fiction contained in the *Letters* (1696) of Mrs. De la Rivière

Manley. What business Susanna had in Exeter, if she actually made the trip, it is impossible to say, unless her acting, an unlikely supposition. In a characteristic vein of mild satire, she describes her traveling companions—a drunken Cornish justice of the peace, a sleeping barrister, an impertinent attorney's clerk, a tailor who had trusted his clients too far, and an arrogant valet to a man who had been elected to Parliament but whose election had been disputed.

In his reply (April 22, 1700) Brown flatters the lady on her conquests in town and advises her to return as soon as possible to make restitution:

> You have been a great *Sinner* in your time, and *four Days Penance* in a *Stage-Coach* will hardly atone for the Sins you have *committed:* . . . Come to *Town*, as soon as you can, and begin to make Restitution in the Place where *you* have done the Mischief.

Brown charges her with killing her lovers who throw themselves at her feet, with stealing hearts even at church from men whose hearts belonged to their wives, with making women guilty of detraction by telling malicious stories of her, and with tempting men to perjury by forsaking their former vows. Undoubtedly he was seasoning his compliment with grains of fact.

The notorious T-m Br-wn seems to have been the center of a considerable group of struggling writers who were willing to collect and publish letters, scandal, or translations as a means to existence. His favor to Briscoe indicates that he was also capable of friendship. How Susanna became acquainted with him and whether the association was less superficial than the letters would indicate it is impossible to say. At any rate Tom probably knew London as well as any man living, and Susanna, through her acquaintance with him and his group, must have added to her insight into men and manners.

Boyer's collection of letters, to which reference has already been made, was published July 22-24, 1701.[4] The names of

4 *Post Man* and *Post Boy*, both for July 22-24.

Samuel Garth, William Burnaby, John Oldmixon, Abel Boyer, Charles Gildon, George Farquhar, Mrs. Carroll (Centlivre), and Mrs. Jane Wiseman probably supply the blanks in the title page. An advertisement in the *New State of Europe* for July 22-26, 1701, adds that the letters by Mrs. Carroll were written under the name of Astraea. The *Post-Angel* for August, 1701, encourages purchasers by saying that "in these letters of Wit and Politicks, we find the Great Men of the Age speaking with Open Heart, and Discovering their True Sentiments." It is difficult to resist the temptation to read the "Letters of Love and Friendship" also as parts of real correspondence.

The Astraea letters[5] include thirty-one items: eleven by Astraea, thirteen by Celadon, two by Chloe, one each by Charles Ustick, Boyer, Damon (Farquhar), and Daphne, and a final one signed *B,* probably Boyer. Mrs. Centlivre no doubt desired to attract attention by imitating Mrs. Behn in calling herself Astraea and her correspondent Celadon. She apparently gave the letters to the editor. In a letter by Celadon dated July 23, 1700, there is this statement, which implies that she had asked to have her letters returned, presumably for publication:

> If I had a mind to return your letters (as methinks at this present writing I could find in my heart to obey any Commands you lay upon me) 'twill be some months before I shall be where they are, and how can I foresee what Revolution may happen in my temper before that time?

Clearly some of Astraea's letters were not returned, and there are resulting gaps in the series.

The correspondence begins as if between two strangers following a flirtation at the theater. The first letter, *"Upon the Drawing Cuts in the Pit, who should write first,"* is Astraea's:

[5] Letters XV-XLVI, pp. 332-74. There is no letter XXX.

If Oracles were now extant, I would consult them, to know what Fortune designs, by thrusting me into an affair of this kind: . . . Well then, what shall I say to you? Why, what can I say to a Man altogether unknown to me, a Man *who will stand or fall, by the general Opinion we have of Mankind?* Now the Sentiments we have of Men in general are very loose; but I am unwilling to entertain such of you; your late Deportment rais'd you above the common level in my Thoughts: This is all I can say in your Commendation, till I know you better, for random Compliments ought to be despis'd by Men of Sense. Pray observe the same Method when you write to me, for I am not so much a Woman as to love to be flatter'd.

The reply, dated June 7, 1700, makes the same kind of trial approach:

Extraordinary Blessings are never merited, but freely given; nor can they come by chance; Fortune therefore shall be quite left out of my Thanksgiving for the double Favour I've been oblig'd with your Letter, and leave to answer it. . . . Should you severely judge my Letters, little reason shall I have to boast, if by 'em I loose that share of your good Graces you was pleas'd in humanity to give to a Stranger. . . .

In the twelfth letter of the series we learn, with reasonable certainty, that Celadon was Captain William Ayloffe. Astraea has discovered that Celadon has a mistress named Chloe, who even joins in the letter writing, and takes him severely to task:

Your whole Sex is scarcely worth the trouble I have given my self about you, and now I dare boldly say, I know Mr. A - - - - - e. I had the curiosity to see if a man of sence could be guilty of the same errors the common stamp of Men are; and now I am convinced that there's no more difference in the honour of Mankind, relating to our Sex, than there is between the King and Beggar in the Grave.

Fourteen letters immediately preceding the Celadon-Astraea sequence are by Captain Ayloffe.[6] Furthermore, Letter LXX (p. 414) is headed "*Captain* Ayloffe *to* Chloe." Then follow Letter LXXI, "*The same to the same*," and four more letters all apparently by Ayloffe to Daphne. Daphne was the name under which, according to Boyer's advertisement, Mrs. [Jane] W[isema]n[7] contributed. In LXXIV Ayloffe calls himself the lady's "adoring faithful *Amintor*." Apparently, then, he is the Celadon[8] to Mrs. Centlivre's Astraea and the Amintor to Mrs. Wiseman's Daphne. Damon, as we shall see, is George Farquhar. Letter XLV, "*Daphne*'s Complaint to *Astraea*," links the four correspondents—Ayloffe, Farquhar, Mrs. Centlivre, and Mrs. Wiseman—because to her friend Astraea, who insists upon her writing, Daphne complains of being torn between Damon, her old love, and Amintor, her new.

[6] In my opinion Mr. Charles Stonehill errs in including the Celadon-Astraea letters with Farquhar's correspondence in *The Complete Works of George Farquhar* (1930). The identification of Celadon with Ayloffe here weakens his reconstruction of the relationship between Farquhar and Mrs. Centlivre and voids his tentative identification of Chloe with Anne Oldfield. Letters I, II, XIII, and XIV, by Ayloffe to "Dick" or "Honest Dick," are apparently to Richard Steele. Letter XLVII, "*Mr.* Farquhar *to Mr.* R---- S-----," is also to Steele. Farquhar says that Mr. Johnson has just told him that Steele is in love and desires the advice of his friends. He is clearly rallying Steele, for he says that he himself has found love "like Chymistry, a knowledge very chargeable in Experiments, and worth nothing in the Enjoyment." He as well as Mrs. Manley knew that Steele had been dabbling in alchemy. These letters are not included in *The Correspondence of Richard Steele*, ed. Rae Blanchard (Oxford, 1941). It is possible that Susanna also knew Steele at this time and that Johnson is Charles Johnson, the playwright, likewise a friend of hers later, if not already.

[7] Mrs. Wiseman's play, *Antiochus the Great; or, The Fatal Relapse*, was printed in 1702 after being acted at Lincoln's Inn Fields.

[8] Ayloffe's *The Government of the Passions, according to the Rules of Reason and Religion* was published in Feb., 1700; *The Miscellaneous Works of the Honourable Sir Charles Sedley*, "from the original manuscripts by Capt. Ayloffe," in 1702; and his *Pocket Companion for Gentlemen and Ladies*, in 1703. The two volumes of *Letters from the Dead to the Living* (1702-3), though commonly referred to as the work of Tom Brown, include Ayloffe's name on the title page as one of the three authors. It is interesting that the correspondence with Ayloffe does not take Susanna outside the bounds of Brown's circle.

Since Celadon's first letter is dated June 7, 1700, and his
sixth, June 13, it is obvious that the affair narrated, even if no
more than an excuse for a literary exercise, developed rapidly.
In general Astraea joins her desire for friendship with raillery,
but Celadon seeks a more intimate relationship. By his second
letter he has reached the point of verbal ecstasy:

> I love you; I doat on you; my passion makes me mad
> when I am with you, and desperate when I am from you.
> Sure of all miseries Love is to me the most intolerable;
> it haunts me in my sleep; perplexes me when waking; nor
> is there a Remedy in Art so powerful to remove its An-
> guish; . . . I would obey you if I could; but when you bid
> me lay aside my Passion, give me leave to write, I find it
> is impossible.

Susanna says his pain is nothing to hers—she has the toothache.
Anyway, she adds, " 'tis as natural for your Sex to write and
make Love, as 'tis for ours to be caught by your flattering
Baits." If they can no longer write as mere friends, she suggests that it is time to stop.

Nevertheless, the correspondence continues on much the
same basis. Celadon insists that he is deeply smitten, and
Astraea rallies him upon pretending to be in love. If he should
flatter her into thinking that he really loves her, she says, he
would really be in trouble:

> If you have my heart, you will certainly have all the train
> of impertinent follies that usually attend a Woman's love:
> and which make a Man study more how to quit, than ever
> he did to obtain———As, *whether go you? where have you*
> *been? when will you come again? who's that Lady you*
> *ogled at the Play? Hey ho! you don't love me*———And
> a thousand things more of this nature. . . .

On June 13, 1700, Celadon, like a country curate preaching
another man's sermon, copies a letter out of a book which

Astraea had lent him. She thereupon charges him with idleness and insincerity; yet she adds in a postscript: *"I fear I shall go to the Play. I believe* Astraea *would be well enough pleas'd to find* Celadon *there."*

Then Chloe, Celadon's mistress, joins in the correspondence after reading one of Astraea's letters. After a time her initial haughtiness vanishes, and she offers to resign Celadon to her rival. Astraea condemns Celadon for his falseness but is attracted by Chloe, and the two women try to arrange a meeting. Then Chloe drops out, Celadon refusing on August 6 to give her name: "she has lately miscarried and is gone out of Town." But he promises to introduce them in the winter if they are both in town at the same time. He adds that "she's but a Girl, not eighteen; she sings tolerably, and you'll allow her to have some Wit, if your Taste and mine are alike."

Meanwhile Celadon receives a challenge from Charles Ustick, whom I have been unable to identify further:

> I accidentally meeting with a Banter on a Gentlewoman in *B* ------ *street,* who, I suppose, is known to you by the name of *Astraea,* the interest I pretend to have in her, commanded your name, which for some time she made a secret of; and since I find you use her so freely as to make your Mistress write to her, I may reasonably suppose you have been pretty familiar with her. . . . If you are a Gentleman you'll give me satisfaction e're you leave the Town, else I shall find you at your return. You'll meet with me at her house, if not, leave a Note at *Tom*'s Coffee-house in *Russel-street* for *Charles Ustick.*

Celadon replies that, whether Ustick is a husband or a happy lover, he has done nothing to Astraea's shame or Ustick's dishonor and regrets that the letter reached him only after he had left London. He promises to keep Ustick's invitation in October. On the same day, July 16, and on July 21, 23, August 6 and 11, Celadon continues to apologize in letters to Astraea.

On July 23 he writes: "Pray let me tempt you to break your word, and continue to write to me, whilst you are in Town, for if I apprehend you right, *Astraea* goes with her friend at *Michaelmass*." Presumably Astraea intended to leave London on September 29, perhaps with Mrs. Wiseman, who, as we shall see, seems to have been planning to visit an aunt about this time. On August 6 he asks in a postscript for a copy of Astraea's play and for any melancholy wit produced by the death of the young Duke of Gloucester on July 30.

The correspondence ends on August 18 with a letter for Ustick to be left with Astraea. Celadon agrees to meet his rival at Ailsbury, which he intends to visit anyway to help "an honest Church-man against the Whig-Party." As soon as the dog days are over and he has dispatched some private business, he will appear for the "Christian Diversion" to which he has been invited. Did Ayloffe fight Ustick (whoever he was) in a duel? If these letters were pure fiction, this question would probably have been answered.

Abel Boyer in his letter written about the middle of May, 1700, explains that he has not yet been able to arrange for the presentation of Astraea's play and that she should write an elegy on the great Dryden, who has just died. He refers to her "Retirement" and to the "Damps of a *Northern* Clime." Perhaps she was visiting relatives in Holbeach. As for the play, Mr. B.------ (who may have been Thomas Betterton or William Burnaby⁹) "thinks the Catastrophe too abrupt." Other persons have a better opinion of it. Boyer expects to have Mr. F------ read it and believes that both he and Mr. W------ "will stand your Friends in this affair." George Farquhar, whose *The Constant Couple: or, A Trip to the Jubilee* had been so popular that overnight he had become an oracle of theatrical taste, and his friend, Robert Wilks, the actor, must have helped,

---

⁹ Burnaby's *The Reformed Wife* was acted about March, 1700. He was also a contributor to Boyer's collection of letters and he is usually credited with the epilogue to Mrs. Centlivre's drama.

for, as we shall see, the play was produced at the beginning of the following theatrical season.

If her letters are to be taken with any degree of literalness, Mrs. Centlivre was in Exeter in April, probably at Holbeach in May, back in London in June, and again out of town on September 29.

In her reply Mrs. Centlivre gives a characteristic early eighteenth-century view of the small town ("the most rational Creatures here are the Beasts of the Field"), mourns for the death of Dryden, and wishes she had the genius of Mrs. Aphra Behn (the earlier Astraea) or Mrs. Katherine Philips (Orinda) to deserve Boyer's nomination of her as Dryden's successor. She herself thinks that Farquhar should claim the bays, because he has pleased best of the living poets. She accepts his view that "the main design of Comedy is to make us laugh." As a matter of fact she favors Farquhar so strongly that she encloses a copy of verses to him. The implication is that she knows Farquhar only by reputation and also that the verses are only for Boyer, but she probably expected her friend to use her poetic epistle *"To Mr.* Farquhar *upon his Comedy call'd* A Trip to the Jubilee" in winning the young Irishman's support for her play. Mrs. Centlivre's poem is highly flattering to Farquhar but it is also significant for showing the uncertainty in the theater following Collier's attack:

Amongst the many friends your Wit has made,
Permit my humble Tribute may be paid; . . .
For since the learned *Collier* first essay'd
To teach Religion to the Rhiming Trade,
The *Comick* Muse in *Tragick* Posture sat,
And seem'd to mourn the Downfall of her State;
Her eldest Sons she often did implore,
That they her ancient Credit would restore.
Strait they essay'd, but quickly to their cost
They found that all their industry was lost.

For since the *Double Entendre* was forbid,
They could not get a Clap for what they did.
At last *Thalia* call'd her youngest Son,
The graceful and the best beloved one: . . .
Go, something Write, my Son, that may atone
Thy Brethren's Faults, and make thy virtues known.
I'll teach Thee Language in a pleasant stile:
Which, without Smut, can make an Audience smile.
Let fall no word that may offend the Fair;
Observe Decorums, dress thy Thoughts with Air;
Go—lay the Plot, which Vertue shall adorn;
Thus spoke the Muse; and thus didst Thou perform.
Thy *Constant Couple* does our Fame redeem,
And shows our Sex can love, when yours esteem.
And *Wild-Air*'s Character does plainly shew,
A man of sense may dress and be a Beau. . . .
Religious Hypocrites thou'st open laid,
Those holy Cheats by which our Isle is sway'd.
Oh! mayst thou live! and *Dryden*'s Place supply,
So long till thy best Friends shall bid thee die. . . .

This poem apparently led to a correspondence between Mrs.
Centlivre (Astraea) and Farquhar (Damon). The next letter
in Boyer's collection shows Astraea apologizing for her absence
when Damon designed her a visit. She explains that she had
brought a pair of rabbits home, christened them George (after
Farquhar) and Suky (after herself), but "*George* no sooner
shar'd your Name, but all your inclinations follow'd, which
made him grow indifferent to his *Suky;* and on *Sunday* whilst
I was at Church he scamper'd away, and left his poor Female
over-whelm'd with Grief." And then the following day while
she was reading Mr. Asgill, "which you lent me," Suky too
disappeared. Either Suky is bent upon pilgrimage to find her
mate, she thinks, or by belief in Asgill's doctrine she has

mounted to the heavens to provide a seat for her former master and mistress.[10]

Farquhar replies that some think him a rabbit in another sense, because they imagine that he has married while in the country. Also, he is busy about the vindication of his honor from the abuses of Mr. ------. Presumably he refers to an attack upon him by John Oldmixon, which he answered in a new prologue to *The Constant Couple* delivered on July 13, 1700.

Then comes the poem which Astraea borrowed in part from a poem to her by Anthony Hammond.[11] Some of the figures are farfetched, and better parts of the poem are reminiscent of better poets. This, for example, suggests a well-watered Donne:

> A sacred Tie unites my Life and Love,
> Both by some hidden Springs and Wheeles do move.
> Each on the other so dependent is
> That what unhinges that, disorders this.
> Like Soul and Body hand in hand they go,
> And Separation gives the fatal blow.
> Nay, as the Soul survives the stroke of Death
> My Love too shall out-live my latest breath;
> And midst the throng of the Seraphick Powers,
> M'enamour'd Soul shall gently seize on yours. . . .

In the end she promises complete constancy to her "dearest G ---- ," her "only welcome Guest."

The next communication is also a set of verses, *"Shut up in a Snuf-Box, wherein was drawn a Woman a-sleep upon a Couch,*

---

[10] The letter was written sometime after June 15, 1700, when John Asgill's best known work was published: "An Argument Proving, That *according to the Covenant of Eternal Life revealed in the Scriptures,* Man may be translated from hence into that Eternal Life without passing through Death, altho the Humane Nature of *CHRIST* himself could not be thus translated till he had passed through Death." His thesis caused the author to be known commonly as "translated Asgill," though in his seventy-nine years (1659-1738) he was philosopher, politician, financier, and humorist as well as eccentric writer.

[11] See p. 10.

with a Cupid shooting at her," in which Astraea advises Cupid
to shoot when Damon opens the box:

> Now *Cupid* shoot, and with thy Dart
> The roving Youth surprise.
> Aim right your Arrow at his Heart,
> And make him feel the subtle smart,
> By which *Astraea* dies.
> Leave trifling with the sleeping Dame,
> Lift up thy drowsie Eyes,
> See *Damon* stands, he's nobler Game
> Wound me him, and immortal Fame
> Shall crown thy Enterprise.
> But if thou'rt deaf to what I say,
> And will no Succour give,
> A Prisoner in this Box you stay
> Untill you sigh your self away,
> Or till I cease to live.

Farquhar was obviously a favorite with the female wits.
The next letter, *"Daphne's* Complaint to *Astraea,"* links him,
as we have seen, with both Mrs. Centlivre and Mrs. Wiseman,
as well as with Captain Ayloffe. Susanna and Jane Wiseman
were clearly good friends, who planned their diversions together and who may have helped one another in writing their
plays. It may be that Jane was the friend with whom Susanna
was to leave London on September 29, since Letter LXXV
indicates that Daphne was planning to visit an aunt about that
time.

The last letter of the Astraea series is signed *B.* The correspondent says that if the country has proved as dull to her
as the town in her absence has been to him, she has not relished
the one more than he has the other; for he too has fallen into
her snare. "You've gain'd a victors Right o're me as well as
Celadon," he adds, "and I expect you'll use me ill because he

abus'd your Mercy." The writer was probably Boyer himself, the editor of the volume.

And so ended for Susanna what must have been a diverting summer. Moreover, Boyer had arranged for the presentation of her tragedy, and by the end of September she could boast of having diverted the town as well as herself. Before considering *The Perjur'd Husband*, however, let us pause long enough to consider two items: another correspondence with Farquhar written during the following winter[12] and published in the second volume of Briscoe's collection of letters, which appeared, along with the third edition of the first volume, between May 1 and 3, 1701; and the elegy on Dryden.

At least seven of the letters in "A Pacquet from *Will's*" in the *Familiar and Courtly Letters*, II, 1701, passed between Farquhar and Mrs. Centlivre. Immediately preceding them are seven letters, the first two credited to Mr. Farquhar, the next four unsigned, and the seventh, "*To a Masque on* Twelfth-day," signed *Wildair*. These may have been intended for Mrs. Centlivre or one of her circle of acquaintances, but there is no means of identifying the lady or ladies. The seven letters between Celadon and Astraea are clearly between Farquhar and Mrs. Centlivre.[13] A final group of *"Seven Passionate Love-Letters written by* Celadon *to his Mistress"* were added to the Farquhar canon by Mr. Stonehill, but there is nothing to connect them with Susanna.

Four of the Celadon-Astraea letters are by Farquhar and three by Mrs. Centlivre. They begin romantically and pleasantly enough, but Farquhar's quickly become coarse, and Susanna breaks off the correspondence. Celadon begins:

> You may be assured, *Astrea*, that neither Grief nor Love will break the Heart of any Man, since neither of them have killed me, though I have been forc'd to be two

[12] Farquhar went to Holland in August and returned to England in November.
[13] In the 1718 edition the double heads over these letters are *"Mr. Farquhar to Mrs. C ---- ll."*

Days without the Honour of seeing You. When I parted from you, to begin this tedious Separation, I remember you promised me a Letter; the Expectation of which was a Comfort to me in my Absence: But when I came to Town this Morning, and found none; if ever you saw or could fancy a Man wild with Despair, just such a thing was I: The mildest of my Thoughts was, that I was forgotten and deservedly slighted; that something of Disadvantage to me had occurr'd since I saw you; and that some body, I don't know who, has been doing, I don't know what, to ruin me in your Esteem: For You are in your Nature generous, and a strict Observer of your Word. Sure, therefor, it must be something extraordinary that could provoke you to be at once both unkind and unjust to

> *Yours,*
>
> CELADON.

Susanna teases him with using a thimble on the seal of his letter but is delighted to hear from him:

> I find we both lay under a Mistake: You expected a Letter *Yesterday*, and I a Visit. I would not stir abroad, nor was I good Company at home. I was as much out of Humour at my Disappointment, as if I had been really in Love with you.

Farquhar's next letter includes a fleshly poem, which he says that he wrote in answer to a poem of hers. Her poem was apparently omitted. Then he adds in prose:

> No more *Poetry*, I beseech you: 'Tis too chargeable a way of writing to be pleasant to a Man that's forc'd to hire: So unlucky am I too at this Juncture, that my Hackney's at Grass, which must serve, both for a Reason why your Answer has been delayed so long, and for the Faintness of his Performance. . . .

P.S. Send me word if I may have leave to visite you to morrow.

Susanna's answer is a lecture on the virtues of modesty:

I guess our Acquaintance will be but of a short Longitude, if your *Pegasus* take such a Latitude in his Stile. I am sorry you misunderstand my Intent, which was only to divert you over a Bottle, and my self from the Spleen.

Thereupon Celadon turns both apologetic and argumentative. His chief defense is that Astraea wrote him verses first and that he can observe decorum only in prose. Susanna admits that she regards Farquhar as "above the common Level of Mankind," but she is unwilling to "indulge the *Folly* of Love." If Celadon wishes, they may continue to write, but she "must never see him more." Farquhar closes the series with an impassioned but immodest appeal to her to reverse her cruel sentence and allow him to visit her.

It is impossible to say to what extent the quarrel (and the emotion which led to it) was real and to what extent it was simulated for literary purposes. Both Farquhar and Mrs. Centlivre had tasted of epistolary publication and must have known that their letters would be printed. Expressing their private feelings was perhaps less important than serving the public taste. The two must have remained friends, for Farquhar furnished Mrs. Centlivre a prologue for *The Platonick Lady* in November, 1706, not many months before his death.

The next item shows Mrs. Centlivre collaborating with a group of literary ladies in a memorial to Dryden. *The Nine Muses. Or, Poems Written By Nine several Ladies Upon the Death of the late Famous John Dryden, Esq;* was printed for Richard Basset in September, 1700.[14] Six women wrote the poems attributed to the nine several ladies.

Mrs. De la Rivière Manley, author of a tragedy and a comedy, seems to have assumed major responsibility for the

[14] Advertised in the *Post Man* for Sept. 24-26.

volume. In addition, she contributed poems for the tragic and
the comic Muses. Lady Sarah Peirce or Piers wrote "Urania:
The Divine Muse." Her friend, Mrs. Sarah Field, also known
as Mrs. Sarah Fyge Egerton, added poems for Erato ("By
Mrs. *S. F.*"), Euterpe ("By Mrs. *J. E.*"), and Terpsichore
("By Mrs. *L. D. ex tempore*").[15] Mrs. Mary Pix, author
of seven plays and later a close friend of Susanna, was re-
sponsible for "Clio: *The Historick Muse,*" and Mrs. Catharine
Trotter, afterward Mrs. Cockburn, produced "Calliope: *The
Heroick Muse.*"

The ninth and last poem, "Polimnia: *Of Rhetorick.* . . . By
Mrs. *D. E.,*" has not previously been identified.[16] It begins:

> Call'd by my Grief, *Melpomene* I come,
> With Radiant Tears, to Grace my *Dryden*'s Tomb.

The twenty-four-line poem, which could hardly have been
worse, may be identified as Susanna's on the evidence of a
somewhat scandalous pamphlet, *A Letter from the Dead
Thomas Brown to the Living Heraclitus* (1704), signed "Tho.
Brown" and apparently published shortly after Brown's death.
The epistle represents Tom as writing from "the Land of Darkness," where "Afra" Behn, his guide, desires to learn from
him concerning the state of English poetry since her decease.
Among the poets, or poetasters, he mentions four women:

> . . . there were abundance of Pretenders to the Sacred
> Mystery of not being understood in unintelligible Metre:
> There were three Gentlewomen in particular that had
> taken the Names of three of the Nine Muses upon 'em,
> and a Fourth, who, in her single Person, had made bold
> with three more of their Names in her Poems, call'd the
> NINE MUSES upon Mr. Dryden's death. The first was
> a lean Gentlewoman, Mrs. *P - x,* Caterer to the Play-

---

[15] Reprinted in *A Collection of Poems on Several Occasions* (1705) by
Mrs. Egerton.
[16] Hugh Macdonald, *John Dryden: A Bibliography* (Oxford, 1939), p.
297.

house in Little Lincolns Inn Fields, the second a thundring piece of Man's Flesh, one Mrs. *T - tt --;* the third, a Lady that never look'd a skew in her Life, one Mr̃s. *C - r - ll,* and the fourth, Madam *F -- l - d . . .*

By a process of elimination we learn that Susanna, still known as Mrs. Carroll, was masquerading as Mrs. D. E.

Since Mrs. Pix, the wife of a city tailor, was notoriously fat and Mrs. Trotter was a small woman, we may conclude that Susanna always "look'd a skew" or squinted. When complimenting her, her contemporaries sometimes referred to her beauty, but more often they commented on her wit and gaiety. They probably felt like Olivia in *The Plain Dealer:*

Olivia. First, can any one be call'd beautiful that squints?
Lord Plausible. Her eyes languish a little, I own.

More indicative of her future career than her letters or her elegy on Dryden, however, was her first play, *The Perjur'd Husband: or, The Adventures of Venice.* Although it was called a tragedy at the time, tragicomedy would be a better name for it. According to the *Post Man,* it was published on October 22, 1700, "As 'twas Acted at the Theatre Royal in Drury Lane"—probably about three weeks before, near the opening of the theatrical season. In her dedication to the Duke of Bedford, she says, with customary effusiveness, that, though she may not have created a Wildair for the humor of the town, she has at least followed mankind in its admiration for the Duke.

The Prologue was written by a gentleman (unidentified) and the Epilogue by Mr. B. - - - - - , probably William Burnaby.[17] In her preface Mrs. Centlivre notes that the play *"went off with general Applause"* and might have brought her *"a Sixth Night"*—a second benefit—except that it was acted at a

[17] Allardyce Nicoll, *A History of Early Eighteenth Century Drama,* (Cambridge, 1925), p. 159 n. 2. Certainly the tone of cynicism with which the poets confess that the stage "has been immoral, and debauch'd the Age" is the same as that in Burnaby's own plays.

bad time, before the town had filled, and without the addition of great actors. The dramatis personae included Mr. Mills, Mr. Norris, Mr. Simpson, Mr. Thomas, Mr. Fairbank, Mrs. Oldfield, still an inexperienced young actress, Mrs. Moore, Mrs. Kent, Mrs. Baker, and Mrs. Lucas. Mrs. Oldfield spoke the Prologue, and the notorious Jo Haines (a product of the strolling companies), not a member of the cast, spoke the Epilogue.

The Perjur'd Husband is not what would now be called a success in technique, since the tragic main plot in blank verse and the comic subplot in prose are entirely distinct. It is the carnival season at Venice, and in two scenes characters from the two plots are on the stage at the same time; but this is the only point of contact. Nevertheless, despite the weakness of the tragic part and the commonplaceness of the comic, some of the lines are pointed and exhibit skill in the use of satire. Although such tragicomedies were condemned by the critics and rarely succeeded on the stage, they were encouraged by what for a time had been Dryden's practice and by the feeling of the authors that unrelieved tragedy would not please the taste of an age of wit.

In general outline the tragic plot suggests at times a modification of Dryden's *All for Love* to the purposes of domestic drama; at other times it recalls plays in the tradition of Fletcher's *The Maid's Tragedy*. But no specific sources have been cited for it.

Bassino, husband of Placentia, with whom he was in love only three months before, is now captivated by Aurelia, who had been betrothed by her father, at her own desire, to Alonzo, brother of Placentia. Bassino is unyielding in his intent to marry Aurelia, though pretending to Placentia and his friend Armando that he has overcome his unlawful desire. Armando learns of his treachery, however, and warns Placentia, who, dressed as a man, tries unavailingly to persuade Aurelia to give up Bassino. Unsuccessful, she stabs Aurelia. Then Bassino enters and, not recognizing his wife, strikes her down. He is himself killed by Alonzo.

In the heroic tradition, Bassino and Aurelia are torn between love and honor, and the tragedy results in each instance from submission to love. But, though simple and clearly told, the story lacks motivation, the reader expecting to the end that the bigamous marriage will be averted.

The subplot[18] is extremely salacious. Lady Pizalta, tired of her husband, falls in love with Ludovico. Her maid Lucy disguises the gallant as herself and admits him to Lady Pizalta's house. Lord Pizalto looks around for Lucy, who has promised to keep a thousand-pistole bargain with him. He discovers the young man in Lucy's clothes, but the maid clears her mistress by explaining that she had brought Ludovico in order to trick Pizalto. Lucy nevertheless demands payment on her bond; and, though Lady Pizalta regrets her husbands's loss, the maid silences her with a threat of further disclosures.

At times the prose of the comic part has a genuine sparkle, as in these epigrams:

'Tis an insufferable Fault, that Quality can have no Pleasure above the Vulgar, except it be in not paying their Debts.

Nothing to be done without a Bribe I find, in Love as well as Law—

Women and Lawyers ne'er refund a Fee:

The satire on lawyers reminds us of one of Tom Brown's chief antipathies, and we wonder whether he may have read Susanna's manuscript for her.

Venice in carnival times calls for "Maskers, Dancers, Singers, and Attendants." There are two masked balls and two special dances, *"A* Spanish *Entry"* and *"An Entry of three*

---

[18] In one part of the subplot Friedrich Hohrman ("Das Verhältnis Susanna Centlivre's zu Molière und Regnard," *Zeitschrift für vergleichende Litteraturgeschichte*, N.F., XIV [1900-1901], 401) has shown a very slight influence of *Le Divorce* (1688) by J. F. Regnard.

Men and three Women of several Nations," as well as music and singing. Undoubtedly the players who accepted the drama felt that the dancing and singing would help to carry the unrealities of plot and that the play might be a means of meeting the competition from French singers and dancers and the strong men and other stage exhibitionists then attracting attention in the theater.

During the period when Mrs. Centlivre was writing, the stage sank pretty low. From 1700, when Congreve's *The Way of the World* appeared, to 1722, when Steele's *The Conscious Lovers* was produced, the whole drama, but particularly the literary drama, struggled for existence. Shakespeare had not been completely vindicated; Jonson was already a little old-fashioned; the Restoration comedy of manners had collided with Collier and the reformation of manners; operas, spectacles, and foreign singers and performers drew income from native actors and dramatists; the popularity of translations and adaptations from the French discouraged thoughtful originality at home; and general uncertainty as to what would emerge as the dramatic form of the eighteenth century to replace the comedy of manners and the heroic tragedy of the latter seventeenth gave the advantage to the dramatic artisan rather than to the literary artist.

The playwrights attacked Jeremy Collier for their difficulties, but the issue of decency had been raised before Collier. On January 24, 1696, Charles Sackville, Earl of Dorset, as lord chamberlain ordered that Charles Killigrew, master of the revels, resume his wonted custom of censoring all new and old plays to remove matter objectionable to religion, morality, and good manners. Acting an unlicensed play, he added, might cause the company to be silenced. The lord chamberlain was trying to reassert the authority he had once had, but long neglect by the master of the revels made his task difficult. On June 4, 1697, the Earl of Sunderland, then lord chamberlain, renewed the order.

On February 18, 1699, King William himself noted that
the playhouses had flouted Sunderland's command ("the Master
of the Revels hath represented that in contempt of the said
order the actors did neglect to leave out such profane and indecent expressions as he had thought proper to be omitted")
and forbade the actors thereafter to "presume to act anything in
any play contrary to religion and good manners." Nevertheless,
in a short while, the order seems to have been neglected.

To what extent if at all the lord chamberlain's office censored
The Perjur'd Husband we cannot say. The prologue to
D'Urfey's *The Old and the New* mentions the censor at work
in 1703. Also Killigrew thoroughly blue-penciled *The Force
of Friendship,* a tragicomedy by Charles Johnson, acted at the
Haymarket on April 20, 1710.[19] He deleted words "reflecting
on religion, church, or the clergy, or inclining to the obscene"
and as a result secured a fair example of "verbal decency."[20]
But it is likely that as early as 1700 the work of the censor was
still very irregular.

At least, it is clear from Mrs. Centlivre's preface that some
of the audience took exception to parts of her play, especially to
speeches by Lady Pizalta. Her answer, though embodying
what had already become a conventional argument, is an artistic
defense of realism:

> *I cannot believe that a Prayer Book should be put into the
> Hands of a Woman, whose innate Virtue won't secure her
> Reputation; nor is it reasonable to expect a Person, whose
> inclinations are always forming Projects to the Dishonour
> of her Husband, should deliver her Commands to her
> Confident in the Words of a Psalm. . . . It is not enough
> that* Lucy *says she's honest, in having denied the Brutal*

---

[19] Edward Niles Hooker, "Charles Johnson's *The Force of Friendship* and
Love in a Chest: A Note on Tragi-Comedy and Licensing in 1710," *Studies
in Philology,* XXXIV (1937), 407-411. On May 1 the tragic and comic
parts were separated and presented as two plays, a tragedy and a farce.

[20] The words deleted were restored in the printed copy, the usual custom.

*Part; whoever thinks Virtue centers in that, has a wrong
Notion of it.* . . .

Frankness is to her not only a necessity in the realistic portrayal of life but also a means to morality, for by being frank
the writer holds life up for improvement. When characters
from the various walks of life have been reformed, the stage
will change too; in fact, it will have to change in order to continue to be realistic. Mrs. Centlivre presents her argument,
partly sound and partly specious, as an answer to Collier, whom
she mentions by name.

The Prologue and Epilogue likewise refer to the movement
against stage vice. The first few lines of the Epilogue sum-
marize the argument that the drama merely copies life:

> *Too long the Poets brought before the Bar,*
> *Have with their bold Accuser wag'd the War;*
> *They now plead Guilty: And Confess the Stage*
> *Has been immoral, and debauch'd the Age.*
> *Nay they will mend—But wish that in their Station,*
> *All Men were pleas'd to forward Reformation.*[21]

Mrs. Centlivre and the gentlemen who wrote the Prologue and
Epilogue for her knew that the audiences, still largely of the
beau monde, expected their fare to be highly spiced, but they
did not realize the extent to which the beau monde was losing
control of public opinion and of the government. On December
19, 1700, the grand jury of Middlesex presented both the play-
houses as nuisances, not only because the plays offered were
sometimes indecent but also because the playhouses provided
a center of operation for vice.

It is noteworthy that the objections mentioned by Mrs.
Centlivre were directed only against the comic scenes of *The*

---

[21] The contrary argument that life copies the drama is presented by *The
Poet Banter'd* (2d ed.; 1702, p. 10):
> For ev'ry Custom on the Stage,
> Descends a Fashion to the Age.

Perjur'd Husband. It was proper for ladies to write tragedies, because the heroic idea that tragedies were moral and uplifting still lingered. Yet none of the ladies and very few of the gentlemen (Rowe and Addison are possible exceptions) were good at tragedy in the early eighteenth century.

Apparently *The Perjur'd Husband* was never revived on the London stage, but the plot of John Hewitt's *Fatal Falsehood: or Distress'd Innocence,* acted at Drury Lane for four times beginning February 11, 1734, is almost identical with Mrs. Centlivre's tragic plot. *Fatal Falsehood* is a blank-verse drama in three acts, adapted to the growing taste for sentimentality in domestic tragedy. The scene is shifted from Venice to Bristol. Belladine (Bassino), though betrothed to Maria (Aurelia), has been forced by his father to marry Louisa (Placentia). Maria, entirely innocent, rejects the addresses of Rainford (Alonzo), the brother of Louisa, and marries Belladine on the death of his father, the action of the play beginning on the wedding night. With the assistance of his friend Manlove (Armando), Belladine hopes to dispose of his affairs and escape abroad with Maria. But when Amanthe, a servant, informs Louisa that Belladine has married again, Louisa, disguised as a man, tells Rainford, who vows to have vengeance on Belladine. Then Louisa, still disguised, accuses Maria of bigamy and draws her sword. Just then Belladine enters, and, taking her for a ravisher, kills her. Rainford thereupon kills Belladine, and Maria goes mad and dies.

The general result of the alterations is to throw sympathy on Belladine, who openly admits his love to his friend, because he sees it as an emotion that he cannot control and because he married Louisa only as a result of his father's threat to disinherit him. He is a victim of circumstances and so the recipient of pity. Louisa calls for pity too, though perhaps her death is to be justified because she married a man who did not love her.

Another significant use of *The Perjur'd Husband* was made by Lessing in *Miss Sara Sampson* (1755), "the first eighteenth-century German domestic tragedy."[22] As Professor Kies shows, *Miss Sara Sampson* is based on Shadwell's *The Squire of Alsatia* (1688), Charles Johnson's *Caelia* (1733), and *The Perjur'd Husband* rather than on Lillo's *The London Merchant*. Lessing was clearly familiar with Mrs. Centlivre's dramas. In 1751 he reviewed a French version of her *A Bold Stroke for a Wife*.[23] His borrowings from the Bassino-Aurelia-Placentia plot of *The Perjur'd Husband* are considerable, including elements of both character and scene.

Though not acted again, *The Perjur'd Husband* was not entirely forgotten. In *The Beauties of the English Stage* (1737) is this trite quotation from it:

> Oh Love! how swiftly fly thy Hours away
> When we are bless'd? How tedious are thy Minutes
> When cruel Absence parts two longing Lovers?

[22] Paul P. Kies, "The Sources and Basic Model of Lessing's *Miss Sara Sampson*," *Modern Philology*, XXIV (1926-27), 65-90.
[23] *Ibid.*, p. 77 n. 1.

"*It Is A Woman's*"

AT THE END of 1700 Mrs. Centlivre was well established in London. Her friends included Tom Brown, Abel Boyer, William Ayloffe, George Farquhar, Mrs. Jane Wiseman, Mrs. De la Rivière Manley, Mrs. Catharine Trotter, Mrs. Sarah Fyge Egerton, Mrs. Mary Pix, Lady Sarah Peirce. She probably had already met William Burnaby, John Oldmixon, Richard Steele, Nicholas Rowe, Charles Johnson, and others with whom she was to be associated later. These names may not seem important in the whole history of English letters, but they were not to be scorned in the year following Dryden's death. She also knew the actors and actresses of the time, and her close friendship with Anne Oldfield and Robert Wilks had probably already begun.

Susanna's first play had been acted with moderate success. Surprisingly enough, the Prologue boasted that it was a lady's:

> *And here's To-night, what doubly makes it sweet,*
> *A private Table, and a Lady's Treat:*

It had been printed also with her name on the title page. But the promise of an easy road to a professional literary career was illusory. She was to be allowed immediate credit for her second play, *The Beau's Duel: or, A Soldier for the Ladies*, which was acted at Lincoln's Inn Fields, about June, 1702,[1] but

---

[1] Advertised in the *Post Boy* for July 4-7, 1702, as to be published on the morrow.

after that she would have to accept varying degrees of anonymity for some years.

Before 1700 women dramatists had sometimes found it to
their advantage to represent their plays as the work of men
when presented in the theater, but for the first two years of the
eighteenth century there seems to have been some relaxation of
the hostility toward women playwrights. Then the propaganda
for improvement in the status of women increased, some even
believing that Queen Anne could be persuaded to found a college for women. The reformers were usually rationalists, often
members of the growing number of Cartesians in England.
The writers of plays, letters, essays, and poetry of wit and gallantry toyed with ideas affecting the status of women, sometimes gallantly, sometimes scornfully, but with an astonishing
demonstration of equality and freedom between the sexes. But
the net result was that immediately following Anne's accession
to the throne in 1702 the dislike of the traditionalists for
women writers was stronger than before. For the time being,
the decision remained securely with the conservatives—the
clergy, the educators, and the moralists—who accepted woman's
traditional inferiority of mind and character and feared what
would happen if she were given an education, a more nearly
equal position in marriage, and a more prominent role in society.

Throughout her literary career Mrs. Centlivre fought a
woman's battle for recognition. Undoubtedly she used hostility
toward women to excuse the failure of some of her works when
a better explanation would have been lack of merit, but her
desire to establish herself as a writer in a man's world was the
governing idea of her life from 1700 until her marriage to
Joseph Centlivre in 1707. During these seven years she wrote
eight dramas. Part of the time she also acted in the provinces.
Since making a living was her chief problem, she was primarily
concerned with her plays, dedications, and benefits.

The cast for *The Beau's Duel* was stronger than for *The
Perjur'd Husband*, though it is unlikely that the play had a

very long run. Pack, as Ogle, a fortune hunter, was the most significant actor. Cory and Booth acted Colonel Manly and Captain Bellmein, two gentlemen paired with Clarinda and Emilia, acted by Mrs. Prince and Mrs. Porter, the distinguished tragic actress. Powell, notorious for his own drinking, was Toper, *"an Enemy to Matrimony, and a Friend to the Bottle,"* Bowman was Sir William Mode, a fop, and Fieldhouse was Carefull, the father. Mrs. Lee acted Mrs. Plotwell, a former mistress of Bellmein.

The comedy was repeated at Lincoln's Inn Fields in the autumn. It is advertised for October 21 in the *Daily Courant*, where it is called the last new comedy, "With the Addition of a New Scene, and a new Prologue and Epilogue, with a Whimsical Song Sung by Mr. Pack." Since all printed copies follow the first edition, there is no way to trace the additions.

The Beau's Duel was revived at Drury Lane on April 11, 1785, for the benefit of Baddeley, who took the part of Carefull, father of Clarinda. King, Dodd, Bannister, Jr., R. Palmer, Palmer, Miss Farren, Mrs. Brereton, Mrs. Ward, and Mrs. Wilson also participated. But except for the nonce presentation the play was dead within a year of its birth.

In the comedy Colonel Manly and Captain Bellmein both think themselves in love with Clarinda, whom her father, Carefull, wishes to marry to a foolish but wealthy fop, Sir William Mode. Sir William and Ogle, a conceited poet and beau who imagines every woman in love with him, are teased into a duel by Toper, but they arrange privately to fight with foils ("files"). Clarinda and her cousin, Emilia, with whom Bellmein is really in love, go to the duel disguised as men in order to get proof that Sir William is a coward. There they egg on the combatants, but they make off when Manly and Bellmein appear.

Carefull has meanwhile come upon a letter from Ogle to Clarinda, and, thinking his daughter in love with the beau, orders her to marry Sir William by six the following day or he will himself marry before twelve. Toper, a friend of Manly

and Bellmein, offers his "cousin," really Mrs. Plotwell, whom
he introduces as a highly virtuous Quaker, to be Carefull's
wife.

At her request, Manly and Bellmein rescue Clarinda from
Sir William as he is taking her to church, and Manly marries
her. (The trick is as old as Dekker's *The Shoemaker's Holi-
day*.) Carefull thereupon marries Mrs. Plotwell. After the
ceremony, however, she lays aside her Quaker demeanor and
begins her persecution. (The situation suggests that in Jonson's
The Silent Woman.) Finally, Carefull agrees to forgive his
daughter for having married Manly if Bellmein and Toper will
free him from his wife. Mrs. Plotwell returns her settlement,
and, since Bellmein rather than a parson had performed the
ceremony, it is revealed that there had really been no marriage.
Bellmein is to marry Emilia.

According to Genest (II, 262) that part of *The Beau's
Duel* relating to "Mrs. Plotwell's marriage and subsequent conduct is stolen from the City Match." Robert Seibt[2] points out
the chief scenes borrowed. The main distinction between the
borrowed scenes and their originals is that Mrs. Centlivre writes
as prose what Mayne had written as blank verse. Yet the
characterization of Mrs. Plotwell as a reformed mistress and
the brains of the plot is new. Also in *The City Match* (1639)
it is the nephew rather than the daughter who is to be disinherited. The changes suggest that Mrs. Centlivre was giving
more prominence to the nature and problems of women than
Mayne had done.

The greater part of *The Beau's Duel* is Mrs. Centlivre's
own. Her satire on beaux and fops is freshly handled, though
the use of cowards who will not fight is not new, as readers of
Shakespeare, Jonson, and Congreve know. In some respects
the play reflects ideas and situations which had already appeared
in her correspondence. For example, Sir William gives it as
his opinion that the use of another man's oath is "as indecent

[2] "Die Komödien der Mrs. Centlivre," *Anglia*, XXXIII (1910), 83 ff.

as wearing his Cloaths." He is very proud of his "Affirmatives" like "Impair my Vigour," "blister me," and "enfeeble me." Bellmein says that he and his mistress pass for Celadon and Chloe, and Emilia, like Astraea in the letters, explains how she met Celadon and was so much entertained by his pretty discourse while sitting next him in the pit that she promised to write to him and could not help keeping her word if she was to be hanged for it. Also, Bellmein's description of himself to Emilia as the pale, wan, and skeleton-like lover is much like that of Celadon to Astraea. In short, similarities between the expressions in the letters and those in the comedy lead us to conclude that Mrs. Centlivre probably borrowed only the marriage of Carefull and Mrs. Plotwell.

Except that the various plots are never completely integrated, *The Beau's Duel* is an acceptable comedy, with realistic comments upon contemporary London life and allusions to popular topics like the prognostications of the astrologers and philomaths. The character of Mrs. Plotwell is well done, and the use of her to unify the action, though not completely satisfactory, shows a genuine dramatic sense. Three brief scenes are worth remembering: one in the first act where Sir William corrects Le Reviere, his supposed French valet, for speaking English without an accent ("Blister me if you don't speak plain *English!*"), another at the beginning of Act II where Sir William in a nightgown, before his mirror, conducts both parts of an imaginary conversation with a lord at the playhouse, and Act II, scene 2, in which Ogle describes his conquests over women's hearts, commenting on the fact that a tradesman fails to appreciate the honor a gentleman does him in making love to his wife and demonstrating how his mistress looks longingly down upon him from her window. These are not so crisp as similar scenes from Congreve, but they are well above the Restoration average in the comedy of manners. Elsewhere the emphasis is predominantly on disguises, mistaken identity, and trickery.

One of the most interesting differences between *The Beau's Duel* and the Restoration comedy results from the new emphasis which Mrs. Centlivre puts on men and women of sense. Both a man and a woman of sense are capable of frankness, truth-telling, and genuine affection. The woman of sense is unlike her Restoration predecessor in that she does not make herself difficult and does not take pride in being pursued. In fact, she is as much the pursuer as the man, but only to learn whether her servant really loves her or to escape a second man who is being forced upon her against her will. She admits that she is in love and that she would like to be married, and she believes that no man of sense would take advantage of a virtuous woman. Men and women of sense would not think of marrying for money or of making love without feeling it regardless of the stakes, though they admit that riches are "the common Chance of Knaves and Fools" and "Fortune is rarely favourable to a Man of Sense." Clarinda and Emilia hesitate to don breeches as a means of showing up Sir William, for they fear that "this masquerade will not be reputable for Women of nice Honour," but they do it as a means of securing justice for themselves. Like the man of sense, the sensible woman is generous, courageous, judicious, and constant in love. She is capable of making her own decisions, and she regards love far more highly than obedience to her parents, a view very disagreeable to the moralists of the time.

The Prologue, by a gentleman, is interesting for showing the early eighteenth-century attitude of the dramatists toward their audience:

> *What Hazards Poets run, in Times like these,*
> *Sure to offend, uncertain whom to please:*
> *If in a well-work'd Story they aspire,*
> *To imitate old Rome's or Athen's Fire,*
> *It will not do; for strait the Cry shall be,*
> *'Tis a forc'd heavy piece of Bombastry.*

If Comedy's their Theme, 'tis ten to one
It dwindles into Farce, and then 'tis gone.
If Farce their Subject be, this Witty Age
Holds that below the Grandeur of the Stage.

The dramatists sometimes, as here, charged the audience with a lack of taste and judgment and so accounted for the popular desire for farce, pantomime, and opera. In their view, the audience lacked a proper respect for the sober forms of tragedy and comedy and in its oversophistication condemned genuine emotion and poetry for flashy wit and superficial adornment. Undoubtedly the audience was changing. The people were becoming more interested in politics, science, and trade. In their interests they had been shifting from the court to the town, from court amusements to party controversies, from leisure to business. The small and select audience had given way to a larger but less cohesive one. Perhaps to this very fact was due the popularity of Mrs. Centlivre's busy comedies of intrigue.

Mrs. Centlivre had a third play ready for production before the year was out. *The Stolen Heiress: or The Salamanca Doctor Outplotted* was acted at Lincoln's Inn Fields for the first time on Thursday, December 31, 1702,[3] and was published anonymously on January 16, 1703,[4] with a dedication to Sir Stafford Fairborn, rear admiral of the fleet. The lady says that she is proud to be the first to make him an offering of this kind.

With *The Stolen Heiress* begins for Mrs. Centlivre the attempt to conceal the sex of the author. Her prologue, spoken by Mrs. Prince, begins:

Our Author fearing his Success to Day,
Sends me to bribe your Spleen against his Play, . . .[5]

[3] *Daily Courant*, Dec. 29, 1702.
[4] *Post Boy*, Jan. 16-17, 1703.
[5] The prologue to Mrs. Pix's *The Conquest of Spain*, acted in May, 1705, is equally positive:

How bold a Venture does our Author make!
And what strange Measures do his Wishes take?
How cou'd he hope the Tragick Scene shou'd please . . .

Though, as we shall see, such deception rankled with her, she could do little to counter the demands of the players and the publisher.

The cast of *The Stolen Heiress* included several players who had acted in *The Beau's Duel*. But it was a far better cast than she had had earlier, for the younger players were becoming more experienced and better known, and, for the first time, Mrs. Barry took a part in one of her dramas. Powell had the part of Palante, the hero of the tragic plot, and Pack was Francisco, the protagonist of the comic plot. Dogget acted Sancho, a ridiculous scholar from the University of Salamanca. Mrs. Barry was Lucasia, the tragic heroine, and Mrs. Prince was Lavinia, the comic heroine. The Epilogue was spoken by Dogget, who, as Sancho, indicates his intention of burning all his books and using his shape, dress, and smiles to gain the ladies' favor.

The story of the play may be briefly summarized. Palante, foster son of Euphenes, is in love with Lucasia, daughter of Gravello. Gravello has circulated a false report of the death of his son Eugenio in order to make it appear that his daughter is an heiress, so that the rich Count Pirro will marry her. But Palante and Lucasia elope and are married. Thereupon Pirro uses his influence with his uncle, the governor of Palermo, to have Palante sentenced to death for stealing an heiress. Irus, really Eugenio himself in disguise, informs Gravello that Eugenio is alive, and then, suspecting the secrecy which his father enjoins upon him, gives the information also to Pirro, who employs him in writing to poison Eugenio. The Governor offers Lucasia Palante's life if she will marry his nephew, and, on her refusal, swears never to pardon him. Palante is discovered in the meanwhile to be the real son of Euphenes. As a last resort, Irus produces his contract with Pirro and then discovers himself in order to free Palante. Pirro is exiled, and Palante and Lucasia are accepted by their fathers, who bury an old feud between the two families.

In the subplot Larich tries to marry his daughter Lavinia to Sancho, but by pretending unchastity she succeeds in getting her father's consent to marry Francisco, though at the expense of being disinherited. Then Francisco receives an estate as a result of his uncle's death, Lavinia convinces her father that she is really virtuous, and all are happy except Sancho, who takes a philosophical view of the events.

The Stolen Heiress was advertised and printed as a comedy. Jacob, however, calls it a tragicomedy, perhaps the best name for it. The comic and the tragic plots are better integrated than in *The Perjur'd Husband,* because Gravello and Larich, the fathers of the two girls, are brothers, and because both plots show fathers trying arbitrarily to dispose of their daughters. To some extent the play is propaganda against the Sicilian (and English) law making it a crime punishable by death to marry an heiress against her father's wishes. In the last scene the Governor of Palermo promises that he will "solicit earnestly the King to mitigate this cruel Law, and make the Thefts of Love admit of Pardon."

Although some writers say that *The Stolen Heiress* was probably taken from one of the old Spanish romances, Genest (II, 263) names the real source as Thomas May's *The Heir,* acted by the Company of the Revels in 1620 and printed in 1633.[6] Sometimes Susanna follows her source in the use of blank verse; at other times she writes the speeches, frequently with no other change, as prose. Nevertheless, she makes some alterations with the obvious intention of strengthening her original. She links the two plots somewhat more closely than May does. She also tries to motivate some of his unreal situations and to humanize his improbable characters. Thus, for instance, she replaces Shallow, who is stupidly persuaded that Lavinia is to bear him a child, with Sancho, who is willing

[6] Hans Strube has made a textual comparison of the two plays in *S. Centlivre's Lustspiel "The Stolen Heiress" und sein Verhältnis zu "The Heir" von Thomas May* (Halle a. S., 1900).

to marry the girl but is under no illusions as to the child's parentage.

Philocles and Leucothoe in *The Heir* develop a sudden passion at first sight, but Palante and Lucasia are in love at·the opening of the play. The rich count is also more plausible. The chief objection to Virro in *The Heir* is his age; in *The Stolen Heiress* it is Pirro's ugly passion, reflected in his appearance, that makes him distasteful.[7]

Much of May's play is in turn based on Shakespeare. The enmity between Polymetes and Euphues comes from *Romeo and Juliet*, as does the story of Philocles and Leucothoe's falling in love at first sight. Mrs. Centlivre shifts the emphasis, however, from the family feud to the stealing of the heiress. The offer of the Governor to pardon Philocles if Leucothoe will give herself to him is from *Measure for Measure*.[8] The arrival of Leucothoe in the grove and her apprehension of ill comes from the Thisbe episode of *A Midsummer Night's Dream*; and the scene of the constable and the watch at the end of Act IV, from *Much Ado about Nothing*.

The Stolen Heiress seems not to have been revived, but Mrs. Cowley used the subplot, *The Salamanca Doctor Outplotted*, in *Who's the Dupe?*, a farce acted with considerable applause at Drury Lane in 1779 and the years following. There

[7] Strube (*ibid.*) thinks that Mrs. Centlivre had Cibber's *Love Makes a Man* (acted at Drury Lane in Dec., 1700) in mind when she created Sancho. It is Cibber's scholar Carlos, however, who wins Angelina from his foppish brother despite the fact that the latter has the support of both their fathers. Cibber, who got the story of Carlos and Sancho from that of Charles and his servant Andrew in Fletcher's *The Elder Brother*, probably took the name of the servant from *Don Quixote*, and Mrs. Centlivre may have done the same, for at the end of Act I she says that Sancho "makes as odd a Figure, Sir, as the famous *Don Quixot*, when he went in Search of his *Dulcinea*."

At one point Mrs. Centlivre changed May's "As if 'twere writ in Gallobelgicus" to "as if they had been Spectators of his End." Disregarding dates, Strube suggests that here Mrs. Centlivre is punning on the title of Addison and Steele's *Spectator*.

[8] In keeping with her attempt to make the character of the Governor more generally consistent, Mrs. Centlivre has him offer Lucasia a pardon for her lover if she will marry his nephew, apparently forgetting that Lucasia and Palante are already married.

are no close verbal parallels. Doiley wants his daughter Elizabeth to marry a scholar named Gradus, but she prefers Granger.
With her approval, Granger teaches Gradus the ways of the
world and makes him drunk. Doiley, horrified, gladly con-
siders another scholar for his daughter's hand. Following a
word combat in which Granger, the new scholar, uses learned
English and Gradus uses Greek, Doiley pronounces Granger
the better Greek scholar and rewards him with his daughter.
Gradus consoles himself with the witty servant Charlotte.

So far Mrs. Centlivre's plays had been presented at bad
times of the year—very early or very late in the season or at
vacation time. Her luck did not change with *Love's Contrivance: or, Le Medecin Malgre Lui,* which was first acted anonymously at Drury Lane on Friday, June 4, 1703. It was not unusual in the advertisements of a new play for no author to be
mentioned, but when *Love's Contrivance* was published, on
June 14, the initials "R. M." were signed to the Dedication.
Two days later the following notice appeared in the *Daily
Courant:*

> Whereas the last New Comedy, call'd, *Love's Contriv-
> ance, or, Le Medecin Malgre Luy,* has the two letters
> R. M. to the dedication. This is to give Notice, that the
> Name of the Author (who for some Reasons is not willing
> to be known at present) does not begin with those two
> Letters. The true Name will shortly be made known.

The real name of the author seems not to have been announced
in the newspapers, but in the dedication of *The Platonick Lady*
(1707) Mrs. Centlivre complains that the publisher of *Love's
Contrivance,* realizing the contempt in which female authors
were held, "put two letters of a wrong name to it; which tho'
it was the height of injustice to me, yet his imposing on the
Town turn'd to account with him; and thus passing for a Man's,
it has been play'd at least a hundred times."[9] The only possible

---

[9] The "hundred times" included acting in the provinces as well as in
London.

deduction is that Bernard Lintot, the publisher, played her a scurvy trick.

Mrs. Centlivre's embarrassment was no doubt due in part to the awkwardness of having her dedication falsely initialed. The inscription of a play was a recognized source of income for the playwright, and she chose her patrons with some care. In this dedication to the old Earl of Dorset, who had a reputation for generosity to writers, she mentions "the courteous affability" with which his Lordship "once received a trifle" from her hand. But the style is so notoriously bad that one is tempted to charge the publisher with altering more than the signature.

The cast of *Love's Contrivance* was strong enough to please the dramatist herself. Wilks had the part of Bellmie, an attractive one for an actor because it provides him with three distinct roles—Bellmie, the "angry doctor," and the "doubting philosopher." Mills was Octavio, Bellmie's friend; Norris (better known as "Jubilee Dicky" from his astounding success in Farquhar's *The Constant Couple: or, A Trip to the Jubilee*) took the part of Martin, formerly the servant of Bellmie, now a fagot maker, and soon to pass for a famous doctor; Johnson played Sir Toby Doubtful, the superannuated lover of Lucinda; Bullock was Selfwill, father of Lucinda; Mrs. Rogers, Lucinda; Mrs. Oldfield, Belliza, her cousin; and Mrs. Norris, Martin's wife. Wilks probably spoke the Epilogue, since it refers to *"this Fortune-telling Play"* and suggests that he end it by telling the fortunes of the audience, presumably as he had told the fortune of Sir Toby.

The comedy ran for three nights, Susanna receiving her benefit on June 7. It was repeated on June 14 for the benefit of the boxkeepers, Lovelace, King, and White, with additions: "In which the Famous Gasperini will perform several Italian Sonatas. Entertainments of Singing by Mr. Leveridge and others, and Entertainments of Dancing by the Famous du Ruell and others, as express'd in the Bills at large." It was also repeated on June 18 and 22, on the second occasion for the benefit of Mrs. Campion and for the entertainment of the Envoy Extraordinary from the King of Denmark and several other foreign ministers and ladies of quality. On July 7 the last act, "the comical Scenes of The Angry Doctor, and, The Doubting Philosopher," was part of a hodgepodge entertainment at Drury Lane, including a comedy, *The Comical Rivals,* the fourth act of *The Old Bachelor,* and a variety of singing and dancing.

Our chief source of information about the early performances is Mrs. Centlivre's preface. She says that the play *"met a Reception beyond* [her] *Expectation"* and she attributes its success to the players:

> *I must own myself infinitely obliged to the Players, and in a great Measure the Success was owing to them, especially Mr.* Wilks, *who extended his Faculties to such a Pitch, that one may almost say he out-play'd himself; and the Town must confess they never saw three different Characters by one Man acted so well before, and I think myself extremely indebted to him, likewise to Mr.* Johnson, *who in his way I think the best Comedian of the Age.*

During the following season it was acted on October 20, February 16, and April 28. On the last occasion it was given at the desire of several persons of quality for the benefit of the author. This second benefit for what was no longer a new play seems unusual, but, since the author had to pay the charges of the house, the theater probably did not lose a great deal. In addition, the last act was used as an afterpiece on January 21, March 28 (for Mrs. Oldfield's benefit), and July 5, and again on June 7, 1705, and February 14, 1706. Tony Aston included it also in a medley which he produced in taverns about London in 1723 and 1724.

Lincoln's Inn Fields revived the full play on July 14 and 17, 1724, and twice in 1726. Apparently *Love's Contrivance* was never produced again. The presentation of Henry Fielding's *The Mock Doctor,* a rather close adaptation of *Le Médecin malgré lui,* in 1732, ended any further usefulness it may have had for the stage.

Yet the list of characters in *The Mock Countess,* an unprinted farce first presented at Drury Lane on April 30, 1733, shows that *Love's Contrivance* had not been forgotten. The farce probably included from Mrs. Centlivre's play the early scene in which Octavio gives Sir Toby advice about matrimony and the scenes between Sir Toby and the philosophers, and added the trick of the mock countess—Betty Kimbow in disguise—from *The Play's the Plot* (1718), by John Durant Breval.

The success of her comedy encouraged Mrs. Centlivre to write a preface in which she explained her method of working and her attitude toward the rules of the critics. It is her most fully developed statement of a dramatic theory:

> *The Criticks cavil most about Decorums, and cry up* Aristotle's *Rules as the most essential part of the Play. I own they are in the right of it; yet I dare venture a wager they'll never persuade the Town to be of their Opinion, which relishes nothing so well as Humour lightly tost up with Wit, and drest with Modesty and Air. . . . I do not say this by way of condemning the Unity of Time, Place, and Action; quite contrary, for I think them the greatest Beauties of a Dramatick Poem; but since the other way of writing pleases full as well, and gives the Poet a larger Scope of Fancy, . . . why should a Man torture, and wrack his Brain for what will be no Advantage to him.*

For the time being, too, she acknowledged the necessity of modesty in style:

> *The following Poem I think has nothing can disoblige the nicest Ear; and tho' I did not observe the Rules of* Drama,

I took peculiar Care to dress my Thoughts in such a modest Stile, that it might not give Offence to any.

Her last three plays, it must be admitted, are relatively clean in comparison with the drama that had gone before, but *Love's Contrivance* is far more objectionable than the other two.

Mrs. Centlivre says that she intended to write a farce and so divided her material into three acts, but *"some very good Judges,"* considering what she had added to the farcical scenes borrowed from Molière, divided it, in spite of her, into five acts, *"believing it might pass among the Comedies of these Times."* In her subtitle she acknowledges one of her sources, but Genest (II, 273) thinks that she tried to "conceal that she has borrowed the scenes, in which Sir Toby is concerned, from Molière's Forced Marriage." It seems unlikely, however, that she expected to hide borrowings from Molière; and, in any case, she deserves some credit for combining several plays into one.[10]

The opening scene of *Love's Contrivance* bears a close resemblance to the first scene in Molière's *Sganarelle, ou le cocu imaginaire,* where the father Gorgibus, asserting his absolute power over his daughter Célie, commands her to give her hand to the rich Valère, leaving her heart, if she pleases, with Lélie. But Mrs. Centlivre does not use any of Molière's language. Furthermore, Lucinda is much more impudent to her father than Célie, and Selfwill is much more tyrannical than Gorgibus. Here the Englishwoman is trying to bring her characters into accord with the contemporary types of the comedy of intrigue. A little later in *Sganarelle* Célie defends her lover from the doubts of her maid. Mrs. Centlivre, on the other hand, makes

[10] Cf. Albert Wüllenweber, *Mrs. Centlivre's Lustspiel "Love's Contrivance" und seine Quellen* (Halle a. S., 1900), and Richard Ohnsorg, *John Lacy's "Dumb Lady," Mrs. Susanna Centlivre's "Love's Contrivance," Henry Fielding's "Mock Doctor" in ihrem Verhältnis zu einander und zu ihrer gemeinschaftlichen Quelle* (Rostock, 1900). Wüllenweber denies the charge of H. van Laun in "Les Plagiaries de Molière" (*Le Moliériste*, Jan., 1881, pp. 304-5) that Mrs. Centlivre was a pure and artless plagiary.

the maid into a friend, Belliza, whom she uses for her second pair of lovers.

Much of *Love's Contrivance* is literally translated from *Le Mariage forcé* and *Le Médecin malgré lui.* Mrs. Centlivre makes a characteristic alteration of the wife-beating scene from *Le Médecin malgré lui.* Molière's husband asks forgiveness of his wife and goes to the woods to make fagots for her. But Martin, despite his wife's plea not to spend the money for which her bones have suffered, starts for the alehouse:

> *Martin.* But it was my Friend gave the Money tho'.
>
> *Wife.* But if I had not cry'd out, your Friend might not have come this way tho'.
>
> *Martin.* That's right——well, Wife, I won't stand with you for little Matters, you shall beat me now, and I'll cry out, if you think that will get you a Guinea; if not, if you'll come to the Alehouse, I'll make you drunk; and so good b'w'ye.

Mrs. Centlivre again employs this method of turning the argument in the second act. There Belliza comes to Bellmie's lodgings with a message for him, finds a man reading, and strikes him on the shoulder with her fan. She is surprised to find that he is not Bellmie, but she likes him at once. He addresses her as Bellmie's mistress, for whom he takes her. The scene is sprightly—the kind of thing Mrs. Centlivre could do well—with some sparkle, a bit of philosophizing, and a touch of the casuistry and lust of the Restoration rake in Octavio. The method is seen in these two selections of dialogue, which turn upon the current arguments for free trade:

> *Octavio.* Ah! Madam, he's the most generous Man in the World; his Mistress and his Pocket are still at his Friend's Service.
>
> *Belliza.* Let his Friends share his Mistress! I'm afraid if his Friends applaud his Generosity, they condemn his Sense.

Octavio. Quite to the contrary, Madam, they admire his Morals! he's a Wellwisher to his Country, and knows that the engrossing any Commodity ruins Trade.

But Octavio is so much taken with Belliza that he finds himself in love, and believes he will be to the end of his life.

Belliza. And how many Friends have you to share, pray?

Octavio. Faith, Madam, none at all. I fancy I should play the Monopolist, were you once at my Disposal.

Belliza. But that would be a Ruin to Trade, you know; you would be reckoned an Enemy to your Country.

Mrs. Centlivre uses the Octavio-Belliza scenes to connect the borrowings from her two chief sources. Octavio, believing Belliza a jealous mistress of his friend, tells her that Bellmie does not really love Lucinda. It then becomes necessary for him to rectify his error. This he does by persuading Sir Toby to seek counsel on marriage from a learned doctor and a philosopher, both acted by Bellmie in disguise.[11]

During the summer of 1703 the players from Lincoln's Inn Fields went to Oxford for a period of vacation merrymaking called the "Act." It is satirically described in *The Players turn'd Academicks: or, a Description (In Merry Metre) of their Translation from the Theatre in Little Lincoln's-Inn-Fields, to the Tennis-Court in Oxford* (1703). Mrs. Centlivre (Carroll) would have liked to accompany them but could not afford the trip:

[11] Wüllenweber *(ibid.)* believes than an incident about the middle of Act III may have been suggested by John Lacy's *The Dumb Lady, or the Farrier Made a Physician* (1672), a compounding of Molière's *Le Médecin malgré lui* and *L'Amour médecin.* In Act IV, scene 3, of *The Dumb Lady* Olinda says:

And at the boot of your coach must be running an orange wench, presenting your lady a sweet lemon with a love letter in't.

This may have given Mrs. Centlivre the idea for the scene in which Martin enters Selfwill's house as a vendor of oranges, the cheapness of which attracts Sir Toby. When Martin insists that Lucinda try an orange and pretends to cut it for her, she strikes it down and a letter drops out.

> The first that took Coach, and had often took ——,
> Was the fam'd Mrs. *B* - - - with *P* - - *x* at her *A* - - -,
> A Tool of a Scribe, and a Poetress great,
> Who was said to *Write* well, because well she could *Treat*,
> And for her sake had written her husband in *Debt*.
> While *Carrol*, her Sister-Adventurer in Print,
> Took her Leave all in Tears, with a *Curt'sie* and *Squint*,
> And would certainly take the same Journey as she,
> Had she not giv'n away *Medecin Malgre Lui*.

Mrs. *B* - - - is the unquestionably famed but notorious actress, Elizabeth Barry, and *P* - - *x* is the fat ("great") Mary Pix. Susanna's squint, because of the wen on her left eyelid, was her hallmark among her enemies.

Mrs. Centlivre's giving away her play sounds like an ironical reminder of the false initials signed to the Dedication, but John Nichols in *Literary Anecdotes of the Eighteenth Century* (VIII, 294) notes that Bernard Lintot on May 14, 1703, paid Mrs. Knight ten pounds for *Love's Contrivance*. Apparently Susanna gave her friend the actress the publication rights. Ten pounds was a common but minimum fee for drama manuscripts at the time.

Mrs. Centlivre's success in adapting *Love's Contrivance* from the French encouraged her to try again with *The Gamester*, which she offered the next season. In this play she professes a complete reversal of her purpose in writing. She has previously taken the view that a play should entertain an audience. This view, of which Farquhar was a chief exponent, seems to go back to Dryden, who wrote in his "Defence of an Essay" that "To please the People ought to be the Poet's Aim." Thomas Shadwell had ridiculed the idea, and Collier had declared that the first intent of plays was "to recommend Virtue, and discountenance Vice." In *The Gamester*, acted at Lincoln's Inn Fields about the first of February, 1705, she comes squarely out with the statement that her intention is to correct a reigning social vice. The unsigned dedication to George, Earl of Huntingdon, after mentioning the "Kind Reception" of her play, asserts her purpose to divert "without that Vicious Strain which usually attends the Comick Muse"; she hopes that, "according to the first intent of Plays," she has succeeded in recommending morality. She must have known that she was practically quoting Collier.

The Gamester was published by February 22, 1705, anonymously.[12] Her friend Nicholas Rowe contributed the Prologue, and another friend, Charles Johnson, wrote a sermonizing epilogue on the vicious effects of gambling for both men and women.[13] The comedy was acted for the benefit of the author on February 22, the twelfth night of the production.[14] This benefit seems unusual, since 1705 is a little early for the custom of giving the author benefits every third night through the first run of the play. A new scene, advertised for the benefit but not included in the printed copy, was probably a gambling scene and of little significance except for advertising.

In the dedication to *The Platonick Lady* Mrs. Centlivre says, on the authority of her bookseller, that when a *"spark"* who had bought a copy of *The Gamester* learned it was a woman's work he threw it down and announced *"he was sure if the Town had known that, it wou'd never have run ten Days."* The anonymity which the players and the publisher maintained undoubtedly helped them, but it hurt Susanna's feelings, for it kept her from receiving credit for a considerable theatrical success. At least Rowe knew the author and hinted at her sex in the Prologue:

[12] *Flying Post*, Feb. 20-22: "There is now published, The Gamester, a Comedy, as it is this Day acted the twelfth time."

[13] Both Prologue and Epilogue were printed in the *Diverting Post* for Jan. 27-Feb. 3, 1705. There the Epilogue is credited to Johnson. It was spoken, according to the same source, by Verbruggen. The 1725 edition of the play, which makes the mistake of having the Dedication signed S. Trotter, gives the speaker as Mrs. Verbruggen. In the complete works the speaker is given as Mrs. Santlow, who spoke an epilogue, presumably this same one. in boy's clothes, at Drury Lane on Feb. 7, 1710.

[14] *Daily Courant*, Feb. 20, 1705.

If all the Midwife says of it [the play] *be true,*
There are some Features too like some of you. . . .[15]

Mrs. Centlivre says that in her comedy she is trying to reform one of the reigning vices of England. Reformation was badly needed, for under Queen Anne and the Georges gambling was a national problem. Valere, the protagonist of *The Gamester*, gambles with dice, but cards and lotteries were also common. A chief attraction of the coffeehouses in the days of Addison and Steele was their provision for gambling. On one occasion Addison is said to have won a thousand pounds in a lottery, and heavy gambling losses were a significant stimulus to Colley Cibber to write new plays. Ladies disposed of their silver and even more precious possessions to pay gambling losses. Lords sometimes lost their estates. Gentlemen like Cibber who enjoyed the company of lords found the gambling places a common meeting ground. Even the speculation in stock and perhaps bribery in elections were parts of the same picture.

Actually the realistic gambling scenes in *The Gamester* probably proved more attractive than the reformation of the gambler, who, as it turns out, eats his cake and has it too. Mrs. Centlivre says in her dedication that she was obligated to the French for the gamester, but, whereas he is entirely ruined in the original, she, "in Complaisance to the many fine Gentlemen that play in *England*," has reclaimed him after discovering "the ill Consequence of Gaming, that very often happen to those who are too passionately fond of it."

Jacob calls her play "an improv'd Translation of one under the same Title in *French*," and Mottley names her source as *Le Joueur* (1696) of Jean François Regnard.[16] In the English

---

[15] Rowe included the Prologue in *The Poetical Works of Nicholas Rowe* (1715) and in other editions of his poetry.
[16] Fritz Grober traces Mrs. Centlivre's use of Regnard in *Das Verhältnis von Susannah Centlivre's Lustspiel "The Gamester" zu Regnard's Lustspiel "Le Joueur"* (Halle a. S., 1900); likewise Hohrmann, though not so fully, in "Das Verhältnis Susanna Centlivre's zu Molière und Regnard" (*Zeitschrift für vergleichende Litteraturgeschichte*, N. F., XIV [1900-1901], 419-25).

comedy, young Valere, in love with Angelica, repeatedly breaks his promise to her and to his father to stop gambling. So she dresses as a man and in a gambling bout with him wins all his money and also a diamond-studded picture which she has given him and from which he was never to be separated on pain of losing her forever. But in the end the gambler is fully repentant and entirely submissive, and they are reconciled. In the subplot Valere gives to Lovewell money which Lady Wealthy, a coquettish young widow, has sent him. She marries Lovewell out of gratitude for protecting her honor.

In general, Mrs. Centlivre follows *Le Joueur* closely,[17] frequently merely translating. But she introduces the character of Lovewell, in order to provide the usual two pairs of lovers expected in an English play, and makes Lady Wealthy, the sister of Angelica, an attractive woman when brought to her senses. In order to make the reclamation of Valere more palatable, she reduces the attractiveness of Dorante, Valere's uncle, who wins Angelique in *Le Joueur*. In her play the uncle wishes to marry Angelica only for her money and does not hesitate to inform his mistress against Valere.[18]

Le Joueur, though not deliberately moral, is nevertheless more fundamentally sound than *The Gamester*. In fact, *The Gamester* is Mrs. Centlivre's chief excursion into the realm of sentimental drama.[19] It was written with a consciously moral

[17] The author of an article on "Mrs. Centlivre's Plays" in *Temple Bar*, LI (1877), 247 ff., remarks: "Massinger supplied the principal incident in 'The Gamester,' viz., the giving of a picture by Angelica to her lover Valere, the hero and the gamester, with stringent instructions not to lose it, on pain of forfeiting her hand." Presumably he refers to Massinger's *The Picture*, in which Baptista, at the request of Mathias, makes a picture of Sophia, the wife of Mathias, of such a nature that it will indicate whether or not she is constant to him during his absence. It is a slight alteration of the magic ring motif of the romances. Obviously Mrs. Centlivre has nothing in common with this story except the fact of a picture.

[18] The early eighteenth-century theater did not like informers. Government informers were particularly useful in the fight against vice.

[19] A good discussion of the type is presented in DeWitt C. Croissant's "Early Sentimental Comedy," *Essays in Dramatic Literature*, ed. Hardin Craig (Princeton, 1935), pp. 47-71.

purpose, and it includes the repentance and conversion of a sinner, his resolution to be good henceforth, and his desire that others may profit by his experience. It shows the forgiving spirit of the persons wronged, asserts the goodness of ordinary human beings, and accepts the view that happiness is morally right. It also introduces pathos and pity and indulges unnaturally in emotion for its own sake. After losing the picture, Valere is filled with remorse, and when Angelica breaks off their engagement and his father disinherits him, he is so contrite that Angelica's heart "beats as if the Strings were breaking." We can only hope that she is right in thinking that he has reformed forever. The subplot is also sentimental, for Lady Wealthy, the widow in whose soul "Honor is center'd," is redeemed from her follies by the generous action of Lovewell.

For the first time Mrs. Centlivre had a star cast. Verbruggen played Valere; Betterton took the role of Lovewell, and spoke the Prologue; and Pack acted Hector, the valet of Valere. Mrs. Bracegirdle was Angelica, and Mrs. Barry, Lady Wealthy. The supporting cast included Freeman, Cory, Fieldhouse, Smeaton, Dickins, Weller, Knap, Francis Lee, Mrs. Parsons, Mrs. Hunt, Mrs. Willis, and Mrs. Fieldhouse.

On April 9, 1705, the company moved from Lincoln's Inn Fields to the Haymarket, opened on that day by Captain John Vanbrugh with a foreign opera. The first play given there was *The Gamester*, produced on April 27 and again on May 23. It was performed twice the following season and once in 1706-7. In January, 1708, the Haymarket was made over to Swiney for operas, the acting company joining the one at Drury Lane. When *The Gamester* was revived for Powell's benefit on March 17, 1709, it was played by the combined company, Pack, Cory, Lee, and Mrs. Willis continuing in their original parts. Powell acted the gamester, Booth replaced Betterton as Lovewell, Cibber replaced Dickins as Count Cogdie, and Mrs. Bradshaw took the part of Angelica. Lady Wealthy became Mrs. Porter's role. During the next few years the play was repeated from time to time, especially for benefits. On May 23, 1710, it was given for the benefit of Booth and Keene, with a prologue by Keene and a new epilogue by Pack "in a Riding Habit, upon a Pad-Nagg representing a Town-Miss Traveling to Tunbridge." The prologues and epilogues, demanded by the audience and vied for by the newspapers of the time, often had little relevance to the play, but this epilogue had even less relevance than usual. Mills and Mrs. Bradshaw acted Valere and Angelica at Drury Lane in 1711 and again in a revival in 1714.

The Gamester was presented on various occasions at the newly opened Lincoln's Inn Fields between 1714 and 1718.[20] The income varied from £13 6s. on January 11, 1715, to £66 19s. on January 29, 1718.[21]

In 1719 a charge of plagiarism from Mrs. Centlivre's comedy was leveled at her old friend Charles Johnson, who had written the Epilogue for her. On January 16, 1719, Johnson's *The Masquerade* was presented at Drury Lane. He was promptly accused of copying her work:

> Thus the Extravagancies of the loosing Gamesters at the *Masquerade* are but faintly copied from a Play of Mrs. *Centlivre's,* call'd the *Gamester,* which she translated from the *French,* and from several other Plays written within these Thirty Years.[22]

But there is little resemblance between the two plays except in the subject treated. *The Masquerade* is really nearer Mrs. Centlivre's *The Basset Table* than *The Gamester.*

Dr. George Sewell's *Sir Walter Raleigh* appeared at Lincoln's Inn Fields on the same night as *The Masquerade* at

[20] John Rich's company advertised itself as "the Company of Comedians under Letters Patent granted by King Charles II."

[21] British Museum, MSS Egerton, 2321. The income on Jan. 29, 1718, was due partly to the new dramatic opera, *Amadis, or the Loves of Harlequin and Columbine.* The managers professed objections to operas and pantomimes, but they were forced by experience to use them.

[22] *Critical Remarks on the Four Taking Plays of this Season; vis. Sir Walter Raleigh, The Masquerade, Chit-Chat, and Busiris King of Egypt* (1719), p. 50.

Drury Lane. In the Epilogue the spectators are told, in the spirit of energetic competition, that if they do not like his play they can go to the other theater and "*see old* SHIRLEY *drest in* MASQUERADE." Thus Shirley rather than Mrs. Centlivre was regarded as the source by the rival company. And, in fact, there are some resemblances between Lady Ombre and Mr. Ombre of Johnson's comedy and Aretina and Sir Thomas Bornwell of *The Lady of Pleasure*.

The *Gamester* was revived at Lincoln's Inn Fields on August 2 and 5, 1726, with Ogden as the gamester and Mrs. Morgan as Angelica. Thereafter it continued to be produced on the average of two or three times a year until 1745. Following the Licensing Act of 1737 there were various attempts to avoid its provisions. One of the most obvious is illustrated in the representations of *The Gamester* at Goodman's Fields. Between December 29, 1740, and December 31, 1741, it was advertised five times as a free performance between the two parts of a concert. On January 31, 1741, for example, the play and *The Imprisonment, Release, Adventures and Marriage of Harlequin, and the Triumphs of Love* were to be performed "Gratis, by Persons for their Diversion." The charge was made for the music!

Covent Garden gave *The Gamester* on February 7, 1741, with Hale as Young Valere and Mrs. Woffington as Angelica. Peg Woffington prided herself on her skill in men's roles. On November 21, 1740, she had attracted much attention as Sir Harry Wildair in Farquhar's *The Constant Couple*. The play was produced ten nights running and frequently thereafter during her career on the stage. The Dorimant-Wildair type of synthetic gallant was already seeming a little dated and more appropriate for an actress than for an actor. The role of Angelica, who puts on breeches and gambles with her lover, provided her with a comparable vehicle in which to reveal her shape and figure.

In 1743-44 Mrs. Woffington returned to the part at Drury
Lane, where she acted Angelica twice in the fall of 1743, four
times the next season, and once in the fall of 1745. The play
was produced at Drury Lane again on October 13, 1756, for the
last known London performance, Palmer and Miss Macklin
taking the parts of Valere and Angelica.

Disregarding chronology, the *Biographia Dramatica*, which
has been followed by several stage historians, finds a complete
source for *The Gamester* in N. Destouches's *Le Dissipateur*
(1753). Joseph Knight, in his article on Mrs. Centlivre in the
Dictionary of National Biography, notes the mistake, but himself errs in stating that *Le Dissipateur* "was in part taken from
Mrs. Centlivre." The only close resemblance between *Le Dissipateur* and *The Gamester* occurs in the opening scenes of the
two plays, where the servant of the mistress comes on an errand
to the gamester and has to console herself with seeing his
servant. But Mrs. Centlivre took that part directly from
Regnard's *Le Joueur*. In its general import *Le Dissipateur*
clearly follows *Le Joueur*, because the gambler is apparently
to be left at the end without money, inheritance, or friends.
His last-minute conversion is merely a trick, in which Julie
manipulates matters as adroitly as the ugly woman in the old
tales of magic transformation. In *The Gamester* the intent
and method of the conversion are different. Angelica does not
know that she is going to forgive Valere—she intends, in fact,
to remain obdurate. The sentimental tendency seen in the final
reformation of the two gamblers proves nothing, for it had become stock in trade in both England and France by 1750.
Destouches may have known Mrs. Centlivre's play, but he certainly knew and used Regnard's.

Thomas Holcroft's *Duplicity*,[23] another sentimental comedy,
appeared in 1781. Professor Nicoll states that "the author
denies any indebtedness either to Destouches' *Le Dissipateur*

---

[23] *Duplicity* ran for ten nights. Holcroft's contemporaries thought that
the opposition of the professional gamblers shortened its run.

or to Mrs. Centlivre's *The Gamester*."[24] Holcroft really denies
in his preface that he has taken anything from the tragedy of
The Gamester—that is, Edward Moore's play (1753). Except
that it is another gaming piece in which a hero loses all his
money and is then converted and happliy married, *Duplicity*
and Mrs. Centlivre's comedy have nothing in common. Her
play was at the head of a tradition in England, but direct borrowings from it are difficult to prove. Even Charles in Sheridan's *The School for Scandal* shows many resemblances to
Valere. In particular, the use of his uncle's picture as the acid
test of his character suggests the use of Angelica's picture to
test her lover, and Lady Sneerwell's love for Charles suggests
Lady Wealthy's love for Valere.

The *Gamester* was not forgotten. It was cut down to a
three-act comedy and produced under the title of *The Pharo
Table*, along with *Marian*, a musical entertainment, for Lewis's
benefit on April 4, 1789, at Covent Garden. The playbill for
the day[25] notes the source. Stephen Jones, editor of the 1812
edition of the *Biographia Dramatica*, probably based his comment on an actual performance:

> This was an alteration of Mrs. Centlivre's *Gamester*,
> with the addition of some new characters, particularly one
> of a pugilist, adapted to the present times. The alterations
> were not inferior to the original performance, and were
> very well connected with it; but the piece, which was acted
> for Mr. Lewis' benefit, was never repeated, nor printed.

It was actually repeated on April 13, 1789, and April 21, 1790.[26]
John O'Keeffe says that he made the alteration at Lewis's request and called it the *Faro Bank*.[27] The *Town and Country*

[24] *A History of Late Eighteenth Century Drama* (Cambridge, 1927), p.
134 n. 3.
[25] Theatre Collection, Harvard College Library.
[26] Playbills, Theatre Collection, Harvard College Library.
[27] *Recollections of the Life of John O'Keeffe, Written by Himself* (1826),
I, 140.

Magazine for April, 1789, thought that the revamped play lacked "any addition of wit, or humour, to render its revival entertaining."

In its title *The Faro Table; or, the Guardians,* a comedy by John Tobin, acted at Drury Lane in 1816, recalls O'Keeffe's revision of *The Gamester,* but it has nothing at all to do with Mrs. Centlivre.[28]

Apparently Susanna turned momentarily from the drama in 1705 to write a complimentary poem for *A Collection of Poems on Several Occasions* by Mrs. Sarah Fyge Egerton.[29] Mrs. Egerton says in her preface that she did not intend her poems for publication, "but an unlucky Accident forc'd them to the Press." She adds that they have been seen by only a few of her own sex, some of whom have sent their compliments. Of the four poems signed "J.H.," "M.P.," "S.C.," and "E.C.," the second and third are almost certainly the work of Mrs. Egerton's collaborators in the *Nine Muses*—Mary Pix and Susanna Centlivre (Carroll). S. C.'s subject, as we might expect, is the abilities of women:

Thou Champion for our Sex go on and show,
Ambitious Man what Womankind can do:
In vain they boast of large Scholastick Rules,
Their skill in Arts and Labour in the Schools.
What various Tongues and Languages acquir'd,
How fam'd for Policy, for Wit admir'd;
Their solid Judgment in Philosophy,
The Metaphysicks, Truths, and Poetry,
Since here they'll find themselves outdone by thee. . . .

Despite our sympathy for her cause, we can hardly help wish-

[28] The list of Mrs. Centlivre's works in French's acting edition of *The Wonder* (1794) includes *The Gamester* under the title of *The Perjured Wife.* There seems to have been no other instance in which *The Gamester* was so called, and although Angelica does perjure herself, she is not a wife. The mistake may have been due to confusion with *The Perjur'd Husband.*

[29] The volume is dated 1706, but the *Term Catalogues* show that it appeared in Nov., 1705.

ing that for the sake of her argument both she and Mrs. Egerton wrote better verse.

Encouraged by the success of *The Gamester* Mrs. Centlivre produced a companion piece the same year. Though not a sequel, *The Basset Table* is another study of gaming, this time among women. It was produced on November 20, 1705, at Drury Lane, where it ran for four nights. The printed play, dated 1706, was published as "By the Author of, The Gamester" in November, 1705. In her unsigned dedication to Lord Altham Mrs. Centlivre continues the theory she introduced in the dedication of *The Gamester*. Poetry, she says, was principally designed to correct and rectify manners by inspiring audiences with noble sentiments and laughing them out of their vices. She has therefore attempted by the main drift of this play "to Redicule and Correct one of the most reigning Vices of the Age."

The theaters recognized the relationship between the two plays. In fact, the Haymarket revived *The Gamester* the day before Drury Lane produced *The Basset Table*. Arthur Bedford in *The Evil and Danger of Stage-Plays* (1706) also groups the two together—as the only recent dramas which attempt to reform "a Vice to which their *Hearers* may be inclin'd."[30]

The name of the author does not appear in the advertisements of the first performance, but the Epilogue, spoken by Estcourt, implies that the author was a woman. The cast was satisfactory. Mrs. Oldfield acted Lady Reveller, and Mrs. Rogers, Mrs. Mountfort, Mrs. Cross, and Mrs. Lucas were adequate for the other female parts. Mills was Lord Worthy, in love with Lady Reveller; Wilks was Sir James Courtly, the lover of Lucy and the gallant of Mrs. Sago, the citizen's wife; and Bickerstaff was Ensign Lovely, the lover of Valeria, the philosophical girl. Bullock, Estcourt, Johnson, and Pinkethman had the male supporting roles. Yet the play was hardly a stage success. Some of the individual scenes are good, but

[30] Pp. 128-29.

THE CARD PLAYERS

(From a plate in Mrs. Centlivre's The Basset Table)

there is no strong thread binding them together. Mrs. Centlivre was ostensibly claiming major attention for the story of
Lady Reveller and her basset table, but the stories of Valeria,
Lady Lucy, and Mrs. Sago—all distinctive types of women—
are individually almost as significant as Lady Reveller's. Sir
James is important in each of the plots, but he is not prominent
enough to bind them together into a semblance of unity.

More specifically, the main plot, which suggests the title,
tells the story of Lady Reveller, a coquettish young widow who
keeps a basset table, and Lord Worthy, who loves her deeply
but hates gambling. Sir James, a man of the world, lays a
stratagem by which she is redeemed from herself. On the
pretext of getting some return for money he has lent her, he attacks her viciously. When Lord Worthy, who has been con-
veniently placed, hears her cry for assistance, he comes heroically
to her rescue, and she rewards him with her person and the
promise to withdraw from all her follies.

Ensign Lovely, an officer of the army, is in love with Valeria,
a learned young woman who returns his love but occupies herself with dissecting animals and speculating on the nature of
the universe. Her father is determined to marry her to a navy
officer, but the captain whom he selects decides that she is too
formidable for him and disguises Lovely as a sea captain so
that he can win her father's consent to marry her.

Sir James is tiring of an intrigue with Mrs. Sago, a drug-
gist's wife, who is passionately fond of gambling and who runs
up heavy debts against her husband in order to get money for
her pastime. In the end Sir James pays the debts on the ground
that he is merely refunding money that he had won from her,
and she persuades her husband, who knows nothing of the
liaison, to take her back. Sir James is glad to get rid of her so
easily. She promises to be good henceforth and to stick to her
own class in society.

Sir James himself is in love with Lucy, a religious young
woman who cares as tenderly for her reputation as for her

virtue. To win her he also gives up gambling and other ex-
cesses.

Most of *The Basset Table* seems to have been original with
Mrs. Centlivre. Hohrmann[31] sees a resemblance between Act
I, scene 2, and Regnard's *Le Divorce,* Act II, scene 2. Doubtless she had Regnard's scene in mind, but there are no identities
of language. On the whole her play is nearer to Shirley's
The Lady of Pleasure. Lady Reveller is a post-Restoration
edition of Aretina. Lord Worthy is Sir Thomas Bornwell, a
lover of his wife and of moderation in conduct. Valeria cor-
responds to Frederick, Aretina's nephew, just come from the
university. Mrs. Sago's intrigue ends in the same way as
Aretina's, and both reveal a shocking example of moral hy-
pocrisy.[32] But Mrs. Centlivre has not borrowed any language
or any particular scene from Shirley.

The fact that she professed to be writing a moral play and
that Arthur Bedford so regarded it raises the question of sentimentality. Professor Ernest Bernbaum[33] says that she avoided
sentimentality in *The Basset Table,* "where a female gamester
is reformed by an amusing stratagem, and in subsequent plays."
But it may be that he overemphasizes the element of plot.
Present are the attempt to correct a social vice, the reformation
of a character who is genuinely penitent, and a sympathetic
treatment of persons who deserve little sympathy in a reasonable world. It must be admitted that the conversion scene is
the result of a stratagem, so that there is no place for the in-
dulgence in moral platitudes and emotional demonstrations that
usually accompany sentimentality. Yet certainly there is here
little genuine comic characterization if it is to be distinguished
from the sentimental by the fact that the comic character, like

[31] "Das Verhältnis Susanna Centlivre's zu Molière und Regnard," pp. 416-
17. His suggestion has in its favor the fact that she had unquestionably used
one scene from *Le Divorce* in *The Perjur'd Husband.*

[32] Mrs. Sago's conversion is due to prudence rather than to morality.
She displays no emotion except in the false show by which she overcomes
her husband's doubts.

[33] *The Drama of Sensibility* (Boston, 1915), p. 100.

Valère in *Le Joueur*, goes off unrepentant, trusting that his fortune will turn with his next attempt.

Aside from Mrs. Centlivre's recognition of the great popularity of basset and piquet in London, the most interesting point in connection with the drama is the feminism of Valeria. She is really a charming young woman, with a true lover whom she intends to marry, but she is so much occupied with scientific experiments that she cannot take time for the usual lover's sighs. Professor Florence M. Smith[34] says that in this role Mrs. Centlivre was satirizing Mary Astell, who had become known by her writings in support of the female sex and its rights to education.[35] Valeria is occupied especially with her microscope, performing experiments on various sorts of frogs, fish, and flies. Despite her youthful foolishness, she is really good fun, as in this passage from Act II:

> *Lady [Reveller]*. . . . Why in such Haste, Cousin *Valeria?* [*Stopping her.*]
>
> *Val[eria]*. Oh! dear Cousin, don't stop me, I shall lose the finest Insect for Dissection, a huge Flesh Fly, which Mr. *Lovely* sent me just now, and opening the Box to try the Experiment, away it flew.
>
> *Lady*. I am glad the poor Fly escap'd; will you never be weary of these Whimsies?
>
> *Val*. Whimsies! Natural Philosophy a Whimsy! Oh! the unlearned World.
>
> *Lady*. Ridiculous Learning!
>
> *Alp[iew]*. Ridiculous, indeed, for Women; Philosophy suits our Sex as Jack-Boots would do.

[34] *Mary Astell* (New York, 1916), pp. 29-30. The first chapters of this book treat the origins of ideas for the education of women in England. Myra Reynolds in *The Learned Lady in England, 1650-1760* (Boston, 1920), p. 389, also discusses the relation of Valeria to the history of female learning. Swift was to satirize Mrs. Astell as Madonella in *Tatler* No. 32, and Steele likewise in *Tatler* Nos. 166 and 253.

[35] Molière had already ridiculed the learned lady in France, but he had made her a *précieuse* rather than a scientist or philosopher.

Val. Custom would bring them as much in Fashion as Furbeloes, and Practice would make us as valiant as e'er a Hero of them all: the Resolution is in the Mind—Nothing can enslave that.

Lady. My Stars! this Girl will be mad, that's certain.

Val. Mad! so *Nero* banish'd Philosophers from *Rome*, and the first Discoverer of the *Antipodes* was condemn'd for a Heretic.

Lady. In my Conscience, *Alpiew*, this pretty Creature's spoil'd. Well, Cousin, might I advise, you should bestow your Fortune in founding a College for the Study of Philosophy, where none but Women should be admitted; and to immortalize your Name, they should be called *Valerians*, ha, ha, ha.

Val. What you make a Jest of, I'd execute, were Fortune in my Power.

Alp. All Men would be excluded: the handsome Ensign, Madam.

Lady. In Love! Nay, there's no Philosophy against Love; *Solon* for that.

Val. 'Pshaw, no more of this trifling Subject; Cousin, will you believe there's any Thing without Gall.

Lady. I am satisfy'd I have one, when I lose at play, or see a Lady address'd when I am by; and 'tis equal to me, whether the rest of the Creation have or not.

Val. Well, but I'll convince you then; I have dissected my Dove———and positively I think the vulgar Notion true, for I could find none.

Lady. Oh, barbarous! killed your pretty Dove. [*Starting.*]

Val. Kill'd it! Why, what did you imagine I bred it up for? Can Animals, Insects, or Reptiles, be put to a nobler Use than to improve our Knowledge? Cousin, I'll give you this Jewel for your *Italian* Greyhound.

Lady. What to cut to pieces? Oh, horrid! he had need be a Soldier that ventures on you; for my Part, I should dream of nothing but Incision, Dissection, and Amputation, and always fancy the Knife at my Throat.

Enter Servant.

Serv. Madam, here's Sir Richard, and a ———

Val. A ——— What, is it an Accident, a Substance, a Material Being, or a Being of Reason?

Serv. I don't know what you call a Material Being, it is a Man.

Val. 'Pshaw, a Man, that's nothing.

Lady. She'll prove by and by, out of *Descartes* that we are all Machines.

When Valeria meets Hearty, a sea captain whom her father wants her to marry, she asks him as a matter of polite conversation whether he is "convinc'd there is a World in every Star." "We," she adds, "by our Telescopes, find Seas, Groves and Plains, and all that; but what they are peopled with, there's the Quere." The captain decides that she is not the woman for him: "The philosophical Gimcrack I don't value of a Cockle-Shell."

On one occasion Lovely tries to make love to her, but she insists instead on demonstrating the marvels of a tapeworm which she found in opening a dog and which she keeps in a box. Ensign Lovely does not care for her studies, but he wants to marry her and so humors her, even to bringing her specimens and helping her to fish her eels out of vinegar, which she uses as a preservative.

Valeria's query about a multiple universe shows her interest in the most popular and influential of the works advancing Cartesianism in England. Le Bovier de Fontenelle's *Entretiens sur la pluralité des mondes* was first printed in 1686 in Paris. Both Aphra Behn and Joseph Glanvil promptly translated it into English. Valeria herself belongs to the same group as the lady whom Fontenelle represents himself as instructing. We know that Mrs. Centlivre later borrowed a copy of Fontenelle from Anne Oldfield, but she may already have read it, as the joking attitude here would suggest.

All in all Valeria seems more like a humorous than a satirical portrait. Only foolish or eccentric people ridicule her, and the effect is that the learned lady, obviously an unpopular object in the theater, comes off as well as could be hoped. If Mrs. Centlivre establishes a thesis at all, it is that, no matter how learned a woman becomes, love will win in a contest with science. The opponents of Mrs. Astell's idea of a college[36] assumed that female education would destroy a woman's charm and her interest in a home. It is this contention, after all, that Valeria, despite her youthful curiosity, her childlike wit and seriousness, refutes. In the beginning of Act III she and Lovely are making some observations. He wishes her to elope with him, since her father is opposed to their marriage, but Valeria cannot think of leaving her microscope and all her collections to be destroyed. A moment later, on the approach of her father, she hastens to throw out some fish and hide Lovely under the empty tub. Sir Richard destroys everything just as she had feared. Despite laughter, our sympathies remain with Valeria. Tennyson in *The Princess* hardly advanced the argument for woman's education beyond the point reached by Mrs. Centlivre.

Ordinarily Susanna's dramatic preference is clearly for the army, but in *The Basset Table* she creates two sailors of the bluff and hearty type. Professor Harold Francis Watson[37] points out that the sailor in the drama from 1660 to 1700 reflects either the influence of *The Tempest* or that of the humors

[36] The Rev. A. G. L'Estrange, in his *History of English Humour* (1878, II, 332 ff.), comments on Mrs. Centlivre's purpose: "She often adopts the tone of the day in ridiculing learned ladies. In one place she speaks as if even at that time the founding of a college for ladies was in contemplation. . . ."

[37] *The Sailor in English Fiction and Drama, 1550-1800* (New York, 1931).

comedy, represented best by *The Plain Dealer* of Wycherley. Mrs. Centlivre's Captain Hearty and Captain Match (Ensign Lovely in disguise) both belong to the plain-dealer school. Hearty proposes to Valeria almost before he is introduced to her, but, after listening to her talk, he is glad enough to have her steer past him and to aid Lovely in winning Sir Richard's consent to marry her. Ensign Lovely's change of identity is also in line with the conventions of the plain-dealing school. When Lord Worthy challenges Captain Hearty for saluting Lady Reveller by kissing her hand, the captain characteristically brushes him aside:

> Look ye, Sir, what you mean by contending, I know not; but I must tell you, I don't think any Woman I have seen since I came ashore, worth fighting for. . . . But, Sir if you have a mind to a Breathing, here, tread upon my Toe, or speak but one Word in favor of the *French,* or against the Courage of our Fleet, and my Sword will start of itself, to do its Master and my Country Justice.

Accompanying the sailor business are demonstrations of hatred for the French, fear of the Pope, and love of England.

The bitterest satire in the play is directed against Mrs. Sago, the citizen's wife. She buys goods and charges them to her husband's account and then sells them to get money with which to gamble, and is received among the quality at the gambling table only because she has money and always loses. Even Sir James is glad to be rid of her. It is this satire which makes the Sago subplot unlike similar plots in the Restoration drama and even the subplot in *The Perjur'd Husband.*

As I have said, Arthur Bedford distinguished *The Gamester* and *The Basset Table* as the only two recent plays attempting to correct a current vice. Bedford, a Bristol clergyman, was Jeremy Collier's chief heir in the fight against the theater. His first treatise, *The Evil and Danger of Stage-Plays* (1706), seems petty in comparison with Collier's, for he generally quotes specific passages out of their context and fails to consider the bent of the whole play. His treatment of *The Gamester*, however, is sounder than usual:

> The *First* of these *Reform'd Plays* was *The Gamester*, design'd to expose this *Vice*, and consequently to aim at a *Reformation of Manners;* at least to impose upon the World, and make them think so. In this *Play* the *Devil* is invok'd in the *first Line* (a very good Beginning) and in *seven* other Places. There are several instances of *profane Swearing* and *Cursing*. The fine *Angelica* is dress'd in Men's Cloaths, as a Jest upon Deut. 23. 5. and *Valere* the *Gamester*, having first pretended a *Reformation*, and broken his solemn Vows, is upon the second Pretence (only by the *Poet* suppos'd to be real) rewarded with this fine *Lady* and *Ten Thousand Pounds*, and makes an honourable Exit, without any Penance. . . .[38]

Bedford also finds fault with *The Gamester* for mocking religion and ridiculing marriage.

Though admittedly written for reformation, *The Gamester* and *The Basset Table*, he says, have entirely the opposite effect. The epilogue of *The Gamester*, he admits, speaks out against gaming, but the play as a whole teaches that "*It is good to have Two Strings to our Bow*," for when Valere fails at gambling he is able to marry a rich fortune. As for *The Basset Table*, Lady Reveller "games and wins, and is afterward married to the *Lord Worthy*, one of the best *Reputation*."[39]

In her next play Mrs. Centlivre returned to the theory that drama should entertain rather than instruct. *Love at a Venture* was published in 1706 "As it is Acted by His Grace, the Duke of *Grafton*'s Servants, at the New Theatre in Bath."[40]

[38] P. 24. Bedford makes voluminous citations, which I omit.
[39] Pp. 128-29.
[40] According to the *Post Man* for April 20-22, 1704, "The New Theatre in Bath will be opened the First Week in May next." Belville S. Penley (*The Bath Stage*, 1892, p. 17) remarks that the theater referred to was

The Prologue, written for delivery at Bath, explains that, like other venturers for success in their callings, the author has strolled "with her Brat a Hundred Mile," "And hopes her Profits will her Charge defray." The Epilogue was spoken by Miss Jacobella Power, possibly the daughter of the John Power who owned the company.[41] According to Mottley, Susanna herself joined the players in Bath and acted in her own comedy.

In their travels about England Power and his company may have gone directly from Bath to Bristol, where they were presented for acting plays without license on August 10, 1706.[42] Since Mottley implies that Susanna continued with the company until she met Joseph Centlivre at Windsor, it is likely that she was one of those against whom the action was taken.

The plots of *Love at a Venture* are difficult to follow. Belair, under the guise of Colonel Revel just returned from Portugal, makes love to Beliza, and, under the name of Mr. Constant, an Oxfordshire gentleman in London for a lawsuit, makes love to Camilla, whom he has rescued from the Thames. Since Beliza and Camilla are cousins, he finds himself in the ridiculous position of trying to convince them that he is two people. His father, who has arranged a marriage for him and whom for that reason he wishes to avoid, learns that he has returned to England. At the same time Camilla's father orders

---

erected in 1705. Defoe in *A Tour through the Whole Island of Great Britain* (1725) notes that it was regarded as mean in both decorations and performances.

[41] See page 11. The epilogue spoken by Pinkethman to Burnaby's *The Modish Husband* (1702) is also included in Mrs. Centlivre's *Works*. It may have been used after her comedy in some of the privincial theaters. Burnaby, with his unmitigated irony, ridicules the attempts to reform the stage. He suggests that disbanding the players would really help them. Those lacking in piety could become physicians. The doorkeepers, *"whose Cheats we can't prevent"* (a common complaint), would thrive in government service. Impudent actors might turn lawyers. The "Under Fry" would need little, *"For by the Laws of England, younger Brothers starve"* anyway.

[42] Penley, *The Bath Stage*, p. 18; Sybil Rosenfeld, "The Players in Norwich, 1699-1709," *Review of English Studies*, XII (1936), 136. The archives at Bristol and at Bath contain nothing on this topic.

her to marry immediately the gentleman he has chosen for her. Imagine the surprise of Belair and Camilla when they learn that they had been intended for one another all along!

Sir William is jealously in love with Beliza, but tries to help Belair in his intrigues because his friend once saved his life in Spain. Imagine his suprise when he learns that Beliza is one of the objects of Belair's pursuit! But Beliza is really in love with Sir William, so that everything ends happily.

Sir William lives at the home of his sister, Lady Cautious, the wife of the wealthy but suspicious old Sir Paul Cautious. In order to assist Belair, he shares his rooms with him. As a result, Belair and Lady Cautious, who condemns Sir William for having helped her father to put her off on Sir Paul without a dowry, are brought together, but after two narrow escapes she decides that she values her reputation too much to see Belair again.

Belair also makes love to Patch, Beliza's maid, when she comes to bring him a message from Beliza, but they are interrupted and the affair is not revived. Robin, given his choice at the end between Patch and Flora, Camilla's woman, chooses Flora as a better type of permanent furnishing for his home.

In *Love at a Venture* the dramatist returns to the Restoration with a vengeance. Belair is Dorimant over again, with the one exception that Mrs. Centlivre always manages to save her women's virtue at the last moment.

Mottley correctly names the source of *Love at a Venture* as *Le Galant doublé* by Thomas Corneille, itself taken from *Hombre pobre todo es trazas* by Calderon.[43] Maximilian Hobohm has studied the relation of Mrs. Centlivre's comedy to Calderon's at great length.[44] In four separate literatures he notes five instances in which the main plot—that of one man's acting the parts of two men with two women—occurs: Plautus's

[43] Nicoll thinks that Dryden's *Secret Love* may also have suggested the plot.—*Early Eighteenth Century Drama* (Cambridge, 1925), p. 142.

[44] *Das Verhältnis von Susannah Centlivre's "Love at a Venture" zu Thomas Corneille's "Le Galant Doublé"* (Halle a. S., 1900).

Menaechmi, the three plays just named, and Colley Cibber's *The Double Gallant.* But he is convinced that Mrs. Centlivre used only Corneille's drama.

She alters somewhat the opening situation. In Corneille Don Fernand has killed his man at Seville and has hidden in Madrid, where he wishes to conceal his presence from Don Diègue, the father of his betrothed. Belair, on the other hand, has been called home to be married, but he desires to keep his arrival secret from his father, whose choice he has no desire to follow. Don Juan, Don Fernand's friend, becomes Sir William, the friend of Belair, and the Sir William-Beliza subplot is new: in *Le Galant doublé* Isabelle has a jealous lover whom she finally accepts, but he does not appear on the stage. The Sir Paul and Lady Cautious episodes are also added. Lady Cautious, an incomprehensible character, is at first a lustful wife, but when all gather at her house for the final pairing off of the various couples, she is a delightful woman and a charming hostess.

Hohrmann[45] thinks that Mrs. Centlivre took her Wou'd-be, a fop who apes Sir William's dress, from Molière's *Le Bourgeois gentilhomme,* but Hobohm believes that she had the project-maker of Jonson's *The Devil Is an Ass* in mind. She could have used no more than a suggestion from either. Hohrmann traces Wou'd-be's "Office for Poetry," which will furnish poets with all sorts of refined words, to the *académie de beaux esprits* which Mascarille wishes to found with the *précieuses (Les Précieuses ridicules)* and to the academy of *Les Femmes savantes.* But the scene in *Love at a Venture,* including also Wou'd-be's scheme for moving the streets of London by clockwork in order to get rid of hackney coachmen, is very brief and can contain no more than an allusion to any other play. Hobohm associates Sir Paul Cautious with Molière's *l'avare* and Hohrmann notices a resemblance between Sir Paul and *le malade imaginaire.* Perhaps it would be better

[45] "Das Verhältnis Susanna Centlivre's zu Molière und Regnard," pp. 73-75.

to say that Sir Paul is really the successor to all the old men
with young and unhappy wives of all the types of comedy
before Mrs. Centlivre.

Colley Cibber was immeasurably embarrassed by accusations
that he used *Love at a Venture* in his own *The Double Gallant*,
produced on November 1, 1707. The charges sometimes implied that he had copied out sections of her play while reading
it for the theater (he had rejected it, perhaps during the season
of 1705-6), though of course he could have used the printed
text.[46] Giles Jacob says that part of Cibber's play was borrowed
from *Love at a Venture*, and Mottley recalls that Mrs. Centlivre "used to complain" that Cibber "had taken in the greatest
Part of her Play." "But," adds Mottley, "Mr. *Cibber* understanding the *French* Language himself, why may we not suppose, that he translated it from the same Original, as she had
done?" In one place the *Biographia Dramatica* (II, 384-85)
copies Mottley literally; in another (II, 173) it speaks more
cautiously, calling *The Double Gallant* an imitation of Mrs.
Centlivre's play or her French source. H. A. Huntingdon[47]
reduces the whole argument to an epigrammatic phrase: "Love
at a Venture, the close resemblance of which to Cibber's Double
Gallant occasioned some controversy between the two authors,
happily terminated by the discovery that both authors knew
French equally ill, was produced at Bath in 1706."

[46] Years later when Cibber as poet laureate was the target of abuse from
various sides, the incident was still remembered: "*Aesopus* had a particular
Knack at stealing *Scenes*. . . . There was at this Time a certain *Poetess* in
Rome, called *Fulvia*, who had sometimes succeeded in Characters of Humour
on the Stage; she offer'd a Play to the Perusal of *Aesopus*; in this Play she
had drawn the Character of a very impudent Fellow, who in the same Play
acted under his own Appearance two different Persons, and persuaded his
Mistress to believe him not to be himself in Opposition to her Senses; this
Character *Aesopus* scouted extremely. Why, Madam, said he, this would
be putting upon the Audience indeed; they will never bear it; 'tis extravagant,
it is outraging Nature, it is silly, and it is not ridiculous. The poor Lady
was beat out of her Design; but as our Corrector had the Play left sometime
in his Hand, he culled out this very Character, mix'd it with some other
Felonies of the same Nature, which he had committed, and had it acted as
his own the very next Year. . . ."—*The Laureat: or, The Right Side of Colley
Cibber* (1740), pp. 111-12.
[47] *Atlantic Monthly*, XLIX (1882), 762.

The relations between the two plays have been studied by various scholars.[48] It is clear that Cibber took his basic story from *Love at a Venture,* that he used only the title from Corneille, and that he did not use Calderon[49] any more than Mrs. Centlivre had done. He consolidated parts of *Love at a Venture* with parts of William Burnaby's *The Ladies Visiting-Day* (1701) and *The Reform'd Wife* (1700). Though he changed the names of all his characters, a good deal of the original language remains. The opening scenes of the second act of *Love at a Venture* and *The Double Gallant* show how perfunctory at times was his rewriting:

Love at a Venture	*The Double Gallant*
Beliza. . . . there's my Hand, instruct me how I may be serviceable.	*Clarinda.* . . . There's my hand, tell me how I can serve you.
Camilla. Thus: I have sent *Flora* to give him an Invitation hither.———	*Sylvia.* Why thus;—— because I wou'd not wholly discover myself to him at once, I have sent him a note to visit me here, as if these lodgings were my own.
Beliza. Hither!—to my Lodgings; 'tis well I sent Colonel *Revel* Word I shou'd not be at home. [*Aside.*	*Clarinda.* Hither! to my lodgings! 'Twas well I sent Col. *Standfast* word I shou'd not be at home. [*Aside.*

· · ·   · · ·

[48] Genest, II, 389-90; Richard Besser, *Colley Cibber's The Double Gallant und seine Quellen* (Halle a. S., 1903); DeWitt C. Croissant, *Studies in the Work of Colley Cibber* (Reprinted from the Bulletin of the University of Kansas, "Humanistic Studies," Vol. I, No. 1, Lawrence, Kansas, 1912); F. W. Bateson, "*The Double Gallant* of Colley Cibber," *Review of English Studies,* I (1925), 343-46.

[49] Moritz Rapp adds *Hombre pobre todo es trazas* as a source for Cibber's play (*Studien über Englische Theater* [Tübingen, 1862], p. 177). Thomas Dibdin notes in *A Complete History of the Stage* (n.d.) that Burnaby's *The Reform'd Wife* is supposed to have been the basis of *The Double Gallant,* but, he says, "this is not true; for the source is Spanish, and Cibber went to the fountain head when the water was clear, Burnaby took his opportunity when the water was muddy."

Beliza. But how if my Lover Sir *William*, shou'd happen to come, who is grown a perfect *Spaniard* since his Travels, and has of late been apprehensive of a Rival, tho' from what cause I know not——the Country Gentleman wou'd be in Danger, I assure you.

Camilla. To prevent his being seen, I have order'd him to be brought in the Back-way . . . Cousin, you'll be at Hand.

Beliza. In the next Room.

Clarinda. . . . I am only afraid, my troublesome lover Mr. Clerimont, should happen to see him, who is of late, so impertinently jealous of a rival, tho' from what cause I know not—not but I lie too [*Aside*] I say, should he see him, your country gentleman wou'd be in danger, I can tell you.

Sylvia. O! there's no fear of that; for I have order'd him to be brought in the back way; . . . Cousin, you'll be at hand.

Clarinda. In the next room.

. *The Double Gallant* aroused a storm of protest when it was first presented.[50] Drury Lane revived *The Reform'd Wife* on Friday, October 31, the eve of the production of *The Double Gallant* at the Haymarket, and repeated it on the following Monday. Also a second edition of *The Ladies Visiting-Day* was issued in 1708. At first Cibber's comedy was acted only twice, and then twice more the first season. But when revived five years later, it became a popular stock piece.

[50] Barton Booth, the actor, wrote Aaron Hill that "as soon as the good-natur'd Town found [Cibber] out, they resented his calling [*The Double Gallant*] a new Play, and *hounded* it in a most outrageous Manner."—*A Collection of Letters, Never before printed: Written . . . To the Late Aaron Hill, Esq.* (1751), p. 80. Booth adds that Cibber's sources were "a Play of *Burnaby*'s and another of *Centlivre*'s," which had both been "heartily damn'd the first Night."

Cibber had earlier been accused, in *Visits from the Shades: or, Dialogues Serious, Comical, and Political* (1704), p. 21, of plagiarizing Lee's *Alexander the Great*.

Cibber attempted to excuse himself in the preface to the published comedy:

> When I undertook to make the following Sheets into a Play, I only propos'd to call it a Revis'd one; but some who had Read it were of Opinion, that the Additions in it were of Consequence enough to call it a New one; and the Actors proposing an Advantage by it, the little Concern I had for it, made me comply with their Desires: Notwithstanding I thought my self oblig'd in the Prologue to own how far other Authors had a Claim to it: But I found even that was not enough to silence the Criticks, who wou'd have the Pleasure of taking it to pieces, as if I had endeavour'd to put it upon 'em for a Correct Entertainment.

In his *Apology*[51] he mentions that *The Double Gallant* was "made up of what little was tolerable in two or three others that had no Success," and thus himself eliminates the possibility of a foreign source.

William Hazlitt liked *The Double Gallant* very much, especially the two central figures, but, as Mr. Bateson points out, his praise really belongs to Mrs. Centlivre and to Burnaby rather than to Cibber. Possibly to smooth over the difficulty with Mrs. Centlivre, Cibber himself accepted a part in her next play, *The Platonick Lady*, which was acted within a month of *The Double Gallant*, and two years later wrote the Epilogue for *The Man's Bewitch'd*.

The Platonick Lady had a run of four nights, November 25-28, 1706, at the Haymarket. Betterton took the role of Sir Thomas Beamont, uncle to Lucinda, and spoke the Prologue, written by Susanna's old friend, George Farquhar. Wilks acted Captain Beamont, who, under the name of Belvil, is

---

[51] Ed. R. W. Lowe (1889), II, 3-4. Cibber adds: "As I was only the Compiler of this Piece I did not publish it in my own Name; but as my having only a Hand in it could not be long a Secret, I have been often treated as a Plagiary on that Account."

Burnaby had died the year before, on November 8, 1706.

in love with Lucinda. Booth played Sir Charles Richley, and Cibber was Sharper, in search of a fortune. Mrs. Bracegirdle was Lucinda; Mrs. Oldfield, Isabella, contracted to Sir Charles but in love with Belvil; and Mrs. Willis, Mrs. Dowdy, a Somersetshire widow in London to acquire breeding. Norris, Pack, Mrs. Bicknell, Mrs. Mills, Mrs. Lee, and Mrs. Bullock took the minor roles.

Thomas Baker, author of *Tunbridge-Walks* (1703) and *Hampstead-Heath* (1705), wrote an epilogue for Mrs. Bracegirdle, but since it "came too late" to be used, Wilks spoke a short piece, printed in the original edition and in the complete works. In the complete works, another epilogue follows, "By Mr. *Norris* as Drawer," but it is not included in the first edition of the play. No mention of the sex of the author is made in the advertisements of the first performance, but the unspoken epilogue by Baker represents the *"scribbling Sot"* who wrote the play as praising *"his own"* sex and ridiculing women. Evidently the theater had again decided to represent the author as a man, but the fact that it was a woman's seems to have become known at the time of production.

Again Mrs. Centlivre had undertaken to write a Spanish comedy. Very few of the so-called Spanish comedies were actually taken from Spanish sources, though eighteenth-century stage historians often thought they were. Sometimes they came indirectly from the Spanish through the French, as in the case of *Love at a Venture;* at other times they were derived from earlier English plays or were created independently in imitation of what was conceived to be the Calderon or Spanish type. Romantic in plot and spirit, they contain far more of the emotions of love and jealousy than the Restoration comedies. In them usually a young woman is intriguing to marry a young man other than the one her father has selected for her, a popular theatrical situation despite the orthodox English view of the family. Usually a young man, though eager to make assignations with every pretty woman he sees, has his heart fixed on the one who is pursuing him. Another young man, deeply smitten, tries unavailingly to hide his jealousy, but his beloved always returns his love in the last act. Disguises are common, and the reputations of the young women are always protected. Duels are much talked of, but the young women discourage dueling, and few duels are actually fought. Both the young men and the young women are wealthy, often in possession of independent fortunes. The audience may find the type interesting because of the situations, often farcical, provoked by the plot of intrigue or because of the ups and downs of the love story. In general it would seem that Mrs. Centlivre's contemporaries were interested especially in the intrigues, but later the actors and actresses placed the stress increasingly on the emotions of the characters. Hence some of the plays written for the cynical post-Restoration audience came, by a mere shift of emphasis, to be also popular with the Romantics and the Victorians.

Genest (II, 329) calls *The Platonick Lady* "on the whole a good C[omedy]." The weaknesses of the play stand out in a brief summary of the plot. Lucinda, a Platonic lady, lives with her uncle, Sir Thomas. Belvil, of unknown parentage, has happened by at a crucial moment and protected them from robbers. He and Lucinda think they are in love, but Belvil has promised Sir Thomas, his good-natured benefactor, that he will not marry Lucinda without permission. Lucinda, a philosophical survival from the first half of the seventeenth century, is also protected by her Platonism.

Sir Charles and Isabella have been contracted by their fathers, but Sir Charles is in love with Lucinda and Isabella is in love with Belvil, who paid court to her when she was in a French convent five years before. Belvil and Isabella actually plighted their faith, but she was called home suddenly and has had no chance to give him her name and address. Now having seen him again she is determined to win him back, and assumes various disguises in order to attract him away from Lucinda.

First she comes masked into his house, fleeing, as she pretends, from an irate husband. Belvil shuts her and her maid in a room while he keeps an engagement with Lucinda, who has become suspicious of his excuses for not inviting her to see his pictures and has followed him home. Isabella and her maid get off masked, but Lucinda is suspicious and her thin veneer of Platonism buckles a little. Then Isabella, who has taken a course in dialect and manners from Mrs. Dowdy, the Somersetshire widow, presents herself to Lucinda as the daughter of a tenant. Later she contrives to have her maid, in fine array, beheld in Belvil's apartment. Again, as Donna Clara from Flanders she pretends to Lucinda and later to Belvil himself that she and Belvil were married and that she has borne him a son. Sir Thomas and Sir Charles arrive as Belvil pretends to treat her as his wife, and she is recognized. Belvil learns that he is really Lucinda's brother and that Isabella is the girl whom he lost in France. Sir Charles is married to Lucinda, and Belvil to Isabella.

In the meanwhile Belvil, by a profession of love, has managed to get some papers from Mrs. Dowdy. Sir Thomas explains that these are the papers to an estate of which Roger Dowdy has defrauded Belvil, whose parentage he concealed until the papers could be secured. Mrs. Brazen, the marriage-maker, puts Sharper off on Mrs. Dowdy as a knight, but loses her fee when he finds that Mrs. Dowdy is no longer as wealthy as he had supposed.

The scenes between Mrs. Dowdy and her milliner, mantua-maker, tirewoman, dancing master, and singing master recall the comedy of manners, as do the appearances of Sharper and his servant. The contrast between real gentlemen and ladies and the would-be kind and the stratagem for getting the estate back also suggest the Restoration type. In other respects the comedy of intrigue and disguises has taken over.

Despite the unpleasantness of the brother-sister relationship, the pointlessness of Isabella's masquerades, the impossibly romantic nature of the plot, and the fact that the Platonic woman was already an old story, *The Platonick Lady* is richer than many of Mrs. Centlivre's comedies in comments on contemporary life and in the variety of manners reflected.

Hohrmann traces parts of the play to Molière and Regnard. Mrs. Dowdy enjoys being called "your Ladyship" just as M. Jourdain of Molière's *Le Bourgeois gentilhomme* likes the titles *"Monseigneur"* and *"votre Grandeur,"* and she receives her singing and dancing masters much as he does. But there are no borrowings of language from Molière. The first scene of *The Platonick Lady* is in part translated from the beginning of Regnard's *Attendez-moi sous l'orme* (1694), a pastoral drama in twenty-four scenes. Dorante settles Pasquin's account by getting a receipt for his wages before making payment, and Sharper in the same fashion beats Equipage out of his earnings.[52] Mrs. Centlivre also uses scene vi of Regnard's play in the construction of the Mrs. Dowdy scenes in Act III. Both plays develop, for example, the opinion that fashions are devised for the hiding of defects:

> *Pasquin.* . . . Falbala par haut pour celles qui n'ont point de hanches; celles qui en ont trop le portent plus bas. Le cou long et les gorges creuses ont donné lieu à la steinquerque; et ainsi du reste.

> *Mrs. Turnup* [the mantua-maker]. . . . our Art lies in hiding the defects of Nature——Furbelows upwards, were devised for those that have no Hips, and two large ones, brought up the full-bottom'd Furbelows.

> *Mrs. Wheedle* [the milliner]. And a long Neck and a hollow Breast, first made use of the Stinkirk.

A final point concerns the country song which Mrs. Dowdy sings following her country dance in Act III. The *Papers* of

[52] Mrs. Centlivre uses the idea again in *The Perplex'd Lovers.*

the Shakespeare Society[53] contain an eleven-stanza ballad, "I'm
to be married o' Sunday," in illustration of the passage in *The
Taming of the Shrew*, II, i:

> We will have rings, and things, and fine array;
> And kiss me, Kate, *We will be married o' Sunday.*

The contributor received the ballad from a former printer at
York, who had it from an aunt. She was over seventy when
she recited it for him.

But in *Notes and Queries*[54] E. F. Rimbault calls attention
to this earlier printed version of five stanzas from *The Platonick
Lady*. He quotes Mrs. Centlivre's song, "with a few verbal
alterations for the sake of the fair writer's reputation."

The first stanza of the Shakespeare Society version is:

> As I walk'd forth one May morning,
> I heard a fair maid sweetly sing,
> As she sat under her cow milking,
> We will be married o' Sunday.

Mrs. Centlivre's first stanza is almost identical:

> *As I walk'd forth one* May *morning,*
> *I heard a pretty Maid sweetly sing*
> *As she sat under the Cow a milking,*
> Sing I shall be marry'd a *Tuesday;*
> I mun look smug upon *Tuesday.*

Her other stanzas are slightly different from the four following stanzas in the Shakespeare Society version. It is conceivable
that Mrs. Centlivre may have composed the song, but it seems
more likely that she merely adapted it from one which she
had heard, perhaps in Holbeach, and which Mr. Wilson, the
printer, had heard in York. Except that it is much too sophisti-
cated, one might be tempted to say that this is the song which,
according to Giles Jacob, she wrote when she was seven and

---

[53] I (1844), 80-82.
[54] Second ser., V (1858), 43.

which, according to the life in her complete works, became a famous country dance.

The Platonick Lady was published in February, 1707. The Dedication, "To all the Generous Encouragers of *Female Ingenuity*," is Mrs. Centlivre's master appeal for a fair consideration of a work on its merits. She makes the present type of address, she avers, "hoping . . . to find some Souls great enough to protect her against the Carping Malice of the Vulgar World; who think it a proof of Sense, to dislike every thing that is writ by Women. I was the more induc'd to this General Application, from the Usage I have met on all sides." She tells how an anonymous play is approved by everyone and makes money for producer and publisher, unless by chance it is discovered to be fatherless, "with this Reason only, *It is a Woman's*." Finally she accuses the critics of malice in inventing the slander that her plays have been given her by some gentleman:

> Some have arm'd themselves with a resolution not to like a Play they paid to see; and if in spite of Spleen they have been pleas'd against their Will, have maliciously reported it was none of mine, but given me by some Gentleman: Nay, even my own Sex, which shou'd assert our prerogative against such Detractors, are often backward to encourage a Female Pen.

No doubt Susanna did on occasion receive help from friendly gentlemen (and ladies too), for, as we shall find, Rowe helped her with *The Cruel Gift* and Mottley with *A Bold Stroke for a Wife*. But in this age of literary clubs and gatherings when the custom was to pass one's compositions around for improvement the remarkable thing would have been for her not to receive suggestions of any kind.

Women writers had a hard time at the beginning of the eighteenth century. They were often ridiculed and nearly always condemned. *The Female Wits: or, The Triumvirate of Poets at Rehearsal* (1704), "Acted some Years since," is a satire on the three women playwrights of the end of the seventeenth century—Mrs. Manley, Mrs. Pix, and Mrs. Trotter. More general in its application is *A Comparison Between the Two Stages* (1702), both attributed and denied to Charles Gildon by present-day scholars, which is very severe on the female wits. Even when allowance is made for the fact that Critick is himself ridiculous, a passage like this[55] shows the view of the time:

> S[*ullen*].   Oh this is a Lady's!
>
> Crit[*ick*].   How's that?——*Audetq; viris contendere virgo?*
>
> R[*amble*].   See how *Critick* starts at the naming a Lady.
>
> *C.* What occasion had you to name a Lady in the confounded Work you're about?
>
> *S.* Here's a Play of hers.
>
> *C.* The Devil there is: I wonder in my Heart we are so lost to all Sense and Reason: What a Pox have the Women to do with the Muses? I grant you the Poets call the Nine Muses by the Names of Women, but why so? not because the Sex had any thing to do with Poetry, but because in that Sex they're much fitter for prostitution.
>
> *R.* Abusive, now you're abusive, Mr. *Critick.*
>
> *C.* Sir I tell you we are abus'd: I hate these Petticoat-Authors; 'tis false Grammar, there's no Feminine for the *Latin* word, 'tis entirely of the Masculine Gender, and the Language won't bear such a thing as a She-Author.

Chiefly against the women writers was the fact, as Mrs. Centlivre says, that they were women, but in addition they early secured a reputation for "writing Bawdy." Peter Anthony Motteux wrote in the prologue which he contributed for Mrs. Pix's *The Innocent Mistress* (1697):

> *Methinks I see some here who seem to say*
> *Gad, e're the Curtain's drawn I'll slip away;*

[55] Pp. 26-27.

No Bawdy, this can't be a Women's Play.
Nay, I confess there's Cause enough to doubt,
But, Faith, they say there was a deal cut out. . . .

Other writers had to endure the ill repute that Mrs. Behn and Mrs. Manley had achieved. In her off moments, it must be confessed, Mrs. Centlivre also contributed to the notoriety of female writers. But writing in a man's world, they were using the standards and accommodating the taste which they found.[56]

[56] The female wits are not above asking chivalry from the critic. Mrs. Pix in her preface to *Ibrahim* (1696) is an instance: "*I am very sensible those that will be so unkind to Criticize upon what falls from a Womans Pen, may soon find more faults than I am ever able to answer.*" They felt that they were entitled to special consideration because inadequate means had been provided for their education. Note, for example, this statement by Mrs. Eliza Haywood in the preface to *Frederick, Duke of Brunswick-Lunenburgh* (1729): "*I depend the candid Reader will forgive the Want of those Embellishments of Poetry, which the little Improvements my Sex receives from Education, allow'd me not the Power to adorn it with.*"

Marriage *and* Recognition

M RS. CENTLIVRE'S ventures in playwriting had obviously not made her self-supporting. Hence she continued to stroll. Having joined Power's Duke of Grafton's Servants at Bath for the presentation of *Love at a Venture,* she continued with them, according to Mottley, until she attracted the attention of Joseph Centlivre at Windsor:

> Entered in the strolling Company, she attended them to several Parts of *England,* and about the Year 1706, the Court being at *Windsor,* she there put on her Breeches again, and acted the Part of ALEXANDER the GREAT, in the Tragedy of that Name. She played this Part, it seems, to great Perfection. How much she was admired by the rest of the Court is, at this Time, uncertain; but she so greatly charmed one Courtier, of inferior Rank indeed, Mr. *Joseph Centlivre,* one of her Majesty's Cooks, that he fell in Love with, and married her.

No doubt the play was Lee's *The Rival Queens, or The Death of Alexander the Great.* Her first acting part, it will be recalled, had been that of Parisatis in this tragedy.

The marriage license, recorded in the Bishop of London's Registry, is dated April 19, 1707:

19th April 1707

Susannah Caroll als Rawkins of the Parish of St. Paul Covent Garden Midd. Widdow and Joseph Cent Livre of the Parish of St. James Westm. Midd. Widower to be married in the Parish Church of St. Clement Danes in Middlesex.

The marriage took place four days later, not at St. Clement Danes, but at St. Bene't.[1]

Centlivre was yeoman of the mouth to Queen Anne, a position which he had held under William and would continue to hold until after Susanna's death in 1723. At this time the employees in the Queen's Privy Kitchen included four master cooks, one yeoman of the mouth, three yeomen who received the same wages as the yeoman of the mouth but were inferior in rank, four grooms, four children, and several less important persons.[2] The yeoman's position annually paid £55 board wages and £5 wages and the master cook's double that amount. The yeoman of the mouth was also due the sum of £1 6s. from each person knighted.

Mottley implies that Susanna swept Joseph Centlivre off his feet.[3] Nevertheless, he maintained sufficient presence of mind to negotiate a marital contract with his bride-to-be. In his will, unchanged following Susanna's death, he allowed her £50, pursuant to an arrangement they had made before marriage. With him she lived, as Mottley says, "in a decent clean Manner." We do not know where they resided at first, but from 1713 until Mrs. Centlivre's death the couple were estab-

---

[1] *The Publications of the Harleian Society, Registers,* Vol. XXXIX, for the year 1910. *The Registers of St. Bene't and St. Peter, Paul's Wharf, London,* ed. Willoughby A. Littledale (1910), p. 67.

For the significance of the name Rawkins see page 13.

[2] John Chamberlayne, *Magnae Britanniae Notitia: or, The Present State of Great-Britain* (1708), p. 605.

[3] Dr. Doran (*Annals of the English Stage,* ed. and rev. by Robert W. Lowe [1888], I, 124) made the same kind of observation. Though he got his dates and titles mixed, he makes the pleasant reminder that her marriage gave her a bond of affinity with Betterton, the son of a king's cook:

"The powers of Mrs. Carroll had such an effect on Mr. Centlivre, one of the cooks to Queen Anne, that he straightway married her; and when, a few months later, Betterton played Sir Thomas Beaumont, in the lady's comedy, '*Love at a Venture*' [Note by Lowe: "Should be Sir Thomas Beaumont in '*The Platonick Lady*' "], his friend, a royal cook's wife, furnished but an indifferent part for a royal cook's son."

lished in Buckingham Court, adjoining Spring Gardens, Charing Cross.

For the first time since she had begun to write Mrs. Centlivre relaxed before trying another play. The effect was good, for this time she demonstrated greater originality than usual and won popular favor. *The Busy Body,* her most successful comedy, was produced on May 12, 1709. It was advertised in the *Daily Courant* for four nights straight and for May 21, 28, and June 4. Mrs. Centlivre received benefits on May 14 and May 21. The second benefit, when the play was given at the desire of "several Ladies of Quality," was probably the sixth performance, although only four known performances had preceded it.[4] The repetition on May 28, "At the Desire of several Persons of Quality," was for the benefit of "Mrs. Pixes Executor."[5] The *Post Boy*[6] says that the benefit was for "the Family of Mrs. Mary Pix, deceas'd" and adds gratuitously that "the greatest part" of *The Busy Body* "and also of that of the Gamester, was wrote by the said Mrs. Pix." Mary Pix had clearly lived beyond her means, but a theatrical benefit for a distressed person or family that had contributed to the stage was not extraordinary. She and Susanna had been good friends, and it may well be that they had helped one another with their plays. Perhaps it was from the older dramatist that Susanna had acquired her belief that extreme business in a play was certain to please.

The original cast was well suited to the needs of *The Busy Body.* Pack took the role of Marplot admirably.[7] Wilks was

---

[4] It was printed on May 31 "as it was *seven* Days acted at the Theatre Royal in Drury-Lane."

[5] *Daily Courant.* The *DNB* says that Mary Pix died about 1720.

[6] May 26-28, 1709.

[7] Chetwood considered Pack "excellent in many Parts, as *Marplot* in the *Busy Body.*"—*A General History of the Stage* (Dublin, 1749), p. 210. A letter from "The Wagg" to either the *Tatler* or the *Spectator* notes that the different players on benefit nights drew crowds like themselves. "Pack had the buisy-bodies, the merry songsters, and all the ladies."—*Original and Genuine Letters sent to the Tatler and Spectator, During the Time those Works were publishing. None of which have been before Printed* (1725), I, 16. He

a delightful Sir George Airy.   Estcourt, Mills, Bullock, and
Bullock, Jr., had developed into first-rate actors.   Mrs. Cross
as Miranda, Mrs. Rogers as Isabinda, Mrs. Saunders as Patch,
in some ways the plot-maker of the piece, and Mrs. Mills as
Scentwell were fully equal to their parts.

Thomas Baker's prologue arrived on time—perhaps he was
atoning for his neglect in the case of *The Platonick Lady*.   Evidently the attempts to preserve anonymity for Mrs. Centlivre's
dramas were over, for he refers to the play as *"a Woman's
Treat."*[8]   Steele promised the author an epilogue.   When it
still had not arrived at the last moment, she sent him a short
verse epistle through "sweet-scented Charles Lillie," a perfumer
and dealer in snuff at whose shop he received communications
for the *Tatler*, reminding him of the obligation.   Steele gave
Lillie the writings which he had not used in his paper, and in
time Lillie was responsible for getting the message into print:

No prologue yet come from sweet-scented Charles Lillie;
Good faith, I begin to look cursedly silly:
If I han't it to night, what full tides of sorrow
Will o're-whelm your poor scribe, at rehearsal to morrow?
Take pitty for once on a woman distressed,
As you hope to be ever by woman caressed:
And if no compassion the Censor will feel,
I'll rank him no more with immortal Dick Steel.
Once more supplicate him with prayers most fervant,
That he would not baulk,
                              Sir,
                              Your most humble Servant,
                              SUSANNAH CENT-LIVRE.[9]

Not even the poem worked.   But Steele, as we shall see, did

---

was well known as a singer of stage songs and of the female parts in singing
dialogues with Leveridge, the famous singing master and entertainer of the
period.

[8] The prologue is largely an attack on Thomas D'Urfey's *The Modern
Prophets.*

[9] *Original and Genuine Letters sent to the Tatler and Spectator*, II, 33.

make handsome amends by praising her comedy in the *Tatler*. Presumably she wrote the Epilogue herself.

Mottley explains that Mrs. Centlivre had a hard time getting her play acted, the players not acting it until late in the season. At rehearsal one morning, he says, Wilks thought so badly of his role of Sir George Airy that "in a Passion he threw it off the Stage into the Pit, and swore that no body would bear to sit to hear such Stuff." He took it up again only when the poetess begged him with tears in her eyes. Those who had heard of the play in advance knew only that "it was a silly thing wrote by a Woman" and that the players "had no Opinion of it." On the first night the few who came yawned at the beginning, but shortly their interest was aroused and they concluded by applauding the comedy roundly. Audiences increased and the play continued till the thirteenth night. The next year when the company divided, he says, "it was acted at both Houses together for six Nights running in Opposition to one another," Pack taking the part of Marplot at Drury Lane and Dogget at the Haymarket.

Genest (II, 419) thinks that, since *The Busy Body* was acted only three times running at the Haymarket in October and twice at Drury Lane in November, the whole story may be false.[10] But to support the statement that Wilks threatened to resign his part there is contemporary evidence in the *Female Tatler*, No. 41 (October 7-10, 1709), on the eve of the three-day run at the Haymarket. Mrs. Cavil opposes the idea that Mrs. Crackenthorpe should write a play, because "the *Treatment Authors* meet with from the *Play'rs*, is too gross for a *Woman* to bear, since at the getting up of so successful a *Comedy* as the *Busy Body*, Sir *Harry Wild-Air* in great *dudgeon* flung his *Part* into the *Pitt* for damn'd *Stuff*, before the *Lady's Face* that wrote it."

The *Biographia Dramatica* tells a similar story of *A Bold Stroke for a Wife* and quotes a remark attributed to Wilks,

---

[10] It was actually presented at the Haymarket on Oct. 11, 13, 15, and Nov. 1 and at Drury Lane on Nov. 26, Dec. 8 and 26.

"*not only her play would be damned, but she herself be damned for writing it.*" But it seems likely that the story developed from this earlier one regarding *The Busy Body*. The *Biographia Dramatica* adds that, in spite of the prejudice of the audience, *The Busy Body* "forced a run of thirteen nights; while Mr. Congreve's *Way of the World*, which perhaps contains more true intrinsic wit, and unexceptionable accuracy of language, than any dramatic piece ever written, brought on the stage with every advantage of recommendation, and when the author was in the height of reputation, could scarcely make its way at all." Lord Byron gives a neat twist to the *Biographia Dramatica's* views and offers them as his own:

> I also know that Congreve gave up writing because Mrs. Centlivre's balderdash drove his comedies off. So it is not *decency*, but Stupidity, that does all this; for Sheridan is as *decent* a writer as need be, and Congreve no worse than Mrs. Centlivre, of whom Wilks (the actor) said, "not only her play would be damned, but Shee too." He alluded to a *Bold Stroke for a Wife*.[11]

The idea that Mrs. Centlivre, whose plays were more popular in Byron's day than those of her contemporaries, in any way influenced Congreve to stop writing seems to us absurd, but Byron stuck to his guns:

> Nothing so easy as intricate confusion of plot, and rant. Mrs. Centlivre, in comedy, has *ten times the bustle of Congreve;* but are they to be compared? and yet she drove Congreve from the theatre.[12]

Perhaps Steele did more than anyone else to neutralize the fact that *The Busy Body* was a woman's play. In *Tatler* No. 15, for May 14, 1709, the day after the comedy was acted for the second time, he gave a naïve rebuke to those would-

[11] *The Works of Lord Byron, Letters and Journals*, ed. R. E. Prothero (1922), IV, 426-27.
[12] *Ibid.*, V, 218-19.

be wits who had condemned this particular piece before it was acted:

> To-night [May 13] was acted a second time a comedy, called THE BUSY BODY: this play is written by a lady. In old times, we used to sit upon a play here after it was acted; but now the entertainment is turned another way; not but there are considerable men in all ages, who, for some eminent quality or invention, deserve the esteem and thanks of the public. . . . if reason is not to be present at our greatest satisfaction, of all the race of creatures, the human is the most miserable. It was not so of old; when Virgil describes a wit, he always means a virtuous man; and all his sentiments of men of genius, are such as show persons distinguished from the common level of mankind; such as placed happiness in the contempt of low fears and gratifications; fears which we are subject to with the vulgar; and pleasures which we have in common with beasts.

By the second night it is clear that the town had begun to change its mind about *The Busy Body*. Steele returned to the subject in *Tatler* No. 19, for May 24:

> On Saturday last was presented THE BUSY BODY, a comedy, written (as I have heretofore remarked) by a woman. The plot and incidents of the play are laid with that subtilty of spirit which is peculiar to females of wit, and is very seldom well performed by those of the other sex, in which craft in love is an act of invention, and not, as with women, the effect of nature and instinct.

Susanna Centlivre never forgot her indebtedness to him.

The play was popular in the library as well as on the stage, two editions appearing the first year. Despite its popularity, however, Lintot paid her the minimum at this time for printing rights—£10.[13] I have examined more than forty editions or

---

[13] Nichols, *Literary Anecdotes* (1812-15), VIII, 294. Cibber received £3 4s. 6d. for *Love's Last Shift* (1696), Rowe, £75 5s. for *Lady Jane Grey*

separate printings between 1709 and 1884, including two from
Boston (1794, 1822), one from New York (1817), and a
German translation, *Er Mengt Sich in Alles,* by T. E. Jünger
(*Deutsche Schaubühne,* Vol. LIV, Augsburg, 1793). For light
entertainment of the general audience *The Busy Body* is a
masterly comedy, which left its impress upon various other
plays and entertainments of the succeeding centuries without
being quite equaled by any of them.

The two plots of *The Busy Body* are relatively simple,
for the Spanish comedy of intrigue. Sir George Airy loves
Miranda, but her old guardian, Sir Francis Gripe, desires to
marry her himself. Charles, son of the miserly Sir Francis,
is in love with Isabinda, intended by her father, Sir Jealous
Traffick, for the son of a wealthy Spanish merchant. Marplot,
also a ward of Sir Francis, wanders about trying to be of service
to his friends, Charles and Sir George, but instead always manages to interrupt one of their stratagems.

Miranda tests Sir George by meeting him in the park
masked. When Sir George tries to find out who she is, she
promises to unmask if he will turn his back, but instead she
steals off. Sir George purchases an hour's conversation with
her from Sir Francis for a hundred guineas, but she refuses to
talk and so to reveal herself as the incognita. By wheedling
Sir Francis into thinking that she will marry him, she gets the
papers to her own and to Charles's estate. Then she invites
Sir George to visit her by telling Marplot to advise Sir George
not to come again to the garden gate at eight o'clock for fear
of a blunderbuss. He comes, recognizes her as both Miranda
and the unknown, accepts her proposal (he insists that her
£30,000 is immaterial), and they are married, much to the
discomfiture of Sir Francis, who refuses to forgive them.

Charles disguises himself as the Spanish suitor who is
supposed to have just arrived, and with the help of Sir George

---

(1715), Addison, 50 guineas for *The Drummer* (1716), Cibber, £105 for
The Non-Juror (1718), Southerne, £120 for *The Spartan Dame* (1719), and
Steele, £40 for *The Conscious Lovers* (1723).

he secures Sir Jealous's consent to marry Isabinda, who finally becomes agreeable when informed of the stratagem. Marplot almost spoils everything by searching for a friend of his in a Spanish disguise, but Sir George holds Sir Jealous and his servants off until the ceremony is completed. Sir Jealous realizes that he has been completely outwitted, accepts the results with good grace, and closes the play with this bit of romantic counsel:

> *By my Example let all Parents move,*
> *And never strive to cross their Childrens Love;*
> *But still submit that Care to Providence above.*

Marplot is an original comic creation of genuine humor who has served as a vehicle for many of the greatest English actors. But in addition to the splendid acting scenes in which Marplot appears there are others equally good which lend variety to the play. Sir George's visit with the masked Miranda in the park, his making love to the silent Miranda in the presence of Sir Francis, and the scene of the Spanish disguise are worth noting.[14]

William Weidler tries to trace *The Busy Body* to Molière's *L'Étourdi*,[15] but he finds no close resemblances between any of the situations. The disguise of Charles as the Spaniard can hardly have been taken, as he supposes, from any one of the three disguises in *L'Étourdi*. If a source for masquerading in an intrigue drama is necessary, Mrs. Centlivre's scene is nearer the disguise of Courtine as Prince Alexander, a Muscovite, in Burnaby's *The Ladies Visiting-Day* or to the disguise of Careless as Prince Alexander in Cibber's *The Double Gallant*.

Weidler also discusses the relationship between *The Busy Body* and Dryden's *Sir Martin Mar-all* (1668), which Hazlitt names as the "origin" of Mrs. Centlivre's comedy. Dryden's

---

[14] Mrs. Centlivre uses half a dozen speeches in Spanish, but it is as hard to accept these as proof that she knew Spanish as it is to take the Horatian motto on the title page as proof that she knew Latin.

[15] *Das Verhältnis von Mrs. Centlivre's 'The Busy Body' zu Molière's 'L'Étourdi' und Ben Jonson's 'The Divell is an Asse'* (Halle a. S., 1900).

play is based on a translation of Molière's *L'Étourdi* by the Duke of Newcastle and on Quinault's *L'Amant indiscret, ou le maître étourdi*. Mrs. Centlivre may have got the name Marplot from Mar-all, but little else.

Other suggested sources may be mentioned. The *Biographia Dramatica* says that she "seems to have borrowed the hint of her Marplot" from Scrutinio in Sir Francis Fane's *Love in the Dark* (1675), but Genest (I, 174) points out that Intrigo rather than Scrutinio is meant. Intrigo and Marplot are similarly described before they appear, but Marplot is genial and, as he thinks, useful to his friends, whereas Intrigo is made the butt of ridicule and satire. Also Sir George, in love with one mistress whom he knows by sight and another whose face he has never seen, is in much the same situation as Trivultio, who, though in love with Aurana, intends to have an intrigue with Bellinganna, the beautiful young wife of the old banker Cornanti. Finally, there is a similarity in the methods by which Miranda invites Sir George to come to the garden gate and Bellinganna dupes her confessor into sending Trivultio to her.[16] But the similarities are not such as to prove borrowing.

It has also been suggested that Mrs. Centlivre may have been imitating *The Husband His Own Cuckold* (1696) by John Dryden, Jr. In the preface to his son's comedy Dryden writes: "The Story he has treated, was an Accident which happen'd at *Rome*, though he has transferr'd the Scene to *England*." In Dryden's play Mrs. Lurch by indirection invites Feewell to visit her, but the maid Betty does not trust to the subtlety of Feewell's intelligence and makes the invitation more specific. Also Mrs. Lurch has provided a rope and ladder which Feewell can use for escaping her bedchamber window in case they are surprised. After Feewell has escaped on the arrival of Lurch, Betty remarks, as does Patch after Charles has escaped, "The Bird is flown," so that the husband's search in

[16] Fane follows the *Decameron*, Day III, Novel 3, rather closely.

Dryden and the father's search in Centlivre is no longer to be feared. But again the similarities are not very exact.

The source of the dumb scene with Miranda and the threat to the young man who may appear at the garden gate, as the *Biographia Dramatica* points out, is apparently Jonson's *The Devil Is an Ass*. The first goes back ultimately to the *Decameron*, Day III, Novel 5, and the second to Day III, Novel 3.[17] Weidler argues convincingly that Mrs. Centlivre takes her scenes from Jonson and not from Boccaccio. Jonson's avaricious Fitzdottrel is as glad to exchange a conversation with his wife for a beautiful cloak as Boccaccio's Signieur Francesco Vergellesi is to exchange a conversation with his wife for a lovely horse. In each instance the wife is true to her husband until commanded by him to grant the interview. Both husbands order their wives not to reply to their visitors' speeches. Miranda, however, who is only the potential wife of Sir Francis and welcomes the adventure, voluntarily requests to be allowed to feign dumbness, since she does not wish Sir George to recognize her voice as that of his incognita. The language is reminiscent of Jonson's, but there is no copying. The way in which Mrs. Centlivre has laundered the scenes by fitting them into romantic love stories indicates a real accomplishment on her part. Her better plays, despite various statements to the contrary, reflect a different attitude toward life than do the comedies of humors or the comedies of manners.

The closest original of Marplot is Pug of *The Devil Is an Ass*. When Wittipol visits Mrs. Fitzdottrel to keep an assignation, Pug, upon whom she has brought a beating when he was really intent upon serving her, maliciously introduces the husband. Marplot, on the other hand, imagining that some

[17] See further *The Devil Is an Ass* by Ben Jonson, ed. W. S. Johnson ("Yale Studies in English," Vol. XXIX, 1905), pp. lxxv-lxxvi. Johnson traces Mrs. Centlivre's scenes to Jonson, but adds that she "seems to have been acquainted with the *Decameron* also." Herford and Simpson say that "she appears to have used Boccaccio rather than Jonson" for Sir George's conversation with the dumb Miranda (*Ben Jonson*, Oxford, 1925, X, 230).

harm may befall Sir George, since he seems to rejoice at being threatened with a blunderbuss, informs Sir Francis in order to have him warn Miranda of the danger of murder. Though Marplot is a gentleman, curious but not malicious, he, like Pug, wanders aimlessly through the play, always desiring to be a part of the action but invariably finding himself left out. Other motifs which may show Jonson's influence are Miranda's trick to have the estate settled upon her, Charles's disguise as a Spaniard, and Traffick's jealous care of Isabinda.[18]

The extent to which scholars have sought sources for *The Busy Body* is surprising. They seem to have assumed that Mrs. Centlivre could not write a play of her own. Except for the two scenes from Jonson, her borrowings are general and no discredit to her.[19] What she has done is to superimpose a Spanish intrigue plot upon a comedy of humors. The continuation of the humors tradition is indicated by the use of names like Airy, Jealous, Gripe, Traffick, Marplot, Whisper, Patch, Scentwell, Meanwell, and Tackum. Within the limitations of the romantic materials, *The Busy Body* is well motivated, the characters are adequately drawn, suspense is excellently maintained, the characters are easily followed, and the episodes are closely knit by the transference of characters from one plot to another and by the omnipresence of Marplot.

During the first half of the eighteenth century *The Busy Body* was Mrs. Centlivre's most popular drama. It was acted more than 250 times before 1750 and over 200 additional times

[18] R. Cumberland in his notes on *The Busy Body* in the *British Drama* (1817, Vol. X) adds Congreve's *Love for Love*, Act V, scene 1, between Angelica and Sir Sampson, as the source of the interview between Sir Francis and Miranda at the beginning of Act II and argues that in the next scene between Charles and his father she is copying Valentine and Sir Sampson under different names. Yet these resemblances are common to the intrigue plots.

[19] The scene between Miranda and Sir George in the park is a variation of a motif common in the Spanish plays. Mrs. Centlivre uses it also in *The Platonick Lady* and *The Wonder*, and it is found in earlier plays like Dryden's *Secret Love* (1668), Fane's *Love in the Dark*, and Ravenscroft's *The Wrangling Lovers* (1677).

before 1800. It continued as a stock piece through the nineteenth century.

On the division of the Drury Lane company at the end of the 1708-9 season, Wilks, Estcourt, Bullock, Mills, Mrs. Cross, and Mrs. Saunders went to the Queen's Theatre in the Haymarket, where they kept their parts and performed the play five times in 1709-10. The role of Marplot went to Dogget, according to Cibber "the most an Original, and the strictest Observer of Nature, of all his Contemporaries."[20] Genest (III, 52) says that Mrs. Margaret Saunders "seems to have been the best Chambermaid of her time." Her role of Patch became one of the key roles in the play. It is she who brings Charles and Isabinda together despite the watchfulness of Sir Jealous Traffick and plans the Spanish disguise.

Drury Lane, which had been silenced because the management had not paid the actors the full receipts from their benefits, was not opened until late in November, 1709. *The Busy Body* was produced on November 26, Pack continuing with Marplot. The rest of the cast took their parts for the first time. Powell acted Sir George Airy; Booth replaced Mills as Charles; Norris was Sir Francis Gripe; and Leigh took the part of Sir Jealous Traffick. Miranda, Isabinda, Patch, and Scentwell were played by Mrs. Moore, Mrs. Bradshaw, Mrs. Cox, and Mrs. Finch. The play had five performances during the season.

Shortly after the opening of the next season Drury Lane was entirely given over to plays and the Haymarket to operas. *The Busy Body* was acted twice, with the important parts taken by the original cast, except that of Miranda, which was acted on the first occasion by Hester Santlow and on the second by Mrs. Bicknell, and that of Isabinda, which was acted by Mrs. Porter. It was repeated once during each of the next two seasons. On September 24, 1713, a special performance was given at Drury Lane for the "Entertainment of his Excellency the Duke d'Aumont, Ambassador extraordinary from the Court of France."

[20] *An Apology for the Life of Mr. Colley Cibber* (1889), II, 158.

On December 18, 1714, John Rich opened the rebuilt Lincoln's Inn Fields Theatre, and some of the Drury Lane actors joined him. He produced *The Busy Body* five times during the season, with Pack, Bullock, Bullock, Jr., Mrs. Cross, and Mrs. Rogers in their original parts. It was acted three times during 1715-16 and three during the next season. Much of the time the earnings were low, this theater having a hard time for a number of years.[21]

"At the particular Desire of several Ladies of Quality," Mrs. Centlivre received a benefit at Drury Lane on May 5, 1715. She provided the entire program, the afterpiece being *The Custom of the Country*, the revived and renamed *A Bickerstaff's Burying*. It looks as if she were being repaid for her support of the Hanoverians. On October 22, 1717, *The Busy Body* was repeated by command of the Prince of Wales instead of *Othello*, which had been advertised for that day, and again on October 23. The King himself commanded a performance on December 14, 1719, and again, this time at least for the benefit of the author, on March 17, 1720. The theater gave her another benefit on April 14, 1722, with Wilks, Norris, Mills, and Mrs. Saunders in their original roles. Miller, who was first advertised for the part in a production at Pinkethman's theater in Richmond on July 28, 1718, was the Busy Body at this time.

Spiller, who had apparently first acted Marplot at Pinkethman's theater in Greenwich on August 7, 1710, took the part at Lincoln's Inn Fields on November 4, 1720. It was his in 1721-22 except on March 10, when Pack played Marplot for Mrs. Bullock's benefit, it being, according to the advertisements, "the first Time of his Acting this Season; and the last Time he will

---

[21] British Museum, MSS Egerton, 2321 gives the income for many performances: Dec. 22, 1714—£60 19s. 6d.; Dec. 30—£30 13s.; Feb. 21, 1715—£66 5s. 6d.; April 7 (benefit of Monsieur du Pre, dancer)—£121 2s.; Sept. 28—£33 18s.; Jan. 16, 1716—£9 10s. 6d.; June 12 (for the benefit of the "Young Actors"—that is, "Young Cibber on account of Arrears")—£94 10s. 6d.; Nov. 23—£24 12s. 6d.; Feb. 6, 1717—£25 10s.; and May 22 (for the benefit of "Mr. White, Box-keeper")—£87 7s.

Act upon any Stage."[22] Spiller returned to the role on April 26, 1728, and Chapman had it on May 3, 1729, when the Prince of Wales commanded a performance for the benefit of Miss Holliday, who took the part of Miranda. The *Daily Post* for the following Monday noted the fine appearance of persons of quality at the theater.

When Drury Lane gave its second performance "these Seven Years" on November 16, 1730, Wilks and Mills still had their original parts. Theophilus Cibber, who was to become one of the great actors in the role, acted Marplot. He conceived the character as a town coxcomb with an abundance of pertness and impudence. Cibber was replaced at Drury Lane by Macklin, who emphasized foolishness and stupidity in the part.[23]

On December 3, 1736, while Giffard's Goodman's Fields company was using the Lincoln's Inn Fields theater, Henry Woodward acted Marplot for the first time. He was to become the greatest interpreter of the part. On September 10, 1748, he appeared as Marplot at Drury Lane, "His first appearance on that Stage these seven Years." But Garrick and Woodward quarreled at the end of the 1757-58 season, and Woodward left Drury Lane to join Barry in Dublin. Partly perhaps to show that he could get along without his great comedian, whose loss he felt greatly, Garrick himself acted Marplot on December 2, 1758. On the same occasion Mrs. Clive made her first appearance as Patch, a character which in her hands became a principal one. Miss Macklin was also advertised to play Miranda for the first time, though she had

---

[22] Pack's name is listed in programs for April 21 and May 7, 1724, on the latter occasion for his own benefit. According to Chetwood (*A General History of the Stage*, p. 211), "Mr. *Pack* left the Stage in the Meridian of Life, and set up a Tavern (the *Globe*) near *Charing-Cross*, over against the *Hay-market*, where he died. . . ."

[23] James Thomas Kirkman, *Memoirs of the Life of Charles Macklin* (1799), I, 242-43. Kirkman says that productions of *The Busy Body* in 1739 brought Macklin before the public in the character of Marplot, but he had taken the role earlier, at Drury Lane on Nov. 21 and Dec. 1, 1733.

acted this part at least five times before, first on September 18, 1756.

Arthur Murphy explains that Garrick took the part as an expedient, expecting to eclipse Woodward in his finest role. But "the deserter to Dublin could put on such a vacant innocent countenance, that all the mischief he did by being busy in other people's affairs, appeared to be the effect of accident; whereas Garrick had so much meaning, such strong intelligence in his countenance, that he seemed to do everything by design," and the town agreed that Garrick failed in his intention.[24] Percy Fitzgerald repeats the opinion that Garrick's face was not vacant enough for the part, though undoubtedly the face of Marplot had through association become identified with the face of Woodward.[25] Garrick, he adds, claimed for himself the merit of having beaten the character into his actor.

By setting the date of his first performance of Marplot on the night of the première at Covent Garden of Dodsley's tragedy *Cleone,* which he had previously rejected, Garrick involved himself in one of the most notable disputes of his career. Fitzgerald mentions the attendance of Dr. Johnson and Lord Lyttelton at the rehearsals of *Cleone* and indicates their feeling that Garrick was doing all he could to minimize his error in having allowed the play to go to the other house.[26] Garrick wrote to Dodsley the next day congratulating him on the success of his drama and offering to support his interest in any way possible without injuring his own.[27] But Dodsley replied in a fury, and a few days later Dr. Warburton assured Garrick that Dodsley was a "wretched fellow." Garrick was charged with acting Marplot to "very slender pecuniary houses," filled out with "quires of orders [to] indulge Marplot's vanity and keep the *secret* of his *impotence.*"[28] In a precarious position

[24] *The Life of David Garrick* (Dublin, 1801), p. 211.
[25] *The Life of David Garrick* (1868), II, 102.
[26] *Ibid.,* I, 377.
[27] *Ibid.,* I, 377-78.
[28] *A Letter to the Honorable Author of the New Farce, called The Rout, To which is subjoined, An Epistle to Mr. G - - - - - k* (1759).

following the withdrawal of Woodward, he had resorted to the
questionable stratagem of postponing *The Busy Body* after
Covent Garden had announced the postponement of Dodsley's
tragedy.

Garrick took the role thirteen times during the season. The
play was also acted three times at Covent Garden with Shuter
in the title role. For March 29 and May 4 at Drury Lane was
advertised an "Epilogue addressed to the Town, in the Character of the Busy Body by Mr. Garrick." Presumably this
epilogue[29] was first spoken on the night of Garrick's first appearance in the character. It became a favorite with the audiences and was frequently announced in the advertisements.

The Busy Body is discussed at great length in the *London
Chronicle* for December 7-9, 9-12, and 19-21, 1758. Included
are an analysis of the character of Marplot and a criticism of
the chief actors who have taken the part. "The Comedy of the
Busy Body being at present the important object of attention,"
the author gives it as his purpose to provide all the possible
materials "to enable the critics to take a round-about view of
the present subject of the debates at the toilet, at breakfast, at
dinner, at supper, at court, and even at the much adored Whist-
table" and to review all the Marplots "down to the present
actor, who fills the Theatre with it three times a week, and has
put the King of Prussia entirely out of every body's head."
First he defines Marplot as he has come "out of the hands of
the poet":

> Marplot, in age, in rank and circumstances, is under
> one and twenty, a gentleman, and of a good fortune; keeps
> the best company; honest in his passions; of manners not
> inelegant, at least not under-bred; no swordsman, good-
> natur'd, and ever eager for opportunities (whether season-
> ably or unseasonably he does not stay to enquire) of proving
> his regard for his friends, and he is ever officious in their
> service. By instigations of this kind his natural curiosity

[29] Printed in *The Theatrical Bouquet* (1780), pp. 183-84.

is quickened: his desire of knowing every thing is constantly spurred on by the pleasure he feels in being of use to those of his acquaintance; and his curiosity perpetually finds the means of gratifying his favourite passion for doing good.

The critic is clearly antagonistic to Garrick, despite the somewhat objective analysis of the play:

The *Busy Body* was again repeated at this Theatre [Drury Lane] to a crowded audience [December 9]: a convincing proof that the Manager can cram the gaping town with his *chapon bouille* as often as he pleases; and as a satire on the public taste we are told at the head of each Play-bill, how often they have been made fools with this old revived New Piece [this had been "The Fifth Day"].

Among the actors who have taken the part of Marplot, he mentions Pack, the creator of the character, as a man of "an agreeable person, a pleasing voice, and an open, vacant, undesigning countenance"; Bickerstaff, who had "neither youth, person, voice, or countenance"; Joe Miller, "very happy in the buffooning way of humour"; Theophilus Cibber, who changed the conception of the role from that of "a downright stupid country booby" "with his shoulders up to his ears" to that of a forward and impudent young gentleman of the town; Macklin, with features too strong and looks too busy for the part; young Bullock, "tall, agreeable in his person," with "a comic kind of voice, which vented itself in a shrillness of tone, but never sunk into meanness," the first to body forth the character as Theophilus Cibber had conceived it; Egleton, a former page at court, "thoughtless, extravagant, good-natured, totally regardless of consequences on all occasions," and perfectly suited for the character; Chapman, from whom little had been expected but whose representation of curiosity was remarkably fine; and then Woodward and Garrick.

The comparison of Woodward and Garrick as Marplot sheds light on a subject of acute controversy in the eighteenth century. Woodward, according to the critic, "has about him some traces of youth; he is loosely genteel in his person; has the air of a gay, giddy, unthinking town coxcomb; though he does not altogether appear the fine gentleman . . . he does not seem mean, or unbred." His bearing, "easy and debonaire," is very well suited "to the strenuous idleness of Marplot," so that the character "seemed to *come to him*." Garrick, on the other hand, looks "much too old for a ward," lacks the necessary "frankness in his mien," and his countenance shows constantly "the pale cast of thought." On the other hand, he represents well Marplot's "eagerness to know every thing that he may be of service to his friends." Woodward's voice has "a comical shrillness," which, "when he pleases, sounds unthinking, and always inspirits every scene, where absurdity and whimsical distress are concerned." Garrick's voice is remarkably "distinct, articulate, and sensible," but his modulation, "very fine in most characters, is here too regularly and significantly harmonious for a silly, empty, giddy, frolicsome fellow," and, like his looks, seems too much affected by a thinking mind.

The criticism, though undoubtedly intended to favor Woodward, seems to reflect the view of the town that in this one character Garrick failed to reach the consistent excellence of his pupil.

The *Theatrical Monitor* for November 7, 1767, accuses Garrick of jealousy toward dramatic authors, stating that he would not permit Arthur Murphy's *The Orphan of China* to be acted until he had been brought to reason by Murphy's "exposing his vain attempt to rival Woodward in the character of Marplot." Since *The Orphan of China* was produced at Drury Lane on April 21, 1759, four months after these articles appeared, we may be assured that Murphy was the author of them.[30]

[30] Murphy had studied Mrs. Centlivre's plays for other purposes as well. His *No One's Enemy but His Own* (acted at Covent Garden, Jan. 6, 1764)

M.ʳ WOODWARD *in the Character of* MARPLOT

"There he goes".

Garrick acted Marplot only once in 1759-60. After the season of 1760-61 he resigned the role to his recruit, O'Brien. Covent Garden took advantage of the discussion of Garrick's acting by reviving *The Busy Body* on March 22, 1759, after a lapse of seventeen years. Shuter had the title role. In the fall of 1762 Woodward returned to London. On October 5, and twelve additional times during the season, he performed Marplot at Covent Garden. He spoke a new occasional prologue, which attracted much favorable attention in London but which the Dubliners did not care for. As a result of his "prodigal prologue" he never again acted in Dublin.

The papers about this time began carrying more theatrical criticism, but Mrs. Centlivre's plays usually received far less attention than the literary classics. The *London Chronicle* for September 27-29, 1766, calls *The Busy Body* "a second rate performance," though a stock piece, but praises the acting of Miss Pope, who took the part of Patch at Drury Lane for the first time on September 20:

> Neither the conduct of the *Drama*, nor the language will stand the test of criticism. The character of *Marplot* (which for a series of years has been generally well acted) seems to have been its principal support.—Miss Pope acquitted herself in the part of *Patch*, with great reputation, especially as it was the first time.

The *Theatrical Register* for 1769[31] calls it a "very entertaining play," which "not only met with great success on its first appearance on the stage, but still continues to be a favourite with the public," despite the indifferent language and the not altogether probable plot.

---

was founded on Voltaire's *L'Indiscret* (1725). The *Universal Magazine* for Jan., 1764, notes that the character of Sir Philip Figurein was adapted from Sir Philip Modelove of *A Bold Stroke for a Wife*. The resemblance is even closer between Murphy's Careless and Mrs. Centlivre's Marplot. Cf. Howard Hunter Dunbar, *The Dramatic Career of Arthur Murphy* (New York, 1946), p. 160.

[31] P. 48.

Francis Gentleman's *The Dramatic Censor; or, Critical Companion* (1770) makes a long examination of the performers in *The Busy Body* and the nature of their parts.[32] Palmer as Sir George Airy, Gentleman says, was too much of the fop; Smith, on the other hand, was entirely satisfactory, having "sufficient vivacity, without diminishing essential elegance." The situations into which Sir Francis Gripe enters "are pleasant, and render him rather an object of laughter, than of the contempt he really deserves." Yates, to be known by a strict adherence to nature in his proper cast," was remarkably chaste as Gripe at Drury Lane, and it is certain that "though Mr. Shuter may make the galleries laugh more, by a luxuriance of humour, yet he never can be so correct." The "inoffensive Charles" has for many years been done "inoffensively enough" at Drury Lane by Packer; Clarke took the part, but it was far beneath his abilities; Hull, the present Charles at Covent Garden, should take only the graver parts of comedy. Sir Jealous Traffick, unlike Sir Francis, commits folly as a result of a deficient head and not of a bad heart. There is "an open bluntness of expression about him, which Mr. Love at Drury Lane is very characteristic in, and we think Mr. Dunstall equally happy." Miranda has "good sense, steadiness and generosity," and no fault except an excess of forwardness in her love affair. Mrs. Palmer, though unequal to the part, acted it without offense because of her amiability. Mrs. Bulkley mended matters, though she was not so good as Miss Macklin. Mrs. Mattocks, though better fitted for Patch, played Isabinda respectably. Patch should be in the hands of Mrs. Green, though the part has been well taken by Mrs. Pitt and Miss Minors. *The Busy Body*, he concludes, is a good stage piece but "scarce worth any body's purchase for the closet."

Covent Garden opened its 1773-74 season with *The Busy Body*, which drew a crowded and polite audience. Woodward spoke a new occasional prologue as well as Marplot's original

[32] II, 365 ff.

epilogue. The play continued to be produced frequently,
Woodward acting Marplot for the last time on April 16, 1776.
He had played the role eighty-six times during the thirteen
years since his return to London.

On September 23, 1782, the renovated Covent Garden
Theatre opened with a new occasional prelude, followed by
The Busy Body and a farce. The *London Chronicle* for September 21-24 says that an opposition developed and prevented
the conclusion of the prelude, which was really a satire against
the malevolence of ignorant pretenders to dramatic criticism
who refused to listen until the last word of the last act. The
"sprightly comedy" of *The Busy Body* "went off with great
éclat." The *London Chronicle* during this period criticizes few
performances unless there was a new play or a riot. Frequently
the two went together, farces especially causing trouble.

Toward the end of the century *The Busy Body* was sometimes reduced to three acts and used as the second part of a
triple bill. It was so acted at the Haymarket on October 18,
1779, and again at Covent Garden on April 14 and 27, 1780.
The *World* for October 21, 1793, says that *The Busy Body*
contains witty dialogue and business, and "when put in competition with modern dramas, has obviously so much merit, that
it is with difficulty the mind can descend to . . . the pretty
shifts of stage-trickery." But a play should be moral as well
as entertaining, and "several popular actors" should be less
"frequent in their profane catch-traps of applause, lest another
COLLIER should vindicate the cause of rectitude, and destroy
that reputation they so shamefully acquire."

The high regard for *The Busy Body* just before 1800 is
shown again in the *True Briton* for August 15, 1796, which
contains a review of a performance at the Haymarket the evening before. The house was not full and all the actors were
not perfect in their parts, but the drama is called "sterling
Comedy," a relief to the town from its surfeit of "O'Keefean

trash." *The Busy Body* had been acted in London every year
from 1709 to 1800 except 1777 and 1786-89.

Mrs. Inchbald in 1808[33] remarks that Marplot is the "sole
support" of the play, but the "busy curiosity, the officious good
temper, and the sheepish cowardice, of this mean atom of human nature, are so excellently delineated, that he allures the
attention and expectation of the auditors, and makes them
bear with patience, the dull, and commonplace dramatic persons
which surround him." She hopes that there are no longer such
unnatural fathers and guardians as are commonly to be found
in the old plays, so that playwrights can now paint "parental
and filial love" from nature.

William Hazlitt expresses his fondness for the play in the
Examiner for Monday, January 8, 1816. The "admirable
Comedy" was brought out, he says, at Drury Lane on Wednesday in order to introduce Mrs. Mardyn as Miranda. "She
acted the part very delightfully, and without overdoing it."
Harley presented in Marplot "a very laughable picture of
blundering vivacity and blank stupidity," but he had one fault:
"The officious *Marplot* is a gentleman, a foolish one, to be sure;
but HARLEY played it like a footman." The complete play
gives him an abundance of satisfaction:

> It is not so profound in wit or character as some other
> of the old Comedies, but it is nothing but bustle and gaiety
> from beginning to end. The plot never ceases. The in-
> genuity of contrivance is admirable. The development
> of the story is an uninterrupted succession of what the
> French call *coups de theatre,* and the situations succeed
> one another like the changes of machinery in a pantomime.

In his preface to *The Busy Body* in *The British Drama*
(1817) Cumberland remarks that Mrs. Centlivre's comedy
is acted several times each season because the "bustle and variety
of the plot, and the easy air of gaiety which runs through the

[33] Preface to *The Busy Body* in the *British Theatre* (1808), Vol. XI.

piece, will attract an audience, on whom the wit of Congreve and morality of Addison can make no impression" and because "the character of Marplot is so unique and excellent in its kind, that it will ever be occasionally chosen to exhibit the graces of some favourite performer, or to aid the debut of some youthful candidate for the sock."

The *Opera Glass* notices performances at Drury Lane on November 24 and December 15, 1826. It praises Harley as Marplot but finds Ellen Tree inadequate as Miranda. It regards Marplot as vastly superior to his "clumsy imitation," Paul Pry, who is funny only because of Liston's "face, breeches, and umbrella."

The *Paul Pry* referred to is a three-act comedy by John Poole, acted for the first time at the Haymarket on September 13, 1825. It was enormously popular with Liston in the title role. All the critics recognized immediately the resemblance of Paul Pry to Marplot, though the drama shows no close borrowings. In Paul Pry Marplot has ceased to be a gentleman and become a mischievous, curious child, peeping through key-holes and snooping around the kitchens, mature only in the sense of his own importance. The type degenerates still further in Douglas Jerrold's *Paul Pry* (1827), which is pure farce.

The Busy Body was successfully revived at the Haymarket in 1844. Oxberry's *Weekly Budget of Plays* notes performances on July 22, 23, 24, 25, 26, 29, 30, 31, August 1, and September 28. Charles Mathews and Madame Vestris gave excellent interpretations of Marplot and Miranda.

On July 27, 1844, Webster, manager of the Haymarket, was presented a formal testimonial because he had kept his theater open four hundred nights straight. He was congratulated for presenting effectively the "comedies of the noblest drama in the world, as the honourable names of Shakspere, Massinger, Congreve, Cibber, Vanbrugh, Goldsmith, Sheridan, Inchbald, Col-man, Centlivre, Murphy, Morton, amongst the dead, and our Sheridan Knowles, with Bulwer, and many others, among the living, whose names have appeared in your bills during the four hundred nights, can successfully and gloriously testify."[34] Mrs. Centlivre was one of six dramatists writing before 1750 who continued to attract attention in the theater.

Though *The Busy Body* remained in the repertory of the theater, the later critics were unwilling to admit that the play was great literature.   For example, Dutton Cook, on the occasion of a production at the Haymarket in November, 1871, remarks that to read the play "is to engage in a very ungrateful employment."[35]   "There is not a witty line in it from the beginning to end," he adds; "the fable is wholly without interest, and the glimpses afforded of the life and manners of a past age are few and imperfect."   Nevertheless, Mrs. Centlivre "thoroughly appreciated the fact that an audience can be sufficiently diverted by a quick march of incidents, by the constant movement of the *dramatis personae,* by characters clearly defined, though of conventional type, and by the general vivacity of the representation."   She desired only to "make the spectators laugh."

[34] Oxberry's *Weekly Budget* for Aug. 5, 1844.
[35] *Nights at the Play* (1883), I, 182 ff.

A Bout With the *Female Tatler*

STILL DAZZLED by her triumph with *The Busy Body*, Mrs. Centlivre on Monday, December 12, 1709, offered another comedy to the public at the Haymarket. But *The Man's Bewitch'd: or, The Devil to Do about Her* ran into trouble from the beginning. The actors omitted it on Tuesday and acted it again on Wednesday and Thursday. Then they laid it aside. The Prologue, written by an unnamed gentleman and spoken by Wilks, suggests that Mrs. Centlivre expected trouble, for it denies that she has written a lampoon against the town, states that she had no intention of teaching reformation, and hopes that she will be spared *"for the* Busie-Body's *sake"*:

> *Our Female Author trembling stands within,*
> *Her Fear arises from another's Sin;*
> *One of her Sex has so abus'd the Town,*
> *That on her Score she dreads your angry Frown:*
> *Tho' I dare say, poor Soul, she never writ*
> *Lampoon, or Satyr on the Box or Pit;*
> *A harmless hum'rous Play is her Extent of Wit.*
> *Tho'* Bickerstaff's *vast Genius may engage,*
> *And lash the Vice and Follies of the Age;*
> *Why shou'd tender* Delia *tax the Nation;*
> *Stickle, and make a Noise for Reformation,*
> *Who always gave a Loose, herself, to Inclination?*

> *Scandal and Satyr's thrown aside to-day,*
> *And Humour the sole Business of our Play,* . . .
> *But if all this can't your Good-Nature wake,*
> *Tho' here and there, a Scene should fail to take,*
> *Yet spare her for the* Busie-Body's *sake.*

Clearly some persons regarded Mrs. Centlivre as the author of the lampoon and she feared in consequence the formation of a party against her play the first night.   In view of later developments, it is likely that a starred "advertisement" in the *Female Tatler* for December 7-9 is the lampoon referred to:

> *Dropt near the* Play-house *in the* Hay Market, *a Bundle of Horse Whips, design'd to belabour the* Footmen *in the Upper Gallery, who almost ev'ry Night this* Winter, *have made such an Intollerable Disturbance, that the Play'rs could not be heard, and their Masters were forc'd to hiss 'em into Silence.   Whoever has taken up the said* Whips, *is desired to leave 'em with my Lord* Rake's *Porter, several Noblemen resolving to Exercise 'em on their Backs the next Frosty Morning.*

If so, it may be significant that the author of the Prologue denies specifically that she wrote a satire on the box or pit.   Or it may be that he is defending her from charges of writing theatrical satire which had been regularly appearing in the *Female Tatler*. Marshaling his best defense for her, he seems to suggest that the real author is "Delia."   Steele, with his *"vast Genius,"* is accorded the privilege of lashing the vices of the age, but Delia is not.   Delia can refer only to Mrs. De la Rivière Manley, who under the name of Delia tells of her mock marriage to John Manley, a cousin, in Volume II of *The New Atalantis*.[1] The conclusion seems inevitable that the author of this prologue, while not denying categorically that Mrs. Centlivre may have contributed, thought Mrs. Manley the editor of the *Female Tatler*.

---

[1] Advertisements of the first performance of the play credit it to "the Author of the Busie Body," so that "Delia" cannot be a pseudonym for Susanna.

The *Female Tatler* had been sniping at the players all fall, accusing them especially of avarice and affectation. In the issue for September 16-19 Cibber is referred to as Captain Brazen; and various plays, it says, have had to give way to *"his* Immortal Xerxes, *and the* Double Dealer, *to his judicious sprightly unborrow'd* Double Gallant." Yet Colley Cibber wrote the epilogue for *The Man's Bewitch'd,* making an appeal for the stage against the popularity of operas, so that he apparently had not previously attributed the satire in the *Female Tatler* to Mrs. Centlivre. It is also to be noted that the Prologue refers with seeming friendliness to Steele—it is difficult to conceive of Susanna's ever attacking him—against whom the *Female Tatler* was to vent its spleen.

Mrs. Centlivre thought that the conditions surrounding the presentation of her play required a preface, which duly appeared in the published copy on December 31. In spite of an opera which interfered with *The Man's Bewitch'd,* she says, it produced *"above Forty Pounds the second Night, which shew'd it had some Merit; for I have known a Play kept up, that fail'd of half that Money the second Night."* According to the rules of the house, it should have been played on, but *"the Actors, according to the Caprice of their Humours, maugre the Taste of the Town, have power to sink the Reputation of a Play"* by resolving not to act in it. Further,

This Play met with a kind Reception in general, and notwithstanding the Disadvantages it had to struggle with, by raising the Prices the first Day, and the Nearness of Christmas, it would have made its way to a sixth Night, if it had had fair Play. Mistake me not, I do not mean from the Representation; for I must do the Players Reason: Had I searched all the Theatres in the World, I could not have selected a better Company, nor had more Justice done me in the Action, tho' they have not dealt honourably by me in my Bargain; for they ought not to have stop'd the Run, upon any Pique whatever.

What happened is that a feature article about her appeared
in the *Female Tatler* for December 12-14 and that she was
thought to have written it. The *"Ingenious* Mrs. *Centlivre"*
is represented as visiting the editor at her lodgings in Greek
Street, Soho, when all the ladies concerned in the paper "written
by a Society of Ladies" and a few others of both sexes were
gathered there. It becomes obvious as the story proceeds why
the actors were piqued:

> . . . her Business then was chiefly to have my Opinion
> of her *New Comedy,* for that she *spy'd* me out the first
> Night in the *Box.* I ask'd her, smiling, whether she took
> the *Title* of her *Play* from the *Characters* she had drawn,
> or from the *Persons* that play'd those *Characters,* since a
> certain *Theatrical Gentleman* is often bewitch'd, and there
> is a *Stage Lady about whom there has been the Devil to
> do:* But letting *Raillery* apart, the whole Company *Con-
> gratulated* her on the *Success* of her *Performance,* and were
> rejoyc'd to see the inimitable Mrs. *Bhen* so nearly reviv'd
> in Mrs. *Centlivre;* some there, who are esteem'd no *ill
> Judges,* were pleased to say, they thought it a Genteel,
> Easy and Diverting *Comedy:* That it had a better *Plot,* and
> as many *Turns* in it as her *Celebrated Buisy-Body;* and tho'
> the two first Acts were not so *roar'd* at as the rest, yet they
> were well Wrought Scenes, tending to Business: The
> *Squire* out did himself throughout the whole *Action;* nor
> is Mrs. *Saunders,* tho' ranked below *Belinda,* to be less ap-
> plauded for her *Natural Trembling and Faultering in her
> Speech,* when she *apprehended Sir Jeffery to be a Ghost.*
> The *Ladies* highly commended the *Author,* as what cou'd
> they expect less from one of their own *Sex,* for the care she
> had taken not to Offend the *nicest Ear,* with the least
> *Double Entendre,* and press'd me to acquaint the *Town,*
> that ev'n Dissenters may be seen at this *Play;* and tho'
> *Emilia* [It was Emilia's day for this issue] has not the
> assurance of some *Tatlers,* to *Licence* one Man to *Ruin* all

the rest of his Trade, yet she wou'd intreat the *Ladies*,
especially those of *Quality*, to engage her such an *Appearance* the *Third* and *Sixth Night*, as to show they have a
Generous Sense of the Pains she is daily taking, so Wittily
and Innocently to Entertain them.

The Society of Ladies had to prevail upon Mrs. Centlivre
to stay for supper:

She complain'd, she was so horribly *Mobb'd*, that she was
enough to fright People; had she imagin'd the Honour
of so much good Company, sh'd have put herself in another guess Trim; but it being a wet Evening, she expected to have found me alone, and coming out in haste,
had n't so much as put on a *Patch*; but assuring her her
Dress needed no *Apology*, or if it had, 'twas her *Conversation* we coveted, she comply'd with our Request.

Then comes the part most offensive to the actors:

The *Society* had the Curiosity of knowing the Nature of
introducing a *Play* into the *House*; Mrs. *Centlivre* told
'em, that 'twas much easier to Write a *Play* than to get it
Represented; that their *Factions* and *Divisions* were so
great, they seldom continued in the same mind two Hours
together; that they treated her, (tho a Woman) in the
Masculine Gender; and as they do all *Authors* with *Wrangling* and *Confusion*, which has made most Gentlemen
that have a *Genius* to *Scribling*, employ their *Pens* another
way; that to show their Judgment in *Plays*, they had actually cut out the *Scene in the Fifth Act, between the Coun-
tryman and the Ghost*, which the *Audience* receiv'd with
that *wonderful Applause*; and 'twas with great strugling
the *Author* prevail'd to have it in again; one made Faces
at his Part, another was Witty upon her's: But as the
whole was very well perform'd at last, she has Condescen-
tion to pass over the Affronts of a Set of People, who have
it not in their Natures to be grateful to their *Supporters*.

After such an article it is surprising that Susanna should pro-
fess entire ignorance of the authorship of the *Female Tatler*, but
she was in a tough spot, and so she did:

*I should not have troubled my courteous Reader with
a* Preface, *had I not lain under the Necessity of clearing
myself of what some People have been pleas'd to charge
me with, viz. of being the Author of a Paper call'd,* The
Female Tatler, *consequently of a Paragraph in that of the
14th Instant, relating to this Comedy; tho' I think no
reasonable Person will believe I could be guilty of so much
Folly.   Tho' Vanity is said to be the darling Vice of
Womankind; yet nothing but an Idiot would express themselves so openly; and I hope the World won't think me
guilty of printing, what I must blush to read, nor imagine
it wrote even by any Friend of mine, for two Reasons:* First,
the Grossness of the Flattery; Secondly, *the Injury it must
of course do me, in the Run of my Play, by putting those
People out of Humour whose Action was to give Life to
the Piece.   I suppose these Reasons are sufficient to convince the judicious Part, that I was no ways concerned in
those Reflections, but own I was treated with all the seeming Civility in the World, till the second Night of my
Comedy.   I willingly submitted to Mr.* Cibber's *superior
Judgment in shortening the Scene of the Ghost in the last
Act, and believed him perfectly in the Right, because too
much Repetition is tiresome.   Indeed, when Mr.* Estcourt
*sliced most of it out, I could not help interposing my
Desires to the contrary, which the rest readily complied
with; and I had the Satisfaction to see I was not deceived
in My Opinion, of its pleasing.   This Passage I happen'd
to mention among my Acquaintance; for 'tis natural to
have a kind of Tender for our own Productions, but especially if they have the Fortune to divert others.   Now, if
from this the Author of the* Tattler *gather'd his Account,*

I am guilty of speaking, but not designedly; for who they are that Write that Paper, or how Distinguish'd, I am perfectly ignorant, and declare I never was concerned either in Writing, or Publishing any of the Tattlers.

I never had the Vanity to think, much less to publish, that any thing I am capable of doing, could support the Stage, tho' I have had the good Fortune to please, or to find the Town willing to be pleased; tho', at present, it seems, a certain Author has enter'd a Caveat against all Plays running to a sixth Night, but his own [another hit at Cibber].

Again a literalist would note that she specifically denies having had anything to do with the *Tatlers*, not the *Female Tatlers*. Professor Paul Bunyan Anderson thinks that Mrs. Centlivre by protesting too much actually reveals herself as one of the editors of the *Female Tatler*, and on the basis of internal evidence attempts to identify her work in it.[2]

The *Female Tatler* was the outstanding rival of the *Tatler*, and, though not the equal of its original, is distinctly worthy of attention. It often pursued topics introduced by the *Tatler*, but it also suggested subjects to the *Tatler*, which it influenced considerably in the development of the essay. Its weakness is in its overindulgence in journalistic gossip, its gross personalities, and its attention commonly to the mechanics rather than the fundamentals of human nature.

The *Female Tatler* Numbers 1-18 (July 8–August 17, 1709) was published by B. Bragge and ostensibly edited by a Mrs. Phoebe Crackenthorpe, *"a Lady that knows every thing."* Numbers 19-44 (August 19–October 17) exist in two separate texts.[3] The editor of the first eighteen issues transferred the paper to the printer A. Baldwin; but Bragge felt that the rights belonged to him, and for a time he published a rival, which

[2] "Innocence and Artifice: or, Mrs. Centlivre and *The Female Tatler*," *Philological Quarterly*, XVI (1937), 358-75.

[3] R. T. Milford, "The *Female Tatler*," *Modern Philology*, XXIX (1931-32), 350-51.

he insisted was the original. Numbers 45-51 (October 19–November 2) were published only by Baldwin, the first editor having won out in the rivalry. Numbers 52-111 (really 52-115 because of faulty numbering, November 4, 1709–March 31, 1710) were published by Baldwin but edited by a "Society of Ladies."

Professor Anderson argues that Mrs. De la Rivière Manley was the real Mrs. Crackenthorpe and that she edited the *Female Tatler* (that is, the Bragge-Baldwin series) from its inception until her arrest on October 29 on a charge of libel in connection with the second volume of *The New Atalantis,* which had appeared on October 20. In Number 51 (November 2) Mrs. Crackenthorpe says that she is giving up her editorship to a society of modest ladies because of an *"Affront offer'd to her by some rude Citizens, altogether unacquainted with her Person,"* which might be read as an allusion, by her coeditor or successor, to the bailiffs who took her to jail. Mrs. Manley and the printer and publisher of *The New Atalantis* were examined on November 1, and the printer and publisher were released. Mrs. Manley was admitted to bail on November 5 and was discharged on February 13, 1710. Professor Anderson contends that the society of ladies who took over the paper with Number 51 was in reality Dr. Bernard Mandeville (who wrote under the names of Lucinda and Artesia) and Susanna Centlivre (who appeared as Emilia, Rosella, Arabella, and Sophronia).[4]

Professor Walter Graham replies that the case for Mrs. Manley is "far from conclusive. It is hard to believe that [Professor Anderson] has presented anything more than a conjecture."[5] After summarizing the evidence, he concludes that the traditional ascription of the editorship to Thomas Baker is justified.[6]

[4] "Splendor out of Scandal: the Lucinda-Artesia Papers in *The Female Tatler," Philological Quarterly,* XV (1936), 286-300.

[5] "Thomas Baker, Mrs. Manley, and the *Female Tatler," Modern Philology,* XXXIV (1936-37), 267-72.

[6] He overlooks one interesting fact. Mottley (*A List of All the Dramatic Authors, with Some Account of Their Lives; and of All the Dramatic Pieces*

There is no reasonable doubt that Thomas Baker was connected with the *Female Tatler*. For example, in Number 24 (August 31) Mrs. Crackenthorpe, under the pretense of satirizing city social climbers, portrayed a city deputy and his two daughters at a party. In recompense Baker received a cudgeling, which the *British Apollo* gleefully celebrated in verse. But it also looks as if Mrs. Manley may have been a coeditor. H. R. Fox Bourne's *English Newspapers*,[7] one of the few works to call Mrs. Manley the editor, cites the first issue of the *General Postscript, being an Extract of all that is most material from the Foreign and English Newspapers, with Remarks upon the 'Observator,' 'Review,' 'Tatlers,' and the Rest of the Scriblers, in a Dialogue between Novel and Scandal*, which appeared on September 27, 1709, for notes on the journalism current in London. The *Female Tatler*, it says, was written "by Scandalosissima Scoundrelia and her two natural brothers." The first could only have been Mrs. Manley, and Baker may well have been one of the other two. The use of three people to gather and process the material would certainly not have been excessive.

Some current allusions, mentioned by Professor Anderson, point to both Mrs. Manley and Thomas Baker rather than to one of them alone. In *Tatler* 229 Addison says that the *Tatler* was "scolded at by a *Female Tatler*, and slandered by another of the same Character under the Title of *Atalantis*." It is tempting to identify these as Baker and Mrs. Manley. Also the *British Apollo*, which feuded interminably with the *Female Tatler*, at times implies joint authorship:

Ever Published in the English Language to the Year 1747, appended to Thomas Whincop's *Scanderbeg: or, Love and Liberty* [1747], p. 166) says that Thomas Baker "was the Anthor [*sic*] of a scurrilous Paper, called *The Female Tatler*, wrote in Imitation of *Isaac Bickerstaff*'s *Tatler*: but which, like most Imitations, was far beneath the Original."

Professor Anderson thinks that Baker may have been the editor of the rival paper.

[7] (1887) I, 68.

> You'll say She is some Mother *Mab* in Disguise,
> Train'd up from her Birth in Abuses and Lies;
> Or else you may think by her scurrilous Tongue,
> From *Billingsgate, Bridewell,* or *Newgate* She sprung;
> Admitting all this (as it seems pretty plain)
> Regard to her *Sex* might have warded the *Cane.*
> But others will swear that this wise Undertaker,
> By Trade's an *At - - - ney,* by Name is a *B - - - r,*
> Who rambles about with a Female Disguise on,
> And lives upon Scandal, as Toads do on Poyson.[8]

The *Female Tatler* had been presented by the grand jury of Middlesex on October 15, along with Defoe's *Review,* as "a great Nusance," but there had been no change in make-up or material. On the other hand, almost immediately following Mrs. Manley's arrest, the fiction of Mrs. Crackenthorpe was dropped, but there was again no noticeable change except in the make-up of the front page. The same kind of libelous caricatures and the same personal animosities (against Thomas D'Urfey, for example) continued. The probability, then, is that Mrs. Manley and Baker were both at work on the paper except for the few days when Mrs. Manley was confined without access to writing materials.

Thomas Baker had written the epilogue which came too late for *The Platonick Lady* (1706) and the prologue to *The Busy Body,* which had been acted on May 12. He and Susanna had been friends for at least three years. Susanna and Mrs. Manley were also friends. Susanna had contributed a poem to the *Nine Muses,* edited by Mrs. Manley, in 1700. She was also a friend of Mrs. Egerton, with whom Mrs. Manley quarreled only after visiting her in Buckinghamshire in the summer of 1704.[9] Mrs. Pix too seems to have been a mutual friend of Mrs. Manley and Mrs. Centlivre. Though politics would

[8] II, 49 (Sept. 14, 1709).
[9] Paul Bunyan Anderson, "Mistress Delariviere Manley's Biography," *Modern Philology,* XXXIII (1935-36), 271.

soon place De la Rivière and Susanna in opposite camps, the parties were only beginning to crystallize among the wits in 1709. Hence it is reasonable to believe that Mrs. Centlivre may have contributed to the *Female Tatler* either by writing for it or by furnishing the editors with literary material, but it is unlikely that she was ever a main editor. The Haymarket actors rightly blamed her for the story about *The Man's Bewitch'd*.[10] Either she wrote it or someone with a good reportorial ear did, and in either case she was responsible. Perhaps her friend, eager to triumph over the players, did not realize in the hurry of meeting the deadline how the article would affect her, but there are no more prologues or epilogues from Baker and there is nothing to connect her and Mrs. Manley again for many years. Perhaps she was sincere in her preface when she entreated *"the Female Tatler to be witty no more at* [her] *Expense."*

Mrs. Centlivre praised the acting. The three couples of lovers were played by Mills (Captain Constant) and Mrs. Oldfield (Belinda), Wilks (Faithful) and Mrs. Cross (Laura), Husband (Lovely) and Mrs. Porter (Maria). Bowman took the part of Sir Jeffrey Constant, the supposedly dead father of Captain Constant; Johnson acted Sir David Watchum, Laura's jealous old guardian; Estcourt was Trusty, steward to Sir Jeffrey and supposedly the father of Belinda; Dogget acted Num, a country squire in love with Belinda, and sang a song by the author in praise of country maidens for wives;[11] and Cross,

---

[10] She took her next play, *A Bickerstaff's Burying*, to Drury Lane, where it was acted on March 27, 1710.

[11] The song is worth quoting:

Wou'd you chuse a Wife for a happy Life,
Leave the Court, and the Country take;
Where Dolly and Sue, young Molly and Prue,
Follow Roger and John, whilst Harvest goes on,
And merrily, merrily rake.

Leave the London Dames, be it spoke to their Shames,
To lig in their Beds till Noon;
Then get up and stretch, then paint too and patch,
Some Widgeon to catch, then look on their Watch,
And wonder they rose up so soon.

Pinkethman, Bullock, Cibber, Harris, Mrs. Saunders, and Mrs. Bicknell took the parts of the servants.

Mrs. Centlivre dedicated her play to William, Duke of Devonshire, Lord Steward of the Queen's Household. She says that since her husband serves her Majesty "under the Command of Your Grace, as he did the late King of pious Memory, under that of your noble Father," she could not be prevailed upon to address her play to another. She was perhaps looking out for her husband's advancement, though it was slow in coming, as much as for her own fee, but it is more likely that she was trying to help him collect back wages due him from William III. He still had not collected them when he died!

The scene of *The Man's Bewitch'd* is laid at Peterborough, not far from Holbeach. At times it seems as if Mrs. Centlivre is trying to work out an original and realistic study of provincial life, but, as we shall see, this is merely a thin veneer with which she covers her borrowing from the French. The lovers of both sexes are people of sense who are careful not to deceive the persons they love. The women are frank and reasonable at all times. But most of the play is farce, and the farce is so broad that it offers little pleasure in the reading, and one wonders whether any except the least critical among the theatergoers were really pleased by it on the stage.

> *Then Coffee and Tea, both Green and Bohea,*
> *Is serv'd to their Tables in Plate;*
> *Where their Tattles do run, as swift as the Sun,*
> *Of what they have won, and who is undone,*
>   *By their gaming, and sitting up late.*
>
> *The Lass give me here, tho' brown as my Beer,*
> *That knows how to govern her House;*
> *That can milk her Cow, or farrow her Sow;*
> *Make Butter, or Cheese, or gather green Pease,*
>   *And values fine Clothes not a Louse.*
>
> *This, this is the Girl, worth Rubies and Pearl;*
> *This the Wife that will make a Man rich:*
> *We Gentlemen need no Quality Breed,*
> *To squander away what Taxes would pay,*
>   *In truth we care for none such.*

There are two main plots, in each of which the devil has a part, and a third to connect the other two. In the first plot Faithful is in love with Laura, an heiress under the strict guardianship of Sir David Watchum, who wants to marry her himself. Constant and Faithful fight a mock duel at the coffee-house just as Sir David enters, and Faithful pretends to be wounded. At their request Sir David orders his coachman to take Faithful *home*. He himself arrives at home a little later and there finds Faithful. Faithful treats Laura as the hostess of an inn and the servants as drawers and chambermaids. Finally, Manage, his extraordinarily clever servant, enters looking for his master. Sir David thinks there has been an honest mistake, and Faithful makes his apologies and leaves after telling Laura that he will return in an hour. He and Manage return as an army officer and his servant, a physician. Having secured her jewels and the writings of her estate, Laura acts as if bewitched, and her old guardian accepts Manage's offer to cure her. Manage assures him that the devil will pass from her to another if they hold hands while he pronounces some incantations. When Laura and Faithful take hands, Laura is cured, but Faithful, now a man bewitched, acts his part with such violence that Sir David allows them to escape, marry, and join their friends.

In the second plot Captain Constant pretends to have lost his father, who has refused him an allowance since he will not marry Mrs. Homebred, a wealthy but unattractive woman. He tricks Trusty, his father's steward, out of rent money and marries Belinda, the steward's daughter. Then Sir Jeffrey, his father, arrives, sooner than expected, and is taken by various persons for a ghost or devil. Ultimately it is discovered that Belinda is the daughter of Lord Belville, and Sir Jeffrey is reconciled.

The third plot includes the courtship of Lovely and Maria, a gentlewoman of fortune, who finally agrees to marry her suitor after Trusty promises to reconcile her father, a violent Tory, with Lovely, a Whig, or to give her a marriage portion himself.

Squire Num, who previously had Trusty's permission to marry Belinda, is encouraged by her ostensibly to keep Trusty favorable to Constant but actually as an excuse to keep the squire on the stage. Roger, a farmer to Sir Jeffrey, succeeds in wooing Dorothy, Belinda's maid. The country characters are something of a relief from the usual diet of gallants and heiresses, and one wishes that Mrs. Centlivre had done more with them.

According to the *Biographia Dramatica, The Man's Bewitch'd* "is little more than a translation of *Le Deuil*, a French comedy, published under the name of Hauteroche, but generally believed to have been written by Thomas Corneille, in 1672." Joseph Knight comments in his sketch of Mrs. Centlivre's life that "This clever farce is said, without much justification, to be indebted to 'Le Deuil' of Hauteroche, which name is in the 'Biographia Dramatica' erroneously supposed to be a pseudonym of Thomas Corneille." Professor Nicoll notes that "Thomas Corneille's *Le Deuil* was utilised by Mrs. Centlivre for *The Man's Bewitch'd*" and adds later that her comedy is "an adaptation, apparently, of *Le Deuil*, a play presumably penned by Thomas Corneille."[12] Whether *Le Deuil* was written by Corneille or Hauteroche, it was printed as "Par le Sieur De HAVTE-ROCHE, Comedien de la Seule Troupe Royale," and the Dedication is signed "De Haute-Roche."[13]

Le Deuil provided Mrs. Centlivre with the second plot, *The Devil to Do about Her*.[14] The plot of Sir David and his ward *(The Man's Bewitch'd)* is taken from Regnard's *Les Folies amoureuses* (1704).[15] Mrs. Centlivre's originality in plot is almost entirely limited to the story of Lovely and Maria, who are friends to both the other pairs of lovers. In setting and in the introduction of supporting characters from Peterborough she makes her chief original contribution.

[12] *Early Eighteenth Century Drama* (Cambridge, 1925), pp. 145, 167.
[13] The Preface mentions the "Contes d'Eutrapel" as the source of the comedy.

[14] Robert Seibt, *Mrs. Centlivre und Ihre Quelle Hauteroche* (Berlin, 1910).
[15] Cf. Friedrich Hohrman, "Das Verhältnis Susanna Centlivre's zu Molière und Regnard," *Zeitschrift für vergleichende Litteraturgeschichte*, N.F., XIV (1900-1901), 419-25.

Mrs. Centlivre follows Regnard more closely than she does Hauteroche. She places the mock duel of the Faithful-Laura story in the coffeehouse, but changes little else. She retains the characters of Hauteroche under different names but alters the function of each considerably. In *Le Deuil* the lovers have been secretly married for six months, so that they are concerned purely with getting the girl's portion. In *The Man's Bewitch'd*, Constant schemes to get some ready cash, but he is primarily interested in winning Belinda. Mrs. Centlivre adds the country scenes in which the tenants of Sir Jeffrey apply for a renewal of their leases and complain of the hardships under which they labor. She adds also the part of Squire Num, for whose hand Belinda feigns a preference, so that Trusty will force her upon Constant. Many of the speeches which Hauteroche gives to the servant Crispin Mrs. Centlivre gives to the friend Lovely. Also Roger, the farmer, is a much more significant person than Nicodème, a servant of Jaquemin, the Trusty of *Le Deuil*. But the chief change which Mrs. Centlivre makes is in the spirit of her comedy. *Le Deuil* is a kind of poetical harlequinade, a short pastoral comedy without the pastoral setting, whereas *The Man's Bewitch'd* is at times very real and very English. In thus naturalizing the fantastic situations of the original, she was courting failure, for some of the highly farcical scenes do not fit against her realistic background.

The Man's Bewitch'd was revived at Goodman's Fields on April 28, 1730. It was acted again that season and once the next. In 1738 an entertainment under the title of "The Man's Bewitch'd; or, The Devil to Do about Her" was produced at Pinkethman's Great Theatrical Booth during the time of Bartholomew Fair. Since the characters were Harlequin, Colombine, Don Furioso, and Diego, it may be that Mrs. Centlivre's comedy was turned into a harlequinade. At Southwark Fair about a month later a series of performances under the same title was given at Hallam's Great Theatrical Booth.

An adaptation of *The Man's Bewitch'd* appeared in *The Strolers Pacquet Open'd, Containing Seven Jovial Drolls or Farces, Calculated for the Meridian of Bartholomew and South-wark Fairs* (1742) under the title of *The Witchcraft of Love: or, Stratagem on Stratagem,* a two-act farce dated 1741.[16] For it the first part of the play was simplified and the Lovely-Maria subplot was omitted.

A second printed adaptation was *The Ghost* (1767), a comedy of two acts, performed at the theater in Smock Alley, Dublin. This time only the plot of Constant and Belinda remains, so that the ghost scenes, however ridiculous, form a unified action. *The Ghost; or, The Man Bewitched* was given at Drury Lane on April 10, 1769, and at the Haymarket on August 28, 1787. *The Ghost; or The Devil to do about her* was acted for the first time at Covent Garden on April 23, 1783, for Quick's benefit. It was repeated not often but regularly to the end of the century. The *Oracle and Public Advertiser* for October 20, 1795, says of a performance at Covent Garden that "Knight's success in one of the characters would have been even greater, and the applause more general, if some of the expressions were not too coarse even for the mouth of a clown." This comment suggests a wide difference of opinion from that held earlier in the century by the *Female Tatler.*

Several persons[17] have noted the similarity between the mistaking of a home for an inn in Goldsmith's *She Stoops to Conquer* and in *The Man's Bewitch'd.* Though Goldsmith is thought to have drawn upon an actual experience for his situation, it is quite possible that he was influenced by Mrs. Centlivre's comedy. In some respects the incidents and even the language are similar.

[16] Nicoll includes this droll in his list of plays at the end of his *Early Eighteenth Century Drama.* In his *Late Eighteenth Century Drama* (p. 329) he writes: "The *Biographia Dramatica* states it [*The Man's Bewitch'd*] was acted in London as *The Witchcraft of Love.* This I have been unable to trace."

[17] Walter and Clare Jerrold, *Five Queer Women* (1929); Mark Schorer, "*She Stoops to Conquer:* A Parallel," *Modern Language Notes,* XLVIII (1933), 91-94, 486.

An Interlude

THE YEARS 1710 and 1711 were a kind of spiritless interlude for Mrs. Centlivre. She no longer had to fight to have her name published, she had no quarrel with a *Female Tatler*, and she had not yet committed herself to an outspoken role in politics. A short farce, a moderately successful sequel to *The Busy Body*, and a complimentary poem probably written at this time were all she had to offer as two years of work.

Regardless of the difficulties over *The Man's Bewitch'd*, she was back in the theater on March 27, 1710, but at Drury Lane rather than at the Haymarket. *A Bickerstaff's Burying; or, Work for the Upholders*[1] was one of three short farces which she wrote for afterpieces. On March 27, however, it was followed by *The Mistake* and on the next evening by *The Woman Captive*. On March 30 it was combined with *The Gamester* for the author's benefit, and on May 11 it was repeated as one of "Three Plays in One" which constituted the entertainment for several foreigners in London.

Norris acted Mezro, an emir of the island of Casgar, and Mrs. Knight, the wife of the emir. The actor Bickerstaff took the part of the shipwrecked English captain; Spiller, Pack, and Miller were the boatswain and two sailors; and Carnaby and Cole were an officer and a servant of the emir. Mrs. Cox

---

[1] The original advertisements call it *A Bickerstaff's Burial*.

acted Isabinda, the niece of Lady Mezro, Mrs. Kent was a lady
of the island, and Mrs. Spiller was Lucy, Lady Mezro's maid.

At "the particular Desire of several Ladies of Quality," *A
Bickerstaff's Burying* was revived as a new farce under the title
of *The Custom of the Country* at Drury Lane on May 5, 1715,
when it was acted along with *The Busy Body* for Mrs. Centlivre's benefit. It was repeated on May 17, June 2, July 6, and
on May 14, 1716.

The title suggests Swift's well-known treatment of the death
of Partridge, the almanac-maker, and Steele's satire against
undertakers in *The Funeral* and the *Tatler*. The Dedication,
"To the Magnificent Company of Upholders, &c.," is one of
the best bits of satire Mrs. Centlivre ever wrote. *"Custom,"*
she says, *"has made some Things absolutely necessary, and
three Sheets without a Dedication, or a Preface, by Way of
Excuse, would be an unpardonable Indecency."* She rejects the
young wives who marry for money and the old men who *"marry Girls of fifteen"* as unworthy and decides that her farce
"could justly belong to none but the Magnificent Company of
Upholders, *whom the judicious Censor of* Great Britain *has so
often condescended to mention"*:

> . . . *to you then, worthy Sirs, whose solemn Train keeps
> up the pompous State of Beauty, beyond the Limits of a
> Gasp of Breath, and draws the gazing World to admire,
> even after Death; to you this Piece I dedicate; 'tis but
> Reason that you should receive some Tribute from us
> living, who so truly mourn us dead. What does not
> Mankind owe to you? All Ranks and Conditions are
> obliged to you; the Aged and the Young, the Generous
> and the Miser, the well descended and the baser born.
> The Escutcheons garnish out the Hearse, the Streamers
> and Wax Lights, let us into the Name of a Man, which,
> all his Life had been hid in Obscurity; and many a Right
> Honourable would fall unlamented, were it not for your*

*decent Cloaks, and dismal Faces, that look as sorrowfully
as the Creditors they leave unpaid.*

Then she begs their leave to remind them *"that in this crouded
Town, there are a prodigious Number of Mr.* Bickerstaff's *dead
Men, that swarm about the Streets,"* men who have done no
good in their lifetime and out of decency ought to be interred.
In conclusion she asks pardon for the liberty she has taken and
hopes that she will not fall into the gentlemen's hands. But she
is not much afraid, since a poet's property is not easily converted and they *"are not over-fond of Paper-Credit."*

The action of *A Bickerstaff's Burying* results from a Cas-
garian law requiring a surviving wife or husband to be buried
with the deceased spouse. It is developed as pure farce, but
the turning of the tables as the wife or husband is threatened
with immolation to the spirit of the other is cleverly contrived.

Genest (II, 438) says that the plot was taken from one of
Sindbad's voyages in the *Arabian Nights,* but Joseph Knight
remarks that this is unlikely, since the publication of Galland's
Les Milles et une nuits (1704-1717) had only recently begun.
"A curious coincidence, hitherto unnoticed," he adds, "is that
'Le Naufrage ou le Pompe funèbre de Crispin' of Lafont, produced in Paris on Saturday, 14 June 1710, is all but identical
with the work of Mrs. Centlivre, who, however, is at least
earlier in date. Parfaict frères, the historians of the French
stage, suggest an origin of the plot earlier than the 'Arabian
Nights.' " But Knight complicates matters unnecessarily. The
Parfaict brothers say that La Font got his idea from the third
volume of the *Arabian Nights* or possibly, if he had a more
recondite source, from reports of travelers that in the kingdom of Malabar a surviving husband or wife is burned on the
grave of the person deceased.[2] Also, Mrs. Centlivre could
easily have used the *Arabian Nights,* for, according to an advertisement in the *Flying Post,* the first four volumes of the English translation had reached a second edition by March 22,

[2] *Histoire du Théâtre Français* (Paris, 1749), XV, 46.

1706. At any rate La Font's plot has in common with Mrs. Centlivre's only the condition that the husband or wife is not allowed to survive the other.

Mrs. Centlivre undoubtedly got the bare idea for her farce from the fourth voyage of Sindbad the Sailor. She follows the *Arabian Nights* in using the grave rather than the pyre, as does La Font, for the disposal of the victim. In her play Lady Mezro, the former Mrs. Take-it of Covent Garden, shipwrecked some years before on her way to Madras, is married to Mezro, who enjoys poor health as the only means of controlling his wife. But when an English boat is driven ashore, she determines to leave the island with the captain, who falls suddenly in love with her niece, Isabinda. Mezro feigns death, but recovers when Lady Mezro becomes more than usually solicitous. Then she feigns death, but just as he is about to be buried alive, according to the custom of the country, it is discovered that his wife has escaped in her coffin and Isabinda with her.

It is likely that La Font independently recognized a dramatic situation in the custom mentioned by the *Arabian Nights*. But to the law sacrificing a surviving husband or wife he added another requiring every woman on the island to marry. Marine, servant of Éliante, takes a husband of Malabar, but her mistress pretends to be married to her servant Crispin, hoping all the while to hear from her lover, Licandre, who was with them on the boat before the shipwreck. When Crispin requests the assistance of the governor in consummating his "marriage," Éliante, on the advice of Piracmon, Marine's husband, feigns death. As Crispin is on the point of being burned on the funeral pyre, Licandre appears, Éliante is given to him, and Crispin is sent to the mines.

As he explains in his preface, J. S. Dodd adapted La Font's one-act farce as *Gallic Gratitude; or, The Frenchman in India* (Covent Garden, April 30, 1779). Captain Atkinson made a three-act opera of the same story and called it *Love in a Blaze,* which was acted at the Crow Street Theater, Dublin, in 1799. Antoin Alarin le Mierre used the idea for *La Veuve du Malabar* (1770), which was turned into a one-act English extravaganza, *You Must Be Buried*, acted at the Haymarket on August 11, 1827, but not printed, and into a two-act English operatic farce, *The Illustrious Stranger, or Married and Buried*, by James Kenney, with music by Nathan, acted at Drury Lane on October 1, 1827. In general, the English cared less than the French for the farcical treatment of the grave.

A Bickerstaff's Burying continues the extraordinary influence of *The Tempest* in the theater.[3] It, too, combines a realistic treatment of sailors with a romantic view of an unknown island. The opening scene suggests the derivation: "*A working Sea seen at a Distance, with the Appearance of a Head of a Ship bulging against a Rock: Mermaids rise and sing: Thunder and Lightning.*" As in *The Tempest*, the ship is only slightly damaged and the spectators discuss the sea tragedy. The sailors report that prayers were mingled with orders aboard ship, the first sailor thinks that he will marry a lady ("And I will be an Ambral too, for all you, and my Master here, shall be my Rear-Ambral") until he learns of the peculiar island custom, and Lady Mezro has been shipwrecked in advance somewhat like Prospero and Miranda on their island. As in *The Basset Table*, where the sailors belong to what Professor Watson calls the *Plain Dealer* school of naval drama, there is a strong note of patriotism, such as the author was likely to introduce whenever she could.

It was natural for Mrs. Centlivre to write a sequel to *The Busy Body*, which had first made her name an asset both to the acting company and to the publisher. The new play, *Mar-Plot, or, The Second Part of the Busie-Body*, was produced at Drury Lane on December 30, 1710, and was published in 1711. Since Cibber and the other actors who had left Drury Lane

[3] Watson, *The Sailor in English Fiction and Drama, 1550-1800* (New York, 1931), pp. 148-50.

for the Haymarket had returned on November 23, 1710, they had obviously forgiven her for the story in the *Female Tatler*. She tells us in her dedication that the play was "kindly receiv'd." At least she received a second benefit, the play being produced seven times before the end of the season.

The Prologue represents the author as trying, despite her ignorance of the rules of writing plays, to entertain the town while the men of wit are engaged in politics and state intrigues. The line between Whig and Tory was already being drawn for the political battle which all foresaw could be decided only with the death of Anne and the placing of her successor on the throne.

In her dedication to the Earl of Portland, for which, according to Mottley, she received the handsome sum of forty guineas, she continues the idea of the Prologue: Since women "are deterred from the Advantages of a Learned Education," she cannot be expected to write according to the rules. She must depend, not on wit and great knowledge, but on her observation of human nature. What she writes will therefore be artless, and her sentiments to that degree will be less disguised than a man's.

The *Tatler* (spurious) for January 9-11, 1711, indicates, in effect, that the play pleased the town but not the *Tatler*. By implication it denies that she was learned in the languages, and it rightly links her to the comic tradition of Ben Jonson:

> The Town has lately been entertained with a Play called *Mar-Plot*, which is a very unfortunate Name, if we should enter into a severe Reflection upon it: But it is enough that it was a Woman's, and one who has made it her Study to divert the *Beaux Monde*, if she could not be so happy as to please the *Beaux Esprits*; and to do her *Justice*, she has succeeded better than some others who have laid Claim, but how justly I will not affirm, to Criticism, Learning and Languages. *Ben Johnson* never appeared to write so well to me, as when I considered the

Nature, Humour and Beauty of his Comedy, compared with the forced and pedantick Affectations and Mimicry of our modern Writers, who make their Characters meer *Pantomimes* of *Ben Johnson*'s.

Pack continued in his old role as Marplot. Wilks was the English officer, Colonel Ravelin, in love with Mademoiselle Joneton (Mrs. Bradshaw), an affected French lady living in Lisbon. Mills continued as Charles Gripe, now the young husband of Isabinda (Mrs. Porter), but already engaged in an intrigue with Dona Perriera, the wife of a Portuguese merchant. Mrs. Willis took the part of Margaritta, Dona Perriera's duenna, Mrs. Cox was Marton, Mademoiselle Joneton's sister, and Mrs. Santlow acted Dona Perriera and spoke the Epilogue. Bowen, Dogget, and Norris were Portuguese in minor roles.

Mar-Plot is by no means the equal of *The Busy Body*. What is most regrettable is the debasing of the character of Marplot. Both his artlessness and his gentlemanliness have gone, and the stupid new Busy Body resorts to all sorts of low contrivances to get information and satisfy his curiosity. The moral tone of the play is also considerably lower. The Charles-Dona Perriera plot hearkens back to the Lady Pizalta business of *The Perjur'd Husband*, the Mrs. Sago affair of *The Basset Table*, and the Lady Cautious plot of *Love at a Venture*. Romantic intrigue has again given way to the intriguing of a rakish gallant and a lustful wife, though Mrs. Centlivre does accept the new moral code to the point of invariably interrupting the assignations in time.

The scene has been shifted to Lisbon, to which Charles has gone to settle the affairs of his father-in-law, Sir Jealous Traffick, now deceased. Marplot has accompanied him. While awaiting some papers, which he has written Isabinda to forward, he attracts the attention of Dona Perriera, who makes an assignation with him, not, however, without being noticed by her brother Don Lopez, who informs Don Perriera. On the advice of Don Lopez, Don Perriera pretends to leave Lisbon for three days. When he is certain that Dona Perriera and her lover are together, he sends for two priests to take their confessions before killing them. But Isabinda, who has brought the papers to Lisbon herself and is now disguised as a man, persuades the priests to help her save Charles. Then two priests, one of them Isabinda in disguise, are admitted to the condemned pair. Without revealing herself, she gets Charles off as a priest, and Don Perriera finds only the two women together. He is berated by his wife for suspecting her, but is greatly relieved to know that she has been faithful.

Charles's friend, Colonel Ravelin, is much in love with the affected Mademoiselle Joneton, whom Marplot calls Mademoiselle Flutter, but he is nevertheless pursuing an affair with a woman who proves to be Marton, Joneton's sister. When he unconcernedly refuses to marry her as the price of her capitulation, Marton goes to a nunnery. Joneton accepts his suit.

Charles, overwhelmed by Isabinda's great goodness in saving his life, is freely forgiven. Dona Perriera is also deeply touched by the excellence of the English wife, and will certainly sin no more:

> *Dona Per.* Oh, Madam, you have set Vice and Virtue in their proper Light, from whence I see the Deformity of one, and the Beauty of the other; your generous Forgiveness is all I want, to raise my Soul above a second Fall. I have injur'd you but ——
>
> *Isab.* No more of that; the good Inclination which you shew wipes out all Faults with me, and your Perseverance will give you as large a Share in my Breast, as if you never had offended.

Many parallels for the characters and incidents of this play may be cited from earlier drama, especially from Mrs. Centlivre's own *The Busy Body*, but it is doubtful that she followed a specific source for it. Colonel Ravelin's relations with Joneton's sister Marton—more callous than are to be expected in a Centlivre play—suggest the cynicism of the Restoration comedy. In most of her other comedies Mrs. Centlivre has as many young men as young women, and brings them all to the marriage altar properly distributed in pairs. The wife's reformation of the much-sinning Charles through kindness reminds us of Cibber's *The Careless Husband*.

Mrs. Centlivre may have got the idea of saving her lovers by duping the husband from Sir Francis Fane's *Love in the Dark*. There Cornanti and his servant come upon Trivultio and Bellinganna, but they are both cowards and retreat, locking the door behind them. Thereupon Trivultio dresses as a duenna, and when the door is opened, he and his mistress deny that a man has been present. Cornanti is finally persuaded to accept their story, and spins a fine yarn of how he ran somebody through and through. It must have been a spirit, he says, which could thus have escaped. Perhaps from the same scene came the idea for Marplot's escape through the locked door. Margaritta lets him out when Don Perriera is not looking and locks the door again, but Don Perriera cannot understand what has happened.

Mar-Plot was revived for the benefit of Williams at the Haymarket on February 18, 1724, Williams himself taking the title role. It was slightly cut and renamed *Marplot in Lisbon* for Woodward's benefit at Drury Lane on March 20, 1755, Woodward acting Marplot. It was repeated twice during the spring, twice in the spring of 1762 at Covent Garden with Cooke as Marplot, and once more at Drury Lane on April 6, 1772, with Dodd in the main role. Then it seems to have disappeared from the stage. *Marplot in Lisbon* rather than the original comedy is included in the complete works of Mrs. Centlivre. No prologue or epilogue is given, and the cast is the one which appeared with Woodward at Dublin in 1759-60.

About the year 1710 or 1711 Mrs. Centlivre interrupted her activities for the stage long enough to write a complimentary poem to the Duke of Newcastle on his daughter, who had just recovered from the smallpox. The Duke was known as the wealthiest man in the kingdom, and Lady Henrietta Holles, his only child, was—as Mrs. Centlivre points out—the wealthiest heiress.[4] She married Edward Harley, later Earl of Oxford, on August 31, 1713. No doubt Susanna found the Holleses attractive for the same reason as Harley. Yet we should not be too critical of either Harley or Susanna, both of whom were acting with the utmost propriety according to the customs of their age—Harley in building a family and Susanna in securing patronage.

So far as I know, "A Poem on The Recovery of the Lady Henrietta Hollis From the Small Pox" exists only in a formally copied manuscript.[5] Its preservation in the great Harleian collection indicates that the Duke and his daughter valued it. Yet some unique manuscripts should be allowed to accumulate the dust of the ages without disturbance, and this is one of them. Other things by Mrs. Centlivre may be as bad, but none is worse. The smallpox, we read, stopped and trembled as he came face to face with the "Beauteous Dame," but then he went on to wage "with Imperial Beauty War." "Not since the pious Great MARIA's Fall" has the nation known such sorrow as when Henrietta was stricken. But Britain's Genius arose, regardful of "the Noblest Patriot Sunk with Greife" as a result of his only child's illness, and called back Health to "Henrietta's Breast." The author also blesses in anticipation the family into which she shall marry.

> Oh happy House, that shall the Nymph Receive,
> And with Her all the Blessings Fate can Give!
> Thrice Happy Youth, whose Smiling Stars decree,
> Virtue, and Truth, Honour, and Wealth for Thee!
> Oh may the destin'd Swain so Faithful prove,

[4] In the *Journal to Stella* Swift says that "the girl is handsome, and has good sense, but red hair."
[5] British Museum, MSS Harleian, 7649.

Worthy the Father's Choice, and Daughter's Love;
Then shall our Joys with his Tryumphant rise,
And our Loud Thanks Ascend the distant Skyes,
Hymen his brightest Saffron Robes shall Wear,
And Lift his Flaming Torch to Bless the Pair.
Fresh Chaplets, shall adorn the Virgin's Head,
And lucky Omens Crown the *Genial Bed.*

Doubtless Mrs. Centlivre's pains did not go unrewarded. Mottley credits her with another poem to the Duke of Newcastle, for which she received a pleasant gratuity:

And the late Duke of *Newcastle,* Uncle to the present, (upon her presenting to him, a little Poem, a kind of Pastoral, which she had wrote upon his purchasing an Estate somewhere, and this was supposed to be a Welcome from the Nymphs and rural Inhabitants of the Place) gave her a large gold Medal in a Shagreen Case, which she kept to the Day of her Death. . . .

Mottley seems not to have seen the poem, nor have I.

A Political *Gambit*

I N HER prologue to *Mar-Plot* Mrs. Centlivre complains that the minds of all the male wits in 1710 were taken up with politics. But Susanna, who never admitted that fields open to men should be closed to women and who rather liked a good scrap, was soon to join them. With *The Perplex'd Lovers*, first produced at Drury Lane on January 19, 1712, her interest in politics became outspoken. For the next five years service to the Whigs and to the House of Hanover was central in her thought. For this reason, as we shall see, she wrote a number of poems. Even in her plays, *The Perplex'd Lovers*, *The Wonder*, *A Gotham Election*, and *A Wife Well Manag'd*, she always introduced in some fashion a declaration of her political zeal.[1]

The Perplex'd Lovers ran for only three nights. In her dedication to Sir Henry Furnesse Mrs. Centlivre charges its failure to her praise of Prince Eugene of Savoy and the Duke of Marlborough. She adds that she "cou'd never have thought it criminal to speak the Praises of those Heroes from a *British* Stage, to whom the greatest Part of *Europe* owes its Safety," and professes to enjoy the honor done her by her enemies in making her "suffer in so glorious a Cause." In a Preface she tells how the managers of the theater did not think it safe to speak the

---

[1] *The Wonder* became a stage favorite of the eighteenth and nineteenth centuries. Except for its political associations at the time it was first presented, it will be reserved for a separate chapter.

Epilogue without a license. But with all the interest she could muster, she was not able to get it approved in time, so that the play was produced with only *"six Lines* Extempore," in which Norris asked the audience to excuse the defect and promised them an epilogue the following night. The audience, convinced that no other epilogue had been intended, hissed. The next day she got the Epilogue licensed by the Vice-Chamberlain, but by that time rumors about town had marked it as a *"notorious whiggish Epilogue,"* and Mrs. Oldfield, *"who design'd me the Favour of speaking it, had Letters sent her to forbear, for that there were Parties forming against it, and they advis'd her not to stand the Shock."* The second night, therefore, Norris spoke an epilogue which implied that the intended one had never been licensed, a ruse which proved unsatisfactory. Norris's epilogue represented him mourning for the poor author, who had been killed by the audience's disdain but who had kindly divided her possessions among her murderers—her spouse to the ladies, *"Copies of soft Billet-doux"* to the beaux unwilling to think for themselves, her wit to the *"pliant Girls, and Gamesters of the Pit,"* her pen to the soldiers for earning their bread in time of peace, and her plots and contrivances to the intriguing citizens' wives.

She included the epilogue intended for Mrs. Oldfield with her printed play so that her readers might judge it. It contains a flattering reference to the Duke of Savoy, whose mission to England really accomplished nothing to help the Allies, and another to Marlborough. The allusion to Marlborough, now out of favor, seems to have caused the trouble. She explains that she owes nothing to his Grace except for what he has done for all England in freeing the country from *"the Insults of a Foreign Power."* As for herself, she knows not the difference between Whigs and Tories; but *"if the Desire to see* [her] *Country secur'd from the* Romish *Yoke, and flourish by a firm, lasting, Honourable Peace, to the Glory of the best of*

Queens, who deservedly holds the Ballance of all Europe, *be
a Whig, then* [she is] *one, else not.*"[2]

Mrs. Centlivre also published with her play a poem "To
his Illustrious Highness Prince *EUGENE* of *Savoy.*" She
welcomes the Allied leader to England after he has aided
Marlborough in scourging the tyrant of Europe and relieving
the oppressed. She has now taken her stand firmly on the side
of the Protestant succession and against Louis XIV:

> Oh! when will *Faction* leave my Native Shore,
> And *Britons* labour to be *Slaves* no more?
> When shall due Merit meet with due Regard,
> And *Friends* to *France,* be *England's Foes* declar'd?
> That once perform'd, my Nation wou'd have Peace,
> And all our Troubles and Distractions cease.

She is convinced too that Eugene will force Louis to discontinue
his attempt to maintain the Bourbon Philip on the throne of
Spain, which will then go to the Austrian House of Hapsburg:

> The *Gallick Tyrant* dreads *thy* vengeful Hand,
> And sees his ill-got *Trophies* tott'ring stand:
> Tho' freed from *Marlbro'* still his *Fears* remain,
> Still *Anjou* trembles on the *Throne of Spain;*
> And if I ought forsee, the *Bourbon Race*
> Shall (*forc'd by thee*) to *Austria's House* give place.

---

[2] Allardyce Nicoll (*Early Eighteenth Century Drama*, Cambridge, 1925,
p. 22) says that "Mrs. Centlivre had a prologue for her *The Perplex'd
Lovers* (D. L. 1712) condemned, for what reason is not known."

Edward Robins's account of the Epilogue (*The Palmy Days of Nance
Oldfield* [1898], pp. 225-26) mingles fact and fiction:

"As for Oldfield, she might have been cautious, too, and with reason, for
she had received letters threatening her with dire pains and penalties if she
spoke the offending words, but Anne stood ready to deliver them at whatsoever time the patentees might name. So when the second night of 'The
Perplex'd Lovers' arrived, and a special licence from the Lord Chamberlain
had been secured, the actress came valiantly forward and spoke the epilogue
with success. Perhaps Eugene of Savoy thanked Mrs. Oldfield—let us hope
that he did—and it is at least certain that after the withdrawal of the play
his Highness sent Mrs. Centlivre an elaborate gold snuff-box."

The poem, at times fairly good, lacks consistency, varying from cheap occasional verse to the formal type of pastoral ode. Mottley says that for it Eugene, "who was just then arrived in *England*," "made her a Present of a very handsome and weighty Gold Snuff-box, on the Rim of which she had engraven *The Present of his Highness Prince* EUGENE *of* SAVOY, *to* SUSANNA CENTLIVRE. This Box was valued at about thirty five Pounds."[3]

In her preface Mrs. Centlivre makes little attempt to defend her comedy. Most of the plot, she says, came from a Spanish drama. Cibber thought the business would carry the play, but Wilks was doubtful, for, though he admitted there was a great deal of business, it was *"not laughing Business."* She argues that she *"cou'd not have dress'd this Plot with much more Humour, there being four Acts in the Dark, which tho'* a Spanish *Audience may readily conceive, the Night being their proper Time of intriguing; yet here, where Liberty makes Noonday as easy, it perplexes the Thought of an Audience too much."* But she promises *"to avoid such Absurdities for the future."*

In the main plot Colonel Bastion is in love with Constantia, the daughter of Sir Roger Merryman—who wants her to marry Lord Richlove—and the sister of Belvil, who has promised her to Sir Philip Gaylove, a friend of his. Lord Richlove, with the bought help of Florella, Constantia's maid, gets into Constantia's presence three times and tries to assault her twice. Each time he is driven off by Bastion. Sir Roger then decides to leave Constantia alone to make her own choice of a husband. In the last act Belvil receives a letter from Sir Philip announcing his marriage, and the brother decides too that his sister may pick for herself. She and Bastion are to be married.

In the minor plot, Belvil is in love with Camilla, his cousin and the confidante of Constantia. As a result of her assistance

[3] Apparently Eugene did not play favorites, for, according to a couplet in James De-La-Cour's *Poems* (Cork, 1778, p. 107), he patronized both Pope and Centlivre—Tory and Whig:

"Lo! Savoy's watch, and Eugene's box of gold,
Pope and Centlivre as a praemium hold."

to her friend, Belvil becomes extraordinarily jealous, but the truth finally resolves their differences.

Mrs. Centlivre had no complaint against the cast. Wilks (Colonel Bastion) and Mrs. Santlow (Constantia) played one pair of lovers, Booth (Belvil) and Mrs. Oldfield (Camilla) the other. Mrs. Saunders was the maid Florella. The additional roles were acted by Mills, Leigh, Bullock, Pack, and Bowen.

The particular Spanish play to which Mrs. Centlivre referred as her source is still unidentified. None of her other so-called Spanish plays came directly from the Spanish, nor, probably, did this one. In one brief episode there is distinctly French influence. As Hohrmann[4] points out, the opening scene varies the situation in which Equipage asks for his wages at the beginning of *The Platonick Lady*, that scene being taken from Regnard's *Attendez-mois sous l'orme*. The despicable Florella, who even introduces Lord Richlove secretly into her mistress's bedchamber, suggests Favourite, who receives gifts from Dorante in *The Gamester*. A lover's jealousy of his mistress, who protects his sister from a match with the man he intends for her, is a common motif in many of the Spanish plots. It is the basis of *The Wonder* and of Ravenscroft's *The Wrangling Lovers*, from which *The Wonder* was taken. It is found too in *Elvira* (1667), adapted by George Digby, Earl of Bristol, from Calderon's *No siempre lo peor es cierto*. When Don Ruis in *The Wrangling Lovers* learns that the man for whom he had intended his sister is dead, he, like Belvil, withdraws his objection to his sister's own choice. But the spirit of *The Perplex'd Lovers* and the details of the plot are different from those in any of the other plays named. Belvil, Colonel Bastion, Lord Richlove, the two girls, and the servants merely stalk about in the darkness and almost as if by conscious contrivance mistake one another for somebody else. Constantia, for instance, mistakes Lord Richlove, his French valet Le Front,

---

[4] "Das Verhältnis Susanna Centlivre's zu Molière und Regnard," *Zeitschrift für vergleichende Litteraturgeschichte*, N.F., XIV (1900-1901), 418.

and her brother Belvil, one after the other, for her lover, Colonel Bastion. Nor is the grossness of various passages a recommendation for the comedy.

Late in 1712 or early in 1713 the Centlivres took up residence in Buckingham Court, Charing Cross, where they resided until Mrs. Centlivre's death. The rate-books of the parish of St. Martin-in-the-Fields show that Joseph Centlivre (spelled throughout St. Liver) was assessed during the first half of 1713. In 1724 a line is drawn through his name and "Empty" is written in the margin. The name Robert Wood appears immediately below, but, since his assessment is only about half the usual amount, he probably did not move in before March. Joseph had left within a few months after his wife's death.

The Centlivres paid a higher rate than anyone else in Buckingham Court except the Admiralty Office, which was situated there part of this time. Apparently they lived on the corner of Buckingham Court and Spring Gardens, itself "a curiously crooked little street, immediately west of Trafalgar Square, connecting Whitehall with the east end of the Mall, and St. James's Park."[5]

During her first year in her new home Mrs. Centlivre, so far as we know, limited herself to the composition of two poems. The first she wrote in a book, Fontenelle's *Plurality of Worlds*, which she had borrowed from Anne Oldfield. She was "so charmed with seeing Mrs. OLDFIELD play the Part of MARTIA in CATO" that she wrote the following poem to her on a blank leaf:

> Plurality of Worlds! *Such Things may be,*
> *But I am best convinc'd by what I see;*
> *Yet tho'* Philosophers *such Schemes pursue,*
> *And* fancy'd Worlds *in every* Planet *view;*
> *They can but* guess *at Orbs* above *the Skies,*
> *And* darkly paint *the Lakes and Hills that rise.*
> *Now* Cupid *skill'd in* Mysteries *profound,*

[5] Laurence Hutton, *Literary Landmarks of London* (1888), p. 41.

> *Points where more* certainty of Worlds *abound;*
> Bright Globes, *that strike the* Gazer *with Surprize,*
> *For* they *are* Worlds *of* Love *and in* Ophelia's *Eyes.*[6]

Mrs. Centlivre undoubtedly approved the doctrine of liberty upheld by Addison in his tragedy. (*Cato* was first acted at Drury Lane on April 14, 1713.) She had already shown an interest in *The Plurality of Worlds*, partly perhaps because of the speculative subject and partly because of Fontenelle's concern for the instruction of women.[7]

The second poem of 1713 was "The Masquerade," which she addressed to the Duke d'Aumont, ambassador extraordinary from the Court of France. Mottley says that she inscribed it to D'Aumont even though she was so "violent a *Whig*," but that "there was nothing of Politics in it." Since the treaty of Utrecht had been signed, Mrs. Centlivre felt that she could forego for a time her hatred of things French and Roman Catholic. Mottley explains that it brought her a Tory snuffbox to match the Whig one Prince Eugene had given her:

> The Duke received her with great Politeness, when she went to wait upon him after sending her Poem, and asked if she had a Snuff-Box; she told him Yes, one that Prince *Eugene* had given her. Oh! said he, that was a *Whig* Box; now I will give a *Tory* Snuff-Box. And accordingly made her a Present of a Gold Snuff-Box with a Picture in the Lid, which, she was told by one of his Domestics, his Excellency had given, to his Knowledge, fifty Pistoles for in *Paris.*

D'Aumont, a thoroughly romantic figure, attracted a good deal of attention at the time. Bishop Burnet[8] notes that the Duke of Shrewsbury went to France as ambassador, following

---

[6] William Egerton, *Faithful Memoirs of the Life, Amours and Performances, of . . . Mrs. Anne Oldfield* (1731), pp. 58-59. "Egerton" was probably a pseudonym for Edmund Curll.

[7] See page 73.

[8] *History of My Own Time* (Oxford, 1833), VI, 141.

Hamilton's death in the duel with Mohun, late in December, 1712. "The same yacht that carried him to Calais, brought over the duke de Aumont, the French ambassador, who was a good-natured and generous man, of profuse expense, throwing handfuls of money often out of his coach, as he went about the streets: he was not thought a man of business, and seemed to employ himself chiefly in maintaining the dignity of his character, and making himself acceptable to the nation."[9]

D'Aumont entertained often with masquerades. Eustace Budgell, Addison's cousin and Mrs. Centlivre's friend, wrote in *A Letter to the Lord * * * * * (2d ed.; 1718) that "The *English*, who have a Genius for *improving* whatever Hint is given them, have, since the Duke *D'Aumont* left *London*, brought *masquerading* to the *highest degree* of *Elegance* and *Perfection* that Diversion seems to be capable of." George I laid aside the cares of state and mixed in the assemblies. George II also favored masquerades, which continued popular until late in the eighteenth century.

The Masquerade, in English and French, was published, according to the *Daily Courant*, on September 3, 1713, by Bernard Lintot. Though printed without the name of the author, this scarce poem is unquestionably Mrs. Centlivre's. It occupies seven pages, the title on page 1, the French version on pages 2, 4, and 6, and the English on pages 3, 5, and 7. The masquerade which is the subject of the poetic epistle was

[9] Oldmixon (*History of England during the Reigns of King William and Queen Mary, Queen Anne, and King George* I [1735], pp. 527-28) adds that D'Aumont arrived in England on Jan. 2, 1713. At first he lodged in Ormond Street, but after the burning of his house on Jan. 26—the Tories said it was burned by the Whigs, who knew that D'Aumont was a friend of the Pretender, and the Whigs said it was burned by the Tories to make an excuse for inviting D'Aumont to Somerset House, from which he could secretly communicate by water with France—the Queen immediately had the finest apartment in Somerset House prepared for him. Oldmixon remarks that it was strongly suspected that the Chevalier de St. George was also in London, lodging in Somerset House, that the Duke d'Aumont gave so many masquerades to make opportunities for him to become acquainted with the English nobility, and that the Chevalier "was often in the Queen's Closet."

celebrated at Somerset House on August 17. The poem begins:

> The Globe with wond'rous Pains Men traverse o'er,
> To learn the Dress and Customs of each Shore;
> From Pole to Pole pursue their trackless Way,
> And run the Dangers of a faithless Sea.

But, says the author, the curious are welcome to visit foreign climes while she beholds the "spacious World" at home. Persons of mythology as well as the inhabitants of foreign lands are represented in the masquerade. All "quit their own, to take a borrow'd Shape"—all, that is, "but the Godlike AU-MOUNT," who alone "Could take no Form so lovely as his own."[10]

On September 24, three weeks after her poem appeared, a special performance of *The Busy Body* was given at Drury Lane for the "Entertainment of his Excellency the Duke d'Aumont." Presumably it was a "command" performance, and it is likely that the Duke rewarded both the players and the author.

Mrs. Centlivre had by this time met with popular stage success in *The Gamester* and *The Busy Body*. Her third important play, which furnished Garrick with a favorite role, was *The Wonder: A Woman Keeps a Secret.* It was acted at Drury Lane on April 27, 1714, and was printed the same year by Edmund Curll with a Dedication, added on a brave but lucky gamble, to the Duke of Cambridge, later George I.[11] As Mottley says, she dedicated her play "to his present Majesty, then Duke of *Cambridge,* and at *Hanover,* just at the Time when a Writ had been demanded, but refused, to call him to his

---

[10] Another rare poem, *A Trip to the Masquerade, or, a Journey to Somerset House,* was printed by J. Read in 1713. It includes more detail about the masqueraders, particularly those who came in the dress of sailors, farmers, chimney sweepers, and the like, and explains that wine, lemonades, and sweetmeats were furnished the motley crowd.

[11] Curll paid her twenty guineas for the rights, twice what she had been accustomed to receive.—Ralph Straus, *The Unspeakable Curll* (1927), p. 227.

Seat in the House of Peers in *England*. Mrs. *Centlivre* did this, to shew her Attachment to the House of *Hanover*, and was rewarded for it when the present Royal Family came to the Throne, who bespoke this Play, which they Honoured with their Presence, and made the Author an handsome Present."

In her Dedication Mrs. Centlivre says that every honest Briton awaits George with impatience. She is pleased that the most accomplished of princes is to perfect himself in the art of government under the eyes of the greatest of queens. His residence in Great Britain will put an end to the expectations of any who would like to see their country become a French province. After the law of nature, he will probably reign over the English, and she is confident that the English religion, laws, and civil rights will then be in no danger. She commends him for the pains he has taken to learn the language, but since the idiom is always difficult, she does not think an English comedy an improper present. In time, she concludes, better pens will pay tribute to him, but in the meanwhile she has the honor of being the first to show her respect in this manner.

A few years later she still remembered that, contrary to the advice of Steele, she had "dedicated" to George of Wales when she knew him hated at the court:

> To GEORGE of *Wales* I Dedicated,
> Tho' then at Court I knew him Hated.
> *Steele* was then in Reputation
> With all true Lovers of my Nation:
> Yet spight of *Steele*'s Advice I did it;
> Nay tho' my Husband's Place forbid it;
> For he these Forty Years has been
> The Servant to a King or Queen:
> Nor will I here the Truth dissemble;
> This Action made his Post to Tremble;
> And he had surely been turn'd out,
> Had not good Fortune wheel'd about.[12]

[12] A WOMAN's CASE: in an Epistle to *CHARLES JOYE*, Esq.; Deputy-Governor of the *South-Sea* (1720).

Her buoyant support of the Protestant House of Hanover might have caused both her and her husband trouble had not Anne died within a few months and the Whigs, ready for the contingency, established George on the throne.

Many of the literary Whigs—Addison, Steele, Philips, Burnet, Budgell, and others—were provided for under the new regime. Unfortunately, however, Susanna was a woman, and the political plums were not thought proper for a woman's table. But the royal family did take an interest in her plays. *The Wonder* was produced by command of his Royal Highness the Prince of Wales on December 16, 1714. *The Cruel Gift* was similarly given at Drury Lane on May 3, 1717, and *The Busy Body* on October 22 and 23, 1717. The performance of *The Cruel Gift* was for the benefit of the author, and the other command performances undoubtedly included gifts for her. The King himself commanded *The Busy Body* at Drury Lane on March 17, 1720, for her benefit. According to the *St. James's Journal* for October 4, 1722, it was rumored that his Majesty intended "to see the New Play call'd the ARTIFICE, on the sixth Night, for the Benefit of the Author," but the play ran for only three nights.

The Prologue to *The Wonder* was written by Thomas Burnet, youngest son of Gilbert Burnet, the bishop and historian. It is included in *Verses Written on Several Occasions, Between the Years 1712 and 1721* (1721), where the author is named as "the son of a very renowned Prelate, to whom this country is indebted for the *History of his Life and Times,* and many other learned and useful works." Burnet is mentioned as one of Mrs. Centlivre's close friends and correspondents, and, like herself, was a determined Whig. He was notorious for debauchery and somewhat distinguished for wit. A lawyer and a minor writer who took his directions from Addison, he was made consul at Lisbon in 1719. Later he became a justice of the common pleas and was knighted. About the twentieth

of April, 1714, Burnet wrote to George Duckett: "I have writ
a Prologue to a Play, which will very speedily be printed, as
well as spoken, and which I design very soon to send you."[13]

The Epilogue was contributed by another Whig, Ambrose
Philips, author of *Pastorals*, who is remembered chiefly as a
rival of Pope. He was a member of Addison's club and a man
of some prominence in Whig circles. Susanna herself was in
the heart of Whigland.[14]

The same year, on October 7, according to an advertisement
in the *Post Boy*, appeared *A Poem Humbly Presented to His
most Sacred Majesty George, King of Great Britain, France,
and Ireland. Upon His Accession to the Throne*, "By Susanna
Centlivre." The six-page work, dated 1715, lauds George as
the deliverer of England from strife and from the self-seeking
Tories who had Anne's confidence during the last years of her
reign:

> The Lark, while she her Gratitude to prove,
> Lauds with her sprightly Notes, immortal Jove,
> Shuts not his Ear against the Sparrows Lays,
> Whose tuneless Pipe can only chirp his Praise.
> Thus I, tho' learned Bards before have strung
> Their sounding Lyres, and most divinely Sung,
> Fear not the Dictates of my Soul to own;
> The less of Art, the more of Love is shown:
> Vouchsafe, Great Prince, to hear my humble Muse,
> And let my Zeal my Want of Skill excuse.

[13] *The Letters of Thomas Burnet to George Duckett, 1712-1722*, ed.
David Nichol Smith (Oxford, 1914), p. 63. Swift wrote to Stella of the
Mohocks in 1712: "The Bishop of Salisbury's son is said to be one of the
gang: They are all Whigs." Burnet told Duckett of the organization of the
Mohocks but denied that he was a member (*ibid.*, pp. 2, 3, 7). The Pro-
logue was also printed in Burnet's *Verses Written on Several Occasions* (1777).

[14] Two lines of the Epilogue show the author defending women from
the charge of pure animalism:

> Some are for having our whole Sex enslav'd,
> Affirming we've no *Souls*, and *can't be sav'd*;

A note in the complete works explains that the allusion was to "an ironical
Pamphlet tending to prove that *Women* had *no Souls*."

Hail! Hero born to rule, and reconcile
The fatal Discords of our *English* Isle!
Our pure *Religion*, long the Mark of *Rome*,
Repriev'd by you Escapes her final Doom. . . .
Delightful *Liberty*, with Fears half dead,
Hears the glad Noise, and rears her pleasing Head;
Her slacken'd Nerves their former Strength regain,
And she her Life redates from GEORGE's Reign. . . .
   By your fam'd Justice, and your prudent Sway,
France shall be taught to Love, or to Obey;
Whilst You the Right of Liberty assert,
And all the Ills of broken Faith avert;
To *Barcelona* may your Succours fly,
Before her Champions 'midst her Ruins dye. . . .
   WELLCOME great Guardian of our *British* Land;
Receive the Nation rescu'd by thy Hand.
A wicked Race of Men, for private Ends,
Had rais'd her baffled Foes, and sunk her Friends,
Dispers'd her Strength, and Royal ANN betray'd,
Whilst in the Sunshine of her Smiles they play'd;
The Ruin rowl'd too fast for her to stem,
Whose greatest Weakness was her Choice of *Them:*
When Heav'n, in Pity to those suppliant Few,
Who own'd its Power, and kept their Vows to You,
Came to our Aid, revers'd our low'ring Fate,
And by thy destin'd ARM retriev'd the State. . . .

One week later the *Daily Courant* announced "AN
EPISTLE TO Mrs. WALLUP, Now in the TRAIN of Her
Royal Highness, The Princess of *WALES*. *As it was sent to
her at the HAGUE. Written by Mrs.* SUSANNA CENTLIVRE."[15]
Again the poem shows Mrs. Centlivre irrepressible in her ela-
tion over the Whig victory. She praises William, Mary, the
King, Carolina Princess of Wales, and Carolina's "Babes," "for
our *Church*'s Safety given." Mrs. Wallup, according to the

[15] The title page bears the date 1715.

poetess, had long since paid her "ardent Vows" to George, but
her zeal was for the good of England:

> When your unweary'd Zeal thrice crost the Sea,
> Nor fear'd what Dangers might obstruct your Way:
> Not led by Int'rest, or Intrigues of State,
> (Avarice and Pride! Faults of the meanly great:)
> No private *End* by you was understood,
> But all your Wishes were the *Publick Good*.

Perhaps the most notable quality of the poem is the deliberate
avoidance of any mention of Queen Anne, a ritualistic neglect
less noticed by the new royal family than by some members of
the Whig party:

> The Sun which set in fair *Maria*'s Eyes,
> In *Carolina*'s does triumphant rise,
> In *her* you'll find *Maria*'s Loss retriev'd,
> That Charming *Queen* for whom so much we griev'd.

And now that Mrs. Wallup is to convey Princess Carolina to
England, she will "our Harvest bring."

On New Year's Day, 1715, Mrs. Centlivre cut out the in-
termediaries and presented a poem directly to the Princess of
Wales. "To her Royal Highness the Princess of WALES.
At her Toylet, on *New-Years Day*" is a trite and dull compliment to the Princess's beauty. It begins:

> Had great *Apelles* once beheld that Face
> When he the Beauteous *Cyprian Goddess* Drew,
> He had neglected all the Female Race,
> Thrown his first *Venus* by, and Copy'd YOU,
> Your Charming Figure had inhanc'd his Fame,
> And Shrines been rais'd to *Carolinas* Name.

The poem was published in the *Patriot* for January 15-18, 1715.
The editor's introduction praising Mrs. Centlivre for her
service to the Protestant succession is more interesting than the
poem:

And since I am now upon the Subject of Female Resolution and Vertue, I cannot forbear mentioning the Name of Mrs. *Susanna Centlivre,* a Woman, whose Good Sense and Noble Passion for the Protestant Succession in the present Illustrious Family, make her an Honour to her Sex, and a Credit to *Our* Country. The Dedication of her Play to his Royal Highness, when Duke of *Cambridge* in *May* last, a time in which it was esteem'd almost a Crime to Name that Family, is a standing Instance that She is Mistress of a True *British* Principle. She has not been wanting since His Majesties Happy Arrival in these Kingdoms, to give us new Marks of her Affection and Zeal for *Him* and his Royal Family: And I shall conclude this Paper with Inserting the Poem which she presented to Her Royal Highness the *Princess of Wales* on *New-Years Day,* as it was Transmitted me (if I mistake not the Hand) by the Lady to whom the Town is oblig'd for those Verses on the Earl of Hallifax's being made Knight of the Garter.

It seems likely that Mrs. Centlivre herself sent a copy of the verses to the *Patriot* and even more certain that she wrote "On the Right Honourable CHARLES Earl of HALLIFAX being made Knight of the Garter," which had appeared in the *Patriot* for November 16-18, 1714. Mottley says that "For some other Poem, the Title of which I know not, the Lord *Halifax* had made her a Present of a fine repeating Gold Watch." The editor's introduction contains high praise of Halifax, compliments to the ladies, and trivia:

Amongst these *Patriots* the Earl of *Hallifax* is one of the first, this Gentleman by the Zeal he has perpetuallo [*sic*] shewn for the Interest of his Country, and the Mild Temper with which he has bore the Insults and Pillages of Prostituted Men, has gained him as many Admirers among his Country Men, who are Honest in their Politicks, as his other Excellent Qualifications have among all

Lovers and Judges of Letters. And thus far one would willingly allow: But that his Lordship should proceed so universally to be admir'd as to make even the Ladies write Panegyricks on him, is what, I fear, some of our fine Gentlemen will ill bear, unless his Lordship will be pleas'd to write something very dull, or do something very trivial in the State, both which are as great Impossibilities to him as it is for his Enemies to have common Sense or common Honesty.

The editor is delighted to have a "fine Lady (for I am sure she must be so by the Goodness of her Poetry and the Badness of her Spelling)" concern herself with national affairs. If he could be certain that the ladies would read him, he would like to give them good intellectual stuff instead of remarks on *"Cloe*'s false Hair" and *"Salley*'s bad Fancy in Dress." The poem itself makes a brief Whig summary of English politics since the time of King William:

> When vicious Statesmen sway'd the Throne of late,
> And to our constant Foes betray'd the State,
> Then *Bourbon*'s Gold flew round our Council Board,
> And Men put Conscience off to put on———Lord!
> Wou'd *Hallifax* have sold his Country so,
> He might have worn the GARTER long ago;
> But his just soul for nobler Actions form'd,
> On such perfidious Terms all Titles scorn'd. . . .
> Him *Williams*'s great unerring Judgment chose,
> And by his Merit (not by Chance) he rose.
> With the same Eye *George* views his mighty Mind,
> And thus fulfils what *William* had design'd.

Dr. Johnson says, on the authority of Pope, that Halifax was "fed with dedications; for Tickell affirms that no dedication was unrewarded. Almost all of the poets except Pope and Steele praised or flattered him."[16]

[16] *The Works of Samuel Johnson*, ed. Arthur Murphy (1806), X, 47. Lintot in 1714 published a poem by Rowe on Halifax: *Mecaenas. Verses*

It was perhaps inevitable that sooner or later Mrs. Centlivre would turn her theatrical gifts directly to the treatment of
political affairs. Her two farces, *A Gotham Election* and *A
Wife Well Manag'd*, were published separately in 1715. They
may also have been published in a single volume, for the Dedication of the former to James Craggs, who became secretary at
war in 1717 and secretary of state in 1718, was obviously intended for both. "Do me the Honour," she says, "to afford
your Protection to these two *Petites* Pieces," and further, "I
wish, Sir, that you may find any thing in either of these little
Comedies, that may entertain you at some leisure Hour." *A
Gotham Election* was republished in 1737 as *The Humours of
Elections*,[17] ironically enough as propaganda against Walpole
and the Whigs, but it seems never to have been acted under
either title. *A Wife Well Manag'd*, in which Mrs. Centlivre
undertook to unlace a Catholic priest, caused as much trouble
as the other, and, despite the statements by modern dramatic
historians that it was probably acted in 1715, was not produced
until 1724.

Mrs. Centlivre believes that the two were persecuted by
people who did not know them. If "they had gone thro' a
legal Course of Theatrical Justice," she would have been satisfied, even though the verdict had been partial. But now she
thinks it necessary to print them in order to show how she
has been maligned:

> The Election, which had the Honour to pass your
> Approbation, was objected against as a Party-Matter:
> I fancy both Sides will agree that there are unreasonable
> Heats and Extravagancies belonging to each of them, which
> deserve to be expos'd, laugh'd at, and exploded by all

---

*Occasion'd by the HONOURS Conferr'd on the Right Honourable EARL OF
HALLIFAX.* It is little better than Mrs. Centlivre's.

[17] F. Pilon may have used the second title in naming his farce, *The
Humours of an Election*, performed fourteen times at Covent Garden between
Oct. 19 and Dec. 16, 1780. There is no further resemblance between the two
pieces.

true Lovers of their Country; since, by such Arts, our Enemies find the Way to poison our Constitution. For the other, it was said there would be Offence taken at the exposing a *Popish Priest*. Good God! To what Sort of People are we chang'd! Are those worthy Gentlemen (the Emissaries of our most irreconcileable Enemy) to be treated with so much tenderness? Is not their Profession Treason in any Subject of *Great Britain?* Have our Neighbours in *France* treated the Clergy of the Reform'd Religion with the same Regard?

She praises Craggs for his loyalty to the Protestant cause and indicates her appreciation of his generously espousing her interest when he knew that she intended to dedicate *The Wonder* to the Duke of Cambridge.

In her Preface she repeats that she had hoped to have *A Gotham Election* acted, so that their Royal Highnesses could see the manner of the English elections and the town could be entertained with a subject entirely new. But the master of the revels would not meddle with anything having to do with elections, and the players would act nothing without his license. Scandalous stories then made her the subject of conversation in every coffeehouse in London. Her friends, who always defended her when they heard her name aspersed, finally advised her to print the farce, especially as it had been maliciously represented as an impudent libel upon Queen Anne. She had attempted in it, she says, to be as natural as possible, with the result that she had put wool in the hats of her Whigs and laurel in those of the Tories, though she cannot see why the Tories should have worn laurel when they were trying to rid England of the benefits of her conquests. A sprig of rosemary would have been a more appropriate emblem to mark the funeral of English religion and liberty that would have occurred if the followers of the Pretender had had their way. If Rowe's *Lady Jane Grey* had represented the heroine as a Papist and

Gardiner as a bishop of the Church of England and had been acted on the French stage, she is sure that no Protestant would have dared to call it a Catholic play without risking the galleys.

Nevertheless, it is little wonder that the lord chamberlain hesitated to license *A Gotham Election.* The pulpit and stage had both been used for the expression of political opinions in 1714, and before the end of December the clergy had been ordered to refrain from politics in their sermons. The elections in January, 1715, had often been violent, and the Riot Act was passed in June, 1715. The government did not care to encourage inflamed opinion.

Mottley says that Craggs rewarded Mrs. Centlivre with twenty guineas, despite Mrs. Bracegirdle's suggestion that he was being overgenerous:

> *The Gotham Election* . . . [was] dedicated to Mr. Secretary *Craggs,* who made her a Present of twenty Guineas, by the Hands of Mrs. *Bracegirdle,* who had got leave for her to dedicate it to him; and when she told him, he was very liberal, and sent the Author more than she could reasonably expect, especially as her Farce had never been acted, he told her, he considered not so much the Merit of the Piece, as what was proper to be done by a Secretary of State.

The witty remark attributed to him has attracted a good deal of attention, but the point of it is blunted by the fact that Craggs did not become secretary of state until 1718.

Genest (X, 154) thinks that the farce "contains a good deal of low humour." In attempting to make a play out of a contemporary problem, Mrs. Centlivre was far ahead of her age, because, although political views were being expressed in prologues and epilogues and developed allegorically in plays like Rowe's *Tamerlane* (1701) and Addison's *Cato* (*The Non-Juror* was yet to come), no one was making a realistic attempt to study social problems in the theater. Mrs. Cent-

livre had shown in *The Platonick Lady* and *The Man's Bewitch'd* some ability to conceive English provincial characters
and to write dialect. *A Gotham Election* is a further development
of the provincial style, with characters whose names indicate their derivation: Tickup, a candidate; Scoredouble, an inn-
keeper; Watt Washball, a barber; Mallet, a carpenter; Scruple,
a Quaker; Last, a cobbler; Tolefree, a miller; Timothy Shallow, a tailor; Ben Blunt; Gregory Gabble; Roger Sly; Goody
Gabble; Goody Shallow; and Goody Sly. If times had been
propitious, Mrs. Centlivre might have contributed realistic
English dramas to the theater instead of the plethora of French
translations and Spanish plots with which she filled her pages.

Tickup, the Tory candidate, and Lady Worthy, the Tory
High-Flyer wife of Sir John Worthy, the Whig candidate, buy
votes as the occasion offers. Friendly, representing Sir Roger
Trusty, a third candidate, and Sir Roger himself are sound
Whigs. Mallet is the means of exposing the Tory method of
making exorbitant pre-election promises. In return for his
vote, Tickup promises him important positions in the government for himself and all his relatives. After the christening of
Mallet's grandson, Lady Worthy shows her true Jacobite colors
by desiring a fiddler to play "The King shall enjoy his own
again." Roger Sly (the republican) refuses to allow it, and
commands "Lillibullera," the Whig tune. Thereupon Lady
Worthy bloodies Sly's nose and a moment later the nose of
Goody Sly. But the defendant avenges himself by publicizing
Lady Worthy's affair with Tickup. The election ends in a
riot, but apparently the Whigs win.

In a romantic subplot Friendly, posing as a Frenchman, gets
Lucy from her Jacobite father, the mayor of Gotham, ostensibly
to take her to her brother in France, where she may be edu-
cated. But Lucy is a Whig to the bone, and, learning of her
father's principles and his intention to send her to a nunnery,
she gives herself sensibly to the man who has rescued her.

One of the best bits of farce results from Tickup's request for the shoemaker's vote. He is received in the cobbler's shop, where he endures the ignominy of kissing the cobbler and having his clothes soiled by the miller in order to prove that he is not proud. Then the shoemaker, after having him parade back and forth in front of the shop, refuses to vote for any man who lacks self-respect.

The language of *A Gotham Election* is by no means poetic. No doubt many of the expressions came from the common people Mrs. Centlivre had actually known. The credulity of men like Mallet who know only the names of state offices is pictured realistically, and the Quaker, Scruple, distinguished by his frankness and honesty, is very different from the stage Quakers introduced in *A Bold Stroke for a Wife*.

A Wife Well Manag'd was printed with a list of the parts as they were *"designed to have been represented by"* Norris, Shepherd, Miller, Mrs. Baker, and Miss Younger. It was finally produced, along with *Jane Shore*, by subscription, on March 2, 1724, at the "new Theatre over against the Opera House" in the Haymarket. In 1732 it was made into *The Disappointment*, "A New Ballad Opera of One Act, Alter'd from a Farce after the Manner of The Beggar's Opera," and was acted at the Haymarket. The Dedication is signed John Randall, probably a pseudonym for Henry Carey. Several names are changed, and the scene is shifted from Lisbon to Madrid, but the recitative is almost identical with Mrs. Centlivre's lines. The twelve songs are in Carey's style.[18] *A Wife Well Manag'd* was itself produced at Hussey's Great Theatrical Booth during the course of Bartholomew Fair in 1747. Its last production seems to have been for the benefit of Edwin at the Haymarket on August 27, 1789, when it was the second piece of a triple bill including *The Young Quaker* and *Duke and No Duke*.

[18] F. T. Wood, "*The Disappointment*," *Review of English Studies*, V (1929), 66-69.

A Wife Well Manag'd is a clever farce. Lady Pizalto
has fallen deeply in love with Father Bernardo, who has also
been attracted to her. She sends him a letter by her Irish
servant Teague inviting him to visit her, but Don Pizalto discovers Teague with the letter. He himself goes to the priest,
borrows a garment from him, and invites him to have supper
with himself and his wife. Then he sends Lady Pizalto a letter
in the name of the priest, and a little later excuses himself to
look after some legal business which will require several hours.
When he reappears in the guise of Father Bernardo, Lady
Pizalto receives him ecstatically. Then he takes a rope's end
from under his cloak and beats her and her maid severely.

When Pizalto returns in his own person, the maid explains
that her mistress has been badly bruised in a fall down the
steps. Pizalto receives Father Bernardo, who comes to keep
his supper engagement, and asks him to visit his wife, who
seems to be possessed by "unclean Spirits." The priest finds
her asleep. When he wakes her with a kiss, she flies up and
pommels him with her fists, and the maid enters and beats
him with a stick, despite his sprinkling of holy water to put
down the fiend. After a time Pizalto rescues him. The husband then shows his wife her letter to Bernardo and threatens
her with a dagger. Lady Pizalto falls on her knees, confesses
her wrong against her dear "Pudsey," and promises to sin no
more.

Genest (II, 559) remarks that Mrs. Centlivre took her
"laughable" one-act piece from *The Husband His Own Cuckold*
(1690), by John Dryden, Jr.; but it must be added that her
alterations agree with the story as told in the thirty-fifth novel
of the *Heptameron*. Dryden's comedy contains a triple plot,
of which Mrs. Centlivre uses only the part relating to Sir John
and Lady Crossit and Dr. Lorman. She changes the doctor
to a priest, reduces the lapse of time from several days to a
few hours, and has the husband beat his wife rather than
scratch her face. Only a few suggestions of Dryden's language

remain. Lady Crossit says to her maid after her husband's departure for the doctor, "I shall tear his Eyes out of his Head, if ever I light on him." Lady Pizalto says under similar circumstances, "if I shou'd see him, I think in my Soul I should tear his Eyes out." Were it not for such passages, I should prefer to think that Mrs. Centlivre used only the *Heptameron*, which she follows in making the lover a priest, in having the husband borrow a habit from her lover, in causing the husband to beat his lady rather than scratch her face, and (with a slight variation) in having the priest sprinkle holy water to mollify the rage of the supposed demoniac.

During the spring of 1716, Robert Walpole, leader of the large Whig majority in the House of Commons, fell seriously ill, and his life was despaired of. On May 19, during his period of forced retirement, James Roberts published a small volume of *State Poems* "By The most Eminent Hands" for Edmund Curll. Susanna Centlivre contributed an "Ode to Hygeia," "The Patriots," and perhaps other poems.[19] The "Ode to Hygeia" is distinctive only for its timeliness and good will. The second of the three stanzas is characteristic:

> Great HYGEIA lend an Ear
> *Britannia*'s pray'r vouchsafe to hear.
> *Britannia* on thy Aid relies,
> Help or else her WALPOLE dies.
> Tho' thou'st frequent cause to blame,
> The Old Ungrateful fickle Dame,
> Yet preserve her *Patriots* life,
> In compassion to his Wife.

[19] Only the "Ode to Hygeia" is credited to Mrs. Centlivre. The volume includes Rowe's "On Mr. Walpole's Recovery," "An Epilogue written for the late celebrated New Play called the Drummer, but not spoke," and Pope's "To the Ingenious Mr. Moore, Author of the Celebrated Worm-Powder." Curll was again printing Pope's poem to embarrass the author. The unspoken epilogue to Addison's *The Drummer* was a new poem also intended to embarrass Pope. Mrs. Centlivre could probably have told him who wrote it.

Calm the tempest in that Breast,
Where great WALPOLE wont to rest.
Bid those Eyes their streams forbear
Whose look gives Pleasure ev'rywhere
Hear us *Health*'s great *Goddess* Hear.

"The Patriots" was really the last three stanzas of another poem, "*Upon the Bells ringing at* St. Martins in the Fields, *on* St. George*'s Day* [April 23], 1716, *being the Anniversary of Queen* Anne*'s Coronation.*" The full work was first published in the *Flying Post* for May 10-12, where it is attributed to "S. C. *a Loyal Female in that Parish.*" It was reprinted in *A Collection of State Songs, Poems, &c. That have been Publish'd since the Rebellion: and Sung in the several Mug-Houses in the Cities of London and Westminster* (1716), in the index to which it is credited to Mrs. Centlivre. She is celebrating, she says, Nancy's coronation day, Nancy by whom the Tory bell-ringers had expected to bring in the young Chevalier of St. George, as the Tories called the Pretender, but Fate that "*pulls down* Queens, and *sets up* Kings" sent a better George:

I.

Pull on, expiring *Tory* Boys,
And please yourselves a while with Noise,
   Y'have lost all other Hopes;
Your Loyalty to *Perkin* seal,
Pull on, ring out your Fun'ral Peal,
   Then *hang your selves i' th' Ropes.*

II.

'Tis *Nancy*'s Coronation-Day,
By whom ye hop'd to bring in play
   Young *George*, the *Chevalier.*
But Fate, who best disposes Things,
And *pulls down* Queens, and *sets up* Kings,
   A better *GEORGE* sent here. . . .

IV.

In spite of Necessary Peers,
Created in those Four Black Years,
   To save that Traytor, *Harley*;
The major Part were firm and true,
And Britain's Int'rest to pursue,
   Did pass the Bill most rarely.[20]

V.

And, maugre all the Tory Hopes,
Of *L* - - - -'s Turn,[21] and *Sh* - - - - *n*'s Tropes,[22]
   'Tis pass'd the Lower House;
And now, a Fig for High Church Daws,
For their King *Perkin*, and his Cause,
   We need not care one Souse. . . .

VIII.

But now they utter loud Complaints,
And curse all Male and Female Saints,
   WALPOLE still lives, their Curb;

[20] On April 13, 1715, a committee of secrecy was announced by the House of Commons to inquire into the late peace of Utrecht and the conduct of the ministers. On June 9 its report was received. The next day were exhibited at the bar of the House of Lords the sixteen articles of impeachment which had been carried in the lower house by large majorities against Robert Harley, first Earl of Oxford, and Earl Mortimer. Most of the articles accused Harley of baseness in arranging the treaty of Utrecht, but the sixteenth accused him specifically of abusing his influence with Queen Anne in creating the twelve new peers in Dec., 1711, to give the Tories control of the House of Lords.—*Journals of the House of Commons*, XVIII, 59, 165; *Journals of the House of Lords*, XX, 99-111.

[21] *L* - - - - was probably Nicholas Lechmere, a member of the committee of secrecy and solicitor-general, 1714-18. He was one of the managers who were appointed in 1710 to conduct the impeachment of Dr. Sacheverell, and, after the uprising of 1715, was engaged in the trial of Lord Derwentwater and the rebel Scots lords at Westminster. As he was an active figure in the House of Commons, the Tories might well have hoped that he would allow some leniency towards Harley.

[22] *Sh* - - - - *n*, or William Shippen, warmly defended Harley in Jan., 1716. One of the most implacable of the Tories, he was sent to the Tower in 1718 following a speech in which he objected to George I on the ground that he did not understand the English government and language.

And four long Years, at least, must come,
E're *French* Pistoles, and Friends to *Rome*,
Our Liberties disturb.[23]

Five weeks later—on May 28—Mrs. Centlivre was back in Holbeach but was still thinking of her beloved House of Hanover. The following *"Verses were writ on King* George's *Birth-Day* [May 28], *by Mrs.* Centlivre, *and sent to the Ringers while the Bells were ringing at* Holbeach *in* Lincolnshire." They were published in the same volume as the preceding poem.

I.

Pull on, be loyal, *Holbeach* Boys,
And gall the *Tories* with your Noise,
    And show you love your King.
King *George* is he that sav'd your Church,
The *Jacks* [Jacobites] had left it in the Lurch,
    At Tyburn may they swing. . . .

III.

Disdain the Artifice they use
To bring in Mass and Wooden Shoes
    With Transubstantiation.
Remember *James* the 2d's Reign,
When Glorious *William* broke the Chain
    Rome had put on this Nation. . . .

V.

Then Weed your Corn, and plough your Land,
And by King *George*'s Interest stand,
    Cast Prejudice away;
To abler Heads leave State Affairs,
Give Railing o'er, and say your Prayers
    For Store of Corn and Hay. . . .

[23] The last election to the House of Commons was held in Jan., 1715. Mrs. Centlivre seems to think that the next election will again be an occasion for Tory bribes and intimidation.

VII.

And when your Leisure will permit
You round the good Ale Pot to sit,
    Your Loyalty proclaim,
And each revolving Month of *May*,
Bless the Eight and Twentieth Day,[24]
    That gave us *George* to reign.

The poem was part of a glorious celebration in which
Susanna invited "all the widows that take Collections of the
Parish, to the tavern to Supper, where she caus'd them to drink
King George's Health on their Knees, then the Prince and
Princess, and all the Royal Family; the Duke of Marlborough,
Lord Townshend, Mr. Stanhope, Mr. Walpole, the Speaker
of the House of Commons, the Duke of Argyle, and Gen.
Cadogan etc. The Musick playing in the Room, and the bells
ringing by her Orders all Supper Time, and the windows of
the Room illuminated; the old Women Danc'd and were ex-
ceedingly rejoyc'd, and the whole Town was in an Uproar."[25]

Engaging as she was in political controversy, Susanna was
courting a reply of some sort. The battle of wits which shortly
developed was not primarily political, but it did have a political
cast, Pope, the chief antagonist on one side, having by this time
severed most of his Whig connections, and Mrs. Centlivre
being one of the Whig group who bore his animosity and returned it as well as they could in kind.

[24] The *DNB* gives the date of George's birth as March 28, 1660, instead
of May 28. Professor J. B. Martin has called my attention to a poem of
Allan Ramsay (British Museum, MSS Egerton, 2023, p. 5) in which a Loyal-
ist designed to have his wife bear him a son on May 29—Charles II's birth-
day—but overlooked the fact that it was leap year, and his wife instead
"George honoured with a Daughter."
[25] *Flying Post*, June 21-23, 1716.

The Wonder:
A Woman Keeps A Secret

*T*HE WONDER is an excellent light comedy. After Garrick had contributed his interpretation of the character of Don Felix, it was often regarded as Mrs. Centlivre's masterpiece. The action is laid in Lisbon. Don Felix, in hiding after wounding Don Antonio in a duel because he would not marry Antonio's sister, secretly visits Donna Violante, with whom he is deeply in love. Violante is allowed a degree of freedom by her father, Don Pedro, because she seemingly accepts his arrangement for her to enter a nunnery the following week. After keeping Isabella's secret as long as necessary, though she meanwhile suffers tortures from Felix's jealousy, she and Felix are married.

In the minor plot, Don Lopez intends on the morrow to marry his daughter, Donna Isabella, to Don Guzman, a wealthy but stupid Spanish grandee, and locks her in her room to secure her until then. She jumps out of a window, but lands in the arms of Colonel Britton, a Scot in Portugal on his way home from Spain following the English peace. He takes her in haste to another house, which proves to be Violante's, and asks that she be cared for. Violante recognizes her as Don Felix's sister and agrees to keep the secret of her presence. Without revealing herself as the lady of the preceding night's adventure, Isabella, veiled, meets Colonel Britton on the Terreiro de passa and decides that if Violante approves she will marry him.

Violante tries him out and learns that he really loves his incognita of the night before and no one else. He and Isabella then meet again on the Terreiro de passa and are married.

Much of the action takes place in Violante's house, where she must conceal Don Felix from her father, hide Isabella from her brother, who might try to return her to her father as a matter of family honor, and keep Don Felix and Colonel Britton apart.

There are a great many plays in French, Spanish, Italian, and English dealing with the same subject as *The Wonder*, but Mrs. Centlivre's chief and perhaps her only definite source was Edward Ravenscroft's *The Wrangling Lovers: or, The Invisible Mistress* (1677).[1] Even the language owes something to Ravenscroft, but in general she has improved what she borrowed. In *The Wonder* Don Felix is an outlaw. Dramatically this complication, recalled possibly from the initial situation in Thomas Corneille's *Le Galant doublé*, is an excellent addition, for it heightens the suspense and contributes atmosphere. The possibility of execution if he is apprehended continues to hang over Felix until it is reported in the fifth act that Antonio is out of danger. Mrs. Centlivre gains unity by reducing the "invisible mistress" plot to a subsidiary position: it is important less for itself than for providing Violante with the secret which she is to keep and for producing the situations of jealous quarreling between her and Felix. Also in *The Wrangling Lovers* Violante's prototype has two suitors, whom Mrs. Centlivre makes into one, the brother of Isabella. The result is that what in both Corneille and Ravenscroft is an ill-jointed combination of two plays becomes in *The Wonder* a carefully conceived and unified whole. In *The Wrangling Lovers* the last act is a concentrated grouping of closet maneuvers. Mrs. Centlivre distributes some of these throughout her play, and, in order to avoid the absurdities for which she apologizes in the Preface to *The Perplex'd Lovers*, eliminates the rest. At the

[1] Genest, II, 526.

same time she develops the servants. Lissardo and Flora are well done. Gibby, the Scots valet of the colonel, is almost equally good; and Inis is a fit opposite for Flora. The third scene of Act III, in which Inis tries to wheedle a diamond ring from Lissardo, who gives her a kiss instead and in turn receives from Flora a box on the ear, and in which Inis and Flora quarrel over Lissardo, Flora accusing Inis of crooked legs, is comparable to the best servant scenes in Molière.

Gerald Langbaine[2] states that Ravenscroft's play was "founded upon a *Spanish* Romance in 8°, translated and called *Deceptio visûs*, or *Seeing and Believing are two things*," but he adds that Thomas Corneille has a play on the same subject, *Les Engagemens du hazard*. The *Biographia Dramatica* mentions the *Deceptio Visus* but adds that "as Corneille has taken the same romance for the groundwork of his *Engagemens du Hazard*, and Molière for that of his *Dépit amoureux*, it is probable that Mr. Ravenscroft might rather set these great dramatic writers before him in forming the model of this piece, than the author of the novel." The *Deceptio Visus*, it is true, tells essentially the same story as *The Wrangling Lovers*, but it was printed after the play and may have been made from it. In any case it is obvious that Ravenscroft did not use it. Even a cursory examination of *The Wrangling Lovers* reveals that Ravenscroft really combined the same two plays which Corneille made into *Les Engagemens du hazard*. Corneille names his sources as Calderon's *Los empeños de un acaso* and *Casa con dos puertas mala es de guardar*; he particularly defends himself from the charge that he has used *L'Inconnue* of Boisrobert, itself adapted from *Casa con dos puertas mala es de guardar*. Ravenscroft probably knew Spanish and may have resorted directly to Calderon, but it is certain that he knew *Les*

---

[2] *An Account of the English Dramatick Poets* (Oxford, 1691). Nicoll (*A History of Restoration Drama* [Cambridge, 1923], p. 242) gives the traditional origin of *The Wrangling Lovers*: "Langbaine traces its source to a novel of that country [Spain], the same to which Mrs. Centlivre was indebted for *The Wonder. A Woman keeps a Secret*."

Engagemens du hazard and had it before him while writing.

As for Molière's *Le Dépit amoureux*, the main story, having to do with Ascagne, supposedly a man but really a woman secretly married to Valère, who believes her to be Lucile, is taken, according to Eugène Despois,[3] from an Italian piece. In the second story, corresponding to that of Don Felix and Violante in *The Wonder*, he finds no direct evidence of borrowing, and concludes with Voltaire that the idea of lovers falling out and then making up is a commonplace for which no specific source is necessary. He notes the resemblance of all such pieces to the charming ode of Horace, *Donec gratus eram tibi*. The third scene of *Le Dépit amoureux* includes the famous lovers' quarrel and reconcilation, but it differs from the corresponding scene in Ravenscroft and Mrs. Centlivre in the significant fact that Éraste and Lucile return their gifts. H. van Laun[4] believes that Ravenscroft was influenced by Molière, but he seems not to have known that *The Wrangling Lovers* is even closer to *Les Engagemens du hazard* and that the ultimate sources of Ravenscroft and Corneille were the Spanish plays of Calderon. Closer to Ravenscroft and Mrs. Centlivre than *Le Dépit amoureux* is Molière's *Dom Garcie de Navarre ou Le Prince jaloux*, which includes a similar study of jealousy. Despois notes that the commentators have spoken of a Spanish original for *Dom Garcie*, but he, although assisted by several scholars in Spain, has not been able to find it. He takes the play from the Italian. The parts of *The Wonder* which resemble *Dom Garcie* Mrs. Centlivre could have got from *The Wrangling Lovers*.

The *Biographia Dramatica* thinks that "there are some circumstances in the concealment of Isabella, Violante's fidelity to her trust, and the perplexities which arise therefrom, that seem to bear a resemblance to one part of the plot of a play of Lord Digby's, called *Elvira; or, The Worst not always true*" (1667).

---

[3] *Oeuvres de Molière* (Paris, 1873), I, 381.
[4] "Les Plagiaries de Molière," *Le Moliériste*, Jan., 1881, pp. 304-5.

Don Pedro is the father of Elvira, a woman who keeps a secret, as Don Pedro is of Violante in *The Wonder*; also a Violante is mentioned in *Elvira* as the mistress of Don Julio, the brother of Blanca, for whom the secret is kept, but she never appears on the stage. Yet, except that a woman keeps a secret and that people enter constantly at the wrong time while others escape by special doors and balconies or go into closets, the plot differs noticeably from that of *The Wonder*. Even the similarity between the servants of *Elvira* and *The Wonder* is no greater than that between those of *Le Dépit amoureux* and *The Wonder*.[5]

John Hewitt's *A Tutor for the Beaus, or Love in a Labyrinth* (1737) resembles both *The Wrangling Lovers* and *The Wonder*, but Hewitt himself accounts for the similarity. He explains in his Preface that he took the plan for the second plot, *Love in a Labyrinth*, from Calderon's *Casa con dos puertas mala es de guardar*.[6]

Mrs. Centlivre was probably familiar with Thomas Corneille's comedy. It is possible, but unlikely, that she was familiar with Calderon's plays in the original Spanish. A basis for all the disguises and misconceptions in her play can be found in Ravenscroft's, though she alters most of them in some fashion.[7] Her play also contains frequent reminiscences of Ravenscroft's language. For example, part of Act V of *The Wrangling Lovers* becomes almost word for word Act IV, scene

[5] *Elvira* is really an adaptation of Calderon's *No siempre lo peor es cierto*. The same story was reworked by Christopher Bullock in *Woman Is a Riddle* (1717) and by Richard Savage in *Love in a Veil* (1719). Both plays suggest *The Wonder* at times, but it is not possible to demonstrate that either Bullock or Savage was imitating Mrs. Centlivre's play or using a common source with it.

[6] He says that he took the hint for the main plot, *A Tutor for the Beaus*, from Boissy's *Le François a Londres*, a short piece first acted in Paris on July 19, 1727.

[7] Violante's attempt to persuade Felix that she has not hidden a man in her bedchamber seems to go back ultimately to Boccaccio, especially to the story (Day VII, Novel 5) in which a wife dupes her husband, who has taken her confession in the habit of a priest.

i, of *The Wonder*. Though this scene of the lovers' quarrel does not stand out unduly in style, it is one of the best scenes in the play. In it Garrick attained special distinction. An engraving frequently met with in editions of the drama shows him seated on a chair slightly behind Violante and beseeching her to give him her hand at parting.

The Wonder was first produced at Drury Lane on April 27, 1714, with Wilks as the jealous Don Felix and Mrs. Oldfield as Violante. The parts of Colonel Britton and Isabella were taken by Mills and Miss Santlow. Gibby, the Scots servant, and Lissardo were played by Bullock and Pack.[8] Mrs. Cox and Mrs. Saunders rivaled each other, at least in the affections of Lissardo, as the two maids, Inis and Flora. The other roles were taken by Norris, Bickerstaff, and Bullock, Jr. Mills spoke the prologue written by Thomas Burnet, and Miss Santlow, the epilogue by Ambrose Philips. The comedy ran at first for six performances, and the next season it was repeated by command of the Prince of Wales on December 16 "for the Entertainment of the Prince and Princess."

To do justice to the actors Mrs. Centlivre wrote a preface complimenting them:

> *I freely acknowledge my self oblig'd to the Actors in general, and to Mr.* Wilks, *and Mrs.* Oldfield *in particular; and I owe them this Justice to say, that their inimitable Action cou'd only support a Play at such a Season, and among so many Benefits. . . .*
>
> *I must again repeat that which I meet with everywhere, I mean the just Admiration of the Performance of Mr.* Wilks, *and Mrs.* Oldfield, *and own that they much outdid in Action the strongest of my Conceptions; for tho' Nature was my Aim in the last Act of this Comedy, yet Nature herself were she to paint a Love Quarrel, wou'd only Copy them.*

[8] According to the advertisement in the *Daily Courant*, Pinkethman was to have a part in the play, perhaps that of Gibby, assigned to Bullock in the cast shown in the printed copy.

According to the life in her complete works, she enjoyed a "great intimacy" with Wilks and Mrs. Oldfield, who frequently acted in her plays and often honored her by speaking prologues and epilogues.

The Wonder is mentioned by "Joseph Gay" in *A Compleat Key to the Non-Juror* (1718), where Colley Cibber is accused of using it along with *Tartuffe*, *The Rape of the Lock*, and other works as the basis of his comedy. Another pamphlet of the same year entitled *The Theatre-Royal Turn'd into a Mountebank Stage* denies Gay's identifications of persons mentioned in the play and perhaps means also to deny the sources suggested. Certainly there is no close resemblance between *The Non-Juror* and *The Wonder*.

The Wonder was not produced again until 1733. In November of that year it was revived at Goodman's Fields, and was acted eleven times running, Giffard and Mrs. Giffard taking the roles of Felix and Violante. It was produced ten times during the next season, and in 1734-35 was acted at the same theater six times and twice at Covent Garden. When the Giffards moved to other theaters, they took their parts with them, acting the play at Lincoln's Inn Fields in 1736-37 and again at Goodman's Fields in 1740-41, "Gratis, by Persons for their Diversion." It was advertised for Drury Lane, "Never acted there before," on January 12, 1744, and, after a lapse of "Twelve Years," for Covent Garden on April 15, 1748.

The Wonder was presented in London more than fifty times before 1750, two-thirds of the time by the Giffards. Between 1750 and 1800 it was given nearly two hundred performances. Garrick became the outstanding Felix, acting the part more than sixty-five times between 1756 and 1776. Even after his retirement only John Philip Kemble seems to have come near him as an interpreter of the role.

Garrick first acted Felix on November 6, 1756. Miss Macklin took the part of Violante; Woodward, who had acted

Frederick at Goodman's Fields for some years beginning on December 4, 1735, was Lissardo; and Mrs. Clive acted Flora. On the following Monday the play was repeated by royal command. It was produced nineteen times during the season. The *London Chronicle* for February 1-3, 1757, reviews a performance on February 2. It repeats the story of Mrs. Centlivre's endangering her life by dedicating the play to the Duke of Cambridge and mentions that the comedy is supposed to have come from the Spanish. The critic rightly notices the author's talent for stage business ("she has contrived to keep the Attention of her Audience alive by a very quick Succession of Scenes") but thinks that the dialogue is "very paltry in general" and that the characters are unmarked by any "separating peculiarities, unless the Jealousy of Don Felix may be accounted such." The acting he regards as excellent:

> Don Felix is admirably performed by Mr. Garrick. His Situation in the last Act is diverting; and the whole Scene between him and Miss Macklin has many Touches in the Execution, very good on the Side of that promising Actress, and exquisite òn the Part of our admired Comedian. Mr. Woodward and Mrs. Clive are, according to Custom, highly pleasant: And upon the whole, this Play is a Proof that what the Players call Business will succeed without Writing, when it is in the Hands of such excellent Performers.

Percy Fitzgerald[9] thinks that Garrick as Kitely in *Every Man in His Humour* and as Don Felix in the "gay *Wonder*" was able to convey the nice distinction between the way jealousy would affect "the plain, sober mind of a merchant" and the way it would affect the mind of "a gayer Spanish nobleman." He adds that there was always a country dance in *The Wonder* and that Garrick danced it "with infinite grace and agility to the end." Arthur Murphy[10] calls *The Wonder* the best of

---

[9] *Life of David Garrick* (1868), II, 97.
[10] *Life of David Garrick* (Dublin, 1801), pp. 201 ff.

Mr GARRICK as DON FELIX.

My passion choaks me, I cannot speak:
Oh! I shall burst! Act V

Published as Act 1773, by T. Lowndes & Partners

Mrs. Centlivre's comedies, the fable being developed with "great dramatic skill" and suspense growing with the "intelligible perplexity." He praises Garrick's acting in it, noting that he "almost excelled himself" in the scene where he comes to take his final leave of Violante.

According to Murphy, Garrick made some suitable alterations in the comedy before producing it, but if the acting editions are to be trusted, his changes were almost negligible. A few expressions were toned down or cut out, but the alterations seem to have served chiefly for advertising purposes, since some apology was needed for acting any play by a person with Mrs. Centlivre's reputation. She had already been thrust back into the Restoration by the critics, who had a knack for forgetting dates. Horace Walpole is representative of the attitude taken: "Wycherley, Dryden, Mrs. Centlivre, &c., wrote as if they had only lived in the 'Rose Tavern'; but then the Court lived in Drury-lane, too, and Lady Dorchester and Nell Gwyn were equally good company."[11] Somewhat later the *Quarterly Review*[12] expresses the same idea: "Macbeth, Hamlet, and Lear were little calculated to please a profligate court that delighted in the declamatory nonsense of Dryden, and the despicable ribaldry of Centlivre."

When Garrick began to act *The Wonder*, the critics were inclined to object to everything except the acting, but their view changed as they became more familiar with the play itself. Taking its cue from a production at Drury Lane on October 7, the *London Chronicle* for October 7-10, 1758, can find very little to compliment either in Mrs. Centlivre or in her drama:

> Mrs. Centlivre, the honest woman who thought proper to scribble this comedy, was, as we may learn from the notes on Pope's *Dunciad*, (in which poem she procured herself a station by some dirty rhymes that she squirted at the

[11] *The Letters of Horace Walpole*, ed. Peter Cunningham (1866), IX, 96.
[12] XII (Oct., 1814), 133.

author and his friends) the wife of one of his Majesty's
yeomen of the mouth, or table-deckers. . . .

And first, as to "what it is," that, I think, is easily
answered by saying, that it is an indifferent play inimitably
acted. However, I can by no means agree to its being so
very wretched a performance, as some people are pleased to
represent it: and for this reason: a good plot is on all hands
allowed to be the principal ingredient towards a good comedy; now that of the Wonder is not only entertaining, but
in some respects exquisitely beautiful. But . . . the language is contemptible to the last degree; and the first act
in particular so lame and ungraceful, that it is hardly to be
borne.

But when the critic comes to the next performance, on November 10, he decides that it is "but an ungrateful office to attempt to put the town out of humor with a representation by
which they have been so often delighted." Garrick, he adds,
"perhaps never performed any character in which he charmed
an audience more than in that of Don Felix, whether we regard
him in his tender or jealous fits." Miss Macklin, as Violante,
"which is prettily imagined and well supported, gives a sensible
delight; and in the scenes with Felix, in which by the way the
dialogue is far from being amiss, she contrasts his jealousy so
agreeably, that we are sorry at every reconciliation for fear
they should not fall out again."

Joseph Knight[13] notes that Felix was "what has been thought
[Garrick's] greatest comic part." Dibdin,[14] who regards this as
certainly Mrs. Centlivre's best drama, remarks that jealousy is
perhaps better depicted in this comedy than in any other but
that probably only Garrick has represented jealousy in Don
Felix to perfection.

Several distinguished actresses played Violante at Drury
Lane during the twenty years that Felix was Garrick's role.

---

[13] *David Garrick* (1894), p. 159.
[14] *A Complete History of the Stage* (n.d.), V, 10.

When Miss Macklin went to Covent Garden in the fall of 1760, Mrs. Cibber succeeded to the part and acted it on several occasions beginning with March 23, 1761. Mrs. Yates was Violante for the first time at Yates's benefit on March 23, 1762, and then it became her role in 1763-64. Miss Pope, Mrs. Abington, Mrs. Barry, and Miss Younge had the part from 1765 until Mrs. Yates resumed it on January 18, 1775. It was one of Mrs. Yates's great roles. After sixty years William Godwin still remembered her acting it with Garrick:

> What I seem best to remember her [Mrs. Yates] in is *Violante*, in "The Wonder"; and though it is sixty years since I saw Garrick and her in that play, I remember a great deal of it, as if it had occurred yesterday. It is an admirable acting play, and the two principal performers seemed to leave nothing to be desired. What I recollect best of Mrs. Yates is the scene in which Garrick, having offended her by a jealousy, not altogether without an apparent cause, the lady, conscious of her entire innocence, at length expresses a serious resentment. *Felix* had till then indulged his angry feelings; but finding at last that he had gone too far, applies himself with all a lover's arts to soothe her. She turns her back to him, and draws away her chair; he follows her, and draws his chair nearer; she draws away further; at length by his whining, entreating, and cajoling, she is gradually induced to melt, and finally makes it up with him. Her condescension in every stage, from its commencement to its conclusion, was admirable. Her dignity was great and lofty, and the effect highly enhanced by her beauty; and when by degrees she laid aside her frown—when her lips began to relax towards a smile, while one cloud vanished after another, the spectator thought he had never seen anything so lovely and irresistible, and the effect was greatly owing to her queen-like majesty. The conclusion, in a graceful and wayward beauty, would

have been comparatively nothing; with Mrs. Yates's figure and demeanour, it laid the whole audience, as well as the lover, at her feet.[15]

The technique which Garrick used to get his effects in the famous reconciliation scene required great assurance. According to Victor,[16] he raised "Laughter and Delight in his Auditors from his *pointed Pauses*," always exercising his judgment to direct him to the second when to resume his speech. In *The Wonder*, "in that entertaining Scene between *Don Felix* and *Violante*, . . . the Pause is near four Minutes; but then, the Marking Eye, and every corresponding Limb, supplies the Want of Words so effectually, as to create repeated Laughs, from the Looks and Actions of that judicious Actor."

When Garrick resumed the character of Felix in 1768-69 after an absence of four years from it, *The Wonder* was called for six times. One of the most notable occasions was the production on April 24, 1769, when Kitty Clive retired from the stage in the part of Flora. Mrs. Clive, a comic genius, had been one of Garrick's favorite performers, especially in the role of chambermaid.

By this time *The Wonder* is consistently treated with respect by the critics. A reviewer of a performance at Drury Lane on December 31, 1771, remarks:

This is one of the best of Mrs. *Centlivre*'s Pieces, for besides, that the Plot is pleasingly intricate, the Conduct and Catastrophe is managed with considerable ingenuity, and the Language is more chaste and correct than in any of her other Comic Pieces. To which we may add, that most of the Characters are justly drawn, and finished with a considerable degree of judgement; which proves her to have been perfectly acquainted with life, and thoroughly intimate with the minds and manners of mankind.[17]

[15] W. Clark Russell, *Representative Actors* [1875], pp. 175-76.
[16] *The History of the Theatres of London* (1771), I, 247.
[17] *The Theatrical Review; or, New Companion to the Playhouse*, by a Society of Gentlemen (1772), I, 335; also *London Chronicle*, Jan. 7-9, 1772.

The Laſt Time of the Company's performing this Seaſon.

At the Theatre Royal in Drury-Lane,

This preſent MONDAY, June 10, 1776,

The WONDER.

Don Felix by Mr. GARRICK,
Col. Briton by Mr. SMITH,
Don Lopez by Mr BADDELEY,
Don Pedro by Mr. PARSONS,
Liſſardo by Mr. KING,
Frederick by Mr. PACKER,
Gibby by Mr. MOODY,
Iſabella by Miſs HOPKINS,

Flora by Mrs. WRIGHTEN,

Inis by Mrs. BRADSHAW,

Violante by Mrs. YATES.

End of Act I. The Grand GARLAND DANCE,
By Signor GIORGI, Mrs. SUTTON,
And Mr. SLINGSBY.

To which will be added a Muſical Entertainment, call'd

The WATERMAN.

The PRINCIPAL CHARACTERS by
Mr. BANNISTER,
Mr. DAVIES,
And Mr. DODD.
Mrs. WRIGHTEN,
And Mrs. JEWELL.

To conclude with the Grand Scene of The RECATTA.

Ladies are deſired to ſend their Servants a little after 5 to keep Places, to prevent Confuſion.

The Doors will be opened at HALF after FIVE o'Clock.
To begin at HALF after SIX o'Clock. Vivant Rex & Regina.

The Profits of this Night being appropriated to the Benefit of
The Theatrical Fund, the Uſual Addreſs upon that Occaſion
Will be ſpoken by Mr. GARRICK, before the Play.

The critics did not always feel that the audiences recognized great acting. For example, the *General Evening Post*, for May 9-12, 1772, points out that the audience on the preceding Saturday had applauded Garrick more loudly when, after dressing up in a woman's riding hood, he hobbled off the stage like an old woman than in those scenes in which his acting was "indeed prodigious." The same paper for December 12-15, 1772, reflects on the nature of dramatic ability. Genius and erudition, it says, did not enable Pope, Fielding, or Dr. Johnson (whose tragedy *Irene* "was stillborn") to produce a living play, whereas Mrs. Centlivre, "with little genius and less education, will be remembered while we have a stage, and gain universal applause from a modest adherence to nature and probability."

The most significant honor that befell *The Wonder* was Garrick's choice of it to close his theatrical career on June 10, 1776. Some have been disposed to criticize him adversely for ending his career in the part of Don Felix, but he chose it over Richard III, in which he had started out, because he desired to be left with the energy to deliver a final word of appreciation to the audience. After giving the prologue which he had written, he went through the part "with great good humour and well-dissembled vivacity."[18] Then, with the actors crowding about the stage and in the wings, he spoke a few heartfelt words, which were heralded in the newspapers and repeated in the magazines of the time. The occasion afforded "one last glimpse of true comedy, the like of which it may be suspected no one has seen since,"[19] and the crowded, magnificent, and responsive audience may be regarded as unique in the history of the English stage.

Following Garrick's retirement *The Wonder* continued to be given, though not so frequently as before. Covent Garden seems never to have found a pair for the two main roles who could challenge the memory of Garrick and Miss Macklin or Garrick and Mrs. Yates. The *Public Advertiser* for January

[18] Murphy, *Life of David Garrick*, pp. 336 ff.
[19] Fitzgerald, *Life of David Garrick*, II, 394 ff.

11, 1783, notes the attendance of a "numerous audience" at Drury Lane the night before to see the comedy, but adds on May 10 that "in these latter Days, the Wonder does not move us much." On December 4, 1784, it explains part of the difficulty—the lack of a satisfactory Felix. Mr. Holman, it says, was not "happy" in the role.

So far as I know, Richard Brinsley Sheridan, who succeeded Garrick as manager of Drury Lane, never acted in *The Wonder*, but he may have drawn upon it for his comic opera, *The Duenna*, first presented at Covent Garden on November 21, 1775. According to the *Biographia Dramatica* he took his plot from "*Il Filosofo di Campagna*, from Molière's *Sicilien*, and from *The Wonder* of Mrs. Centlivre." Don Ferdinand and Clara correspond to Don Felix and Violante of *The Wonder*, and Don Antonio and Louisa to Colonel Britton and Isabella. Louisa is the sister of Ferdinand, and Louisa and Clara are friends, as are Isabella and Violante. Ferdinand and Antonio are also friends, but Ferdinand is jealous of Antonio as is Felix of Colonel Britton. There can be little doubt that Sheridan had *The Wonder* in mind, though the language is entirely his own.

Next to Garrick, John Philip Kemble was probably the most satisfactory performer of Felix. He and Miss Farren, as Violante, made an excellent team in the play. This highly complimentary notice of their acting is characteristic:

> Perhaps there is no play represented on the English stage which affords a greater scope for fine acting; *Kemble* and Miss *Farren* are inimitable throughout; it is worth the whole of the admission money to see them only. The passions of love and jealousy are pourtrayed in their strongest colouring; and we, who well remember *Garrick*, think the acting of Kemble very little inferiour to him.[20]

[20] Clipping in a Haymarket scrapbook, Theatre Collection, Harvard College Library.

Kemble gave the play rather frequently while he was manager. If anything went wrong with the rest of his repertory, he could be sure that *The Wonder* would always draw at least a partial house. One of his chief difficulties was the illness, real or assumed, of Mrs. Dora Jordan. In his *Memoranda* for January 1, 1789, he notes that "Mrs. Jordan pretends to be ill again."[21] This time the audience paid £88 7*s*. 6*d*. to see Kemble and Miss Farren in *The Wonder*. On February 2, Dodd, Bensley, and Mrs. Jordan are marked ill, and *The Wonder* was repeated, this time producing £138 1*s*.

It is interesting that *The Wonder*, written in an age of prose and reason, continued to be popular in an age of increasing romanticism. Such popularity was partly due to the fact that the characters do not hide their feelings and that the situations spring from their emotions. Undoubtedly there had been a change in the attitude of the audience, Mrs. Centlivre's own times desiring especially manners and clever intrigue and the late eighteenth century desiring love and romance, but by shifting the emphasis the actors were able to please the audiences of both periods. As a play of jealousy in high life, *The Wonder* was regarded as supreme during the second half of the century:

> The Wonder is clearly the most entertaining play built upon the domestic Caution and irrational Jealousy, which so long marked the Spanish Character. The character of Don Felix is in the highest degree natural and pleasing—His quick succession of doubts and tenderness—His angry departure, merely to return more enslaved—His ready sensibility and impatience of affront—are not peculiarly national and local; they are the feelings of most men in situations any way similar.
>
> The lower Characters of the Play are natural, and constructed with much knowledge of stage effect.—The

[21] *Memoranda of J. P. Kemble*, British Museum, Additional MSS, 31,972.

Theatre has, perhaps, few pieces which so completely can be considered as freeholds of Dramatic forms.[22]

I have made no attempt to count the number of performances of *The Wonder* in England and America after 1800. It continued, however, to be regarded as a sterling acting comedy, and the number of editions would indicate that it was often read as well. I have examined eighteen separate editions or printings before 1800 (including one translation into French, *Le Prodige* [1785]) and twenty-four after 1800 (including one translation into Polish, *Kobieta dotrzymuiaca sekretu* [1817]).

From its first production *The Wonder* enjoyed a reputation for natural scenes of love, jealousy, quarrels, repentance, and forgiveness. The love scenes, in fact, are as natural and kindly as those of Tom Robertson which set the fashion for the second half of the nineteenth century. Mrs. Centlivre apparently thought that she was writing another comedy of intrigue, but more than any other playwright of her age she gave her characters natural human emotions, so that later ages could forget the intrigue pattern after a few of the looser expressions had been excised.

Perhaps because Garrick had been so outstanding as Felix, in the eighteenth century the part of Violante was considered of minor importance, but during the following century the relative importance of Felix and Violante was frequently reversed. In the early part of the century Dora Jordan, despite her frequent illness, was one of the great Violantes. Leigh Hunt liked her very much:

> ... her laughter is the happiest and most natural on the stage; ... her laughter intermingles itself with her words, as fresh ideas afford her fresh merriment; ... it increases, it lessens with her fancy, ... This is the laughter of the feelings; and it is this predominance of heart in all she

[22] *The Wonder,* 1792 edition, later bound up in Bell's *British Theatre,* XXI; reprinted also in Jones's *British Theatre* (Dublin, 1795), and in the New York edition (1812).

says and does that renders her the most delightful actress in the *Donna Violante* of the *Wonder*, the *Clara* of *Matrimony*, and in twenty other characters, which ought to be more ladylike than she can make them, and which acquire a better gentility with others.[23]

William Macready also praised Mrs. Jordan as Violante:

The moving picture, the very life of the scene was perfect in her mind, and she transferred it in all its earnestness to every movement of the stage.

. . . I have seen many Violantes since, but where was there one, who could, like her, excite the bursts of rapture in an audience, when she recovered from the deadly agony into which her fears and discovery had thrown her, and prepared herself for her triumph over her jealous lover?[24]

The Wonder is included in the *British Theatre* (1808), prefaced with biographical and critical remarks by Mrs. Inchbald, whose career is sometimes compared to that of Mrs. Centlivre. Mrs. Inchbald regards Mrs. Centlivre as an excellent practical playwright:

Mrs. Centlivre . . . ranks in the first class of our comic dramatists: for though she does not possess the repartee of Congreve or Wycherley, and her dialogue, in general, is not equal even to Farquhar's, yet she discovers such happy invention in her plots, incidents, and characters; such skill in conducting the intrigues of a comedy; such art in exciting the curiosity, the anxiety, or the mirth of her auditors, that she foils both the scholar and the wit when the comparison is limited to dramatic effect. . . .

Most comic writers of the present time accomplish the tedious labour of a five act drama by having recourse, alternately, to sentiment and drollery: here a long play is sustained without excursions to either; . . .

[23] *Critical Essays on the Performers of the London Theatres,* by the Author of the Theatrical Criticisms in the News (1807), pp. 165-66.
[24] *Macready's Reminiscences,* ed. Sir Frederick Pollock (1875), I, 63-64.

Among the most interesting criticisms of *The Wonder* are two by William Hazlitt. In the *Examiner* for Monday, September 16, 1816, he reviews a performance at Covent Garden on the preceding Saturday:

> *The Wonder* is one of our good old English Comedies, which holds a happy medium between grossness and refinement. The plot is rich in intrigue, and the dialogue in *double entendre*, which however is so light and careless, as only to occasion a succession of agreeable alarms to the ears of delicacy. This genuine comedy, which is quite as pleasant to read as to see (for we have made the experiment within these few days, to our entire satisfaction) was written by an Englishwoman, before the sentimental, Ultra-Jacobinical German School . . . had spoiled us with their mawkish Platonics and maudlin metaphysics. The soul is here with extreme simplicity considered as a mere accessary to the senses in love, and the conversation of bodies preferred to that of minds as much more entertaining. We do not subscribe our names to this opinion, but it is Mrs. CENTLIVRE'S, and we do not chuse to contradict a Lady. The plot is admirably calculated for stage-effect, and kept up with prodigious ingenuity and vivacity to the end. . . . The time for the entrance of each person on the stage is the moment when they are least wanted, and when their arrival makes either themselves or some body else look as foolish as possible.

Hazlitt does not overlook the fact that *The Wonder* teaches a moral in the rare example of a woman's keeping a secret and being rewarded in the end by the triumph of her friendship and love. Miss Boyle, he adds, as Violante was wrong in her tendency to sentimentalize a purely comic part, for the dialogue in genteel comedy should not come "laboring up all the way from the heart." Charles Kemble was guilty of the same error, playing Felix in much the same style that he might have been expected to use for Macduff.

The second criticism is found in the *Times* for October 9, 1819. In this review Hazlitt reports that Miss Brunton was mediocre as Violante in a performance at Covent Garden the night before, since she failed to unite the "extreme spirit" with the "extreme delicacy" that together make the character. But he now regards Charles Kemble's Don Felix as one of his best parts.

The British Drama (1817) includes *The Wonder* with a criticism by R. Cumberland. Cumberland says that the woman dramatist of Mrs. Centlivre's period was prevented by her education and the habits of her sex from seeing life at first hand in those diversified scenes open to the male dramatists, so that her love scenes are merely copied from those written by the other sex. The result, he concludes, is that her lovers become libertines and her "ladies mistake easy virtue for easy manners." Nevertheless, he praises the play immoderately:

> A more interesting situation can hardly be imagined, nor scenes more ingeniously devised to display the persevering fidelity of Violante, the impassioned character of Felix, and at the same time be contrived to furnish such apologies for his jealousy, as serve to keep the audience in perfect good-humor with him. . . .
>
> . . . few plays of its date have been so frequently before the public; and very few, I believe, who have been present at its representation, ever departed from the theatre dissatisfied with the writer of it.

Wallack was the Felix at Drury Lane in 1826 and 1827. The performances of the play seem to have been well received, but Wallack was generally disapproved, not the least objection to his Felix being his failure to act the part as a gentleman. Ellen Tree made her debut on the London boards as Violante at Drury Lane on the first day of the 1826-27 season.[25] Mac-

---

[25] She had achieved considerable distinction at Bath and had appeared once before in London, for the benefit of her sister, Miss M. Tree, better known as Mrs. Bradshaw. A third sister appeared with Ellen for the first time on Sept. 23.

ready performed Felix at Covent Garden on January 27, 1838. He thought he acted the part "with spirit and self-possession," but he had not had the time to prepare a finished representation of it.[26]

The Wonder was a favorite play with the Hanoverians, as indeed it should have been. George II patronized it both as Prince of Wales and as King, and George III commanded it on at least five occasions. Even Queen Victoria called for a performance at Covent Garden on March 24, 1840. She and her beloved Albert received an ovation. Though sixty-four years old, Charles Kemble is said to have taken the role of Felix admirably.

The comedy continued to attract attention. Mr. and Mrs. Charles Kean (the former Ellen Tree) acted Felix and Violante in a three-act version at Drury Lane on March 22, 1862. One of the last revivals of the play was made in 1897 at Daly's Theater in New York, with Ada Rehan as Violante. It was a spirited production, evoking plenty of laughter and applause. By this time it was regarded distinctly as a woman's play. The audiences seem not to have regarded *The Wonder* as great literature, but they did enjoy Violante's "innocent fooling of her impulsive lover."

[26] *Macready's Reminiscences*, I, 63-65.

The Catholick Poet and "The Cook's Wife"

ABOUT the end of March, 1716, Pope issued *A Full and true Account of a Horrid and Barbarous Revenge by Poison on the Body of Mr. Edmund Curll, Bookseller*, a pamphlet in which he explains how he, with the aid of his publisher, Lintot, gave Curll an emetic. Pope was taking revenge upon Curll for publishing three scandalous pieces called *Court Poems*, two of which had probably been written by Lady Mary Wortley Montagu, whose fascination had caught Pope at the time, and the third by John Gay. Into the account Pope gratuitously introduced Mrs. Centlivre, who was to profit from Curll's imaginary will:

> He clos'd the Book, fetch'd a Groan, and recommended to Mrs. *Curll* to give Forty Shillings to the Poor of the Parish of St. *Dunstan*'s, and a *Week's Wages* Advance to each of his Gentlemen Authors, with some small Gratuity in particular to Mrs. *Centlivre*.

Mrs. Centlivre was naturally beneath the contempt of Pope. As a member of the struggling new democracy among letters, as a Whig and Protestant, as a friend of Addison's circle, as a writer of popular plays without great literary quality, as a woman without formal education or high social position, in his eyes she was merely despicable. That Mrs. Centlivre hated and distrusted Pope and most of his crowd is also obvious. To her

Pope was a Tory, a Catholic, a Jacobite, a man tolerated only because of his friends and his literary gifts. But it is difficult to see why Pope should have introduced her at this point in his quarrel with Curll, unless to imply that the *Court Poems*, which had been attributed to a lady of quality, might have been written by Mrs. Centlivre, and so to scatter the attack against Lady Mary.

Not content, he added *A Further Account of the most Deplorable Condition of Mr. Edmund Curll, Bookseller*, which was published shortly after.   In his *"Instructions to a Porter how to find Mr.* Curll's *Authors"* he includes *"The Cook's Wife* in *Buckingham* Court," and adds, "bid her bring along with her the *Similes* that were lent her for her next new Play." Through his friendship with the laureate, Pope apparently knew that Rowe had helped her with *The Cruel Gift*, which was to appear at Drury Lane on December 17. When Curll's authors appear following his summons, they draw up certain resolutions, including these two: *"Resolv'd*, That a *Ballad* be made against Mr. *Pope*, and that Mr. *Oldmixon*, Mr. *Gildon*, and Mrs. *Centlivre* do prepare and bring in the same" and *"Resolv'd*, That all our Members, (except the Cook's Wife) be provided with a sufficient Quantity of the *vivifying Drops*, or *Byfield's Sal Volatile."*

The ballad, *The Catholick Poet; or, Protestant Barnaby's Sorrowful Lamentation*, to be sung to the tune of "Which no Body can deny," duly appeared on May 31. Pope immediately attributed "this scurrilous attack" on his Homer to Mrs. Centlivre; it rankled in his mind for years after her death and gained for her a niche in *The Dunciad*. In Book II, line 365, of the 1728 edition she is one of the dunces who finally talk themselves to sleep:

> At last *C ------ re* felt her voice to fail.

In the Variorum edition (1729) the blank is supplied and this note is added:

Mrs. *Susanna Centlivre*, wife to Mr. *Centlivre*, Yeoman of the Mouth to his Majesty. She writ many Plays, and a Song (says Mr. *Jacob*, vol. I. p. 32.), before she was seven years old. She also writ a Ballad against Mr. *Pope*'s *Homer*, before he begun it.

In the 1728 edition, Book III, lines 149 ff., he continued:

> See next two slip-shod *Muses*, traipse along,
> In lofty madness meditating song,
> With tresses staring from poetic dreams,
> And never wash'd, but in Castalia's streams.
> *H* ------ and *T* ------, glories of their race!

In 1729 the last line became:

> Haywood, Centlivre, Glories of their race!

In the appendix to *The Dunciad, Variorum* Pope includes among those works which abused him "The Catholick Poet, or Protestant Barnaby's Sorrowful Lamentation; a Ballad about Homer's Iliad [by Mrs. *Centlivre* and others] 1715. Price 1*d*." That the date is wrong by a year and that the sale price is reduced from three pence to a penny are probably of no significance. But Pope is in more serious error in attributing the ballad to Mrs. Centlivre at all. *The Curliad* (1729), presumably written by Curll, contains a complete and probably satisfactory exoneration of her (page 27):

> In the Note upon this Verse, Mrs. *Centlivre* is said to have *writ a Ballad* against Mr. *Pope*'s Homer *before he begun it*. The *Fact* is *true*, but the *Person* on whom it is charged, is falsely accused. The Ballad, here referred to, being wrote by Mr. *Oldmixon*.

Later (page 31) he gives among the "*Falshoods* in the *true Names* of *Authors*" in Pope's appendix, "I. The *Catholick Poet*, &c. a Ballad, the whole by Mr. *Oldmixon*, not one Word by Mrs. *Centlivre*." It is to Pope's credit that in later editions of *The Dunciad* he removed the second reference to her.

A few years after *The Dunciad* appeared Pope is reported to have made another allusion to Mrs. Centlivre. In his *First Satire of the Second Book of Horace*, published in February, 1733, the lines about Sappho had been applied by the town—probably with reason—to Lady Montagu, with whom Pope was no longer friendly. At the lady's request, Lord Peterborough asked Pope to explain them, and then wrote to her:

> He said to me . . . what I had taken the liberty to say to you, that he wondered how the town would apply these lines to any but some noted common woman; that he would yet be more surprised if you should take them to yourself; he named to me four remarkable poetesses and scribblers, Mrs. Centlivre, Mrs. Haywood, Mrs. Manley, and Mrs. Ben (Behn), assuring me, that such only were the objects of his satire.[1]

But perhaps more significant than any of these remarks is the fact that in recent years various scholars[2] have considered the identification of Phoebe Clinket, the female playwright in *Three Hours after Marriage*, with Mrs. Centlivre. As we have seen, Pope in believing her the author of *The Catholick Poet* had the requisite motive for satirizing her, but that Mrs. Centlivre sat for the main portrait to the exclusion of the Countess of Winchilsea, with whom Pope's contemporaries connected the part, is unlikely.

Three Hours after Marriage, by Gay, Pope, and Arbuthnot, was acted continuously for seven times beginning January 16, 1717. The farce is built around a Dr. Fossile, who is a self-

---

[1] Pope, *Works*, ed. Elwin-Courthope (1861), III, 279. The editors in the index to Vol. V represent Mrs. Centlivre as both "novelist and dramatist."

[2] George Sherburn, "The Fortunes and Misfortunes of *Three Hours after Marriage*," *Modern Philology*, XXIV (1926-27), 91-109; George Sherburn, *The Early Career of Alexander Pope* (Oxford, 1934), pp. 193-99; Lester M. Beattie, *John Arbuthnot: Mathematician and Satirist* (Cambridge, Mass., 1935), pp. 229-38; Dane Farnsworth Smith, *Plays about the Theatre in England from The Rehearsal in 1671 to the Licensing Act in 1737* (Oxford, 1936), pp. 101-8; William Henry Irving, *John Gay: Favorite of the Wits* (Durham, N. C., 1940), pp. 147-64.

centered old doctor, a collector of ancient rarities, and a jealous husband. No sooner has he brought home Mrs. Townley as his bride than various of her former lovers try to make assignations with her. In particular, Plotwell and Underplot, who have made a bet on the honor of being the first to "dub" the doctor, attempt by various disguises to get by the suspicious Fossile, finally decking themselves out as a mummy and a crocodile. Phoebe Clinket, Fossile's niece, a female playwright, who lives with her uncle, adds to the complications by introducing into her uncle's house Plotwell, who is to father her play, Sir Tremendous, a horrendous critic, and two players to listen to a tragedy which she hopes the players will produce. In the end Mrs. Townley's child by a previous marriage is forced upon Plotwell, whose marriage to Townley nevertheless evaporates because she was already married to a sailor, and Clinket thriftily gathers up the pieces for the plot of a new comedy.

Of the contemporary attempts to identify the dramatis personae, three pamphlets are sufficiently specific to be considered. "A Complete Key to the New Farce, call'd *Three Hours after Marriage*," by E. Parker, was published on February 2, 1717, and *The Confederates, a Farce*, by Captain John Durant Breval under the pseudonym of Joseph Gay, appeared on March 30, 1717. The third is a key, apparently written in 1717 but not published until later: "Three Hours after Marriage, a comedy, by Gay, Pope, and Arbuthnot: To which is added, never before Printed, a key, explaining the most difficult passages in this comedy. Also a letter, giving an account of the origin of the quarrel between Colley Cibber, Pope, and Gay" (Dublin, 1761).[3]

There is no question that Fossile represents Dr. John Woodward, a man of original mind and a significant contributor to the study of geology despite some of his absurd speculations and his quarrelsome nature. Sir Tremendous, the paltry critic,

[3] The key had previously been printed in *A Supplement to the Works of Alexander Pope, Esq; . . .* (Dublin, 1757).

is John Dennis, Plotwell is Colley Cibber, and the two players are Cibber's comanagers at Drury Lane, Wilks and Booth. Difficulties of interpretation arise in connection with Mrs. Townley and Phoebe Clinket. Mrs. Townley is so obviously an inmate of a bordello that it seems impossible to identify her from internal evidence. But Breval notes that Mrs. Oldfield, who acted the role, mimicked Mrs. Mead, the wife of Dr. Richard Mead, a distinguished Whig physician. Parker says that she represented the wife of "another Eminent Physician." The Dublin key is slightly more exact: "But they say another eminent physician's wife sat for that picture; and the painters have done her justice in all but the catastrophe; for the poor man has her still, nor feels he yet any pain in the forehead; therefore shall be nameless, for I think it hard, a man's head should be laden, for the lightness of his wife's heels." Since the authors were present at rehearsals, they were at least jointly responsible for any mimicry introduced by Mrs. Oldfield.

Although she died in February, 1719, the various attacks on Dr. Mead during the following spring include reflections on his wife. In *An Account of a strange and wonderful Dream, Dedicated to Doctor M - - d* (printed about the middle of May, 1719), Mulso (Mead) acquires horns and becomes an ox after finding his wife unfaithful. Again *Tauronomachia: or a Description of a Bloody and Terrible Fight between two Champions, Taurus and Onos, at Gresham-College* (1719) recounts the story of a street fight between Dr. Mead and Dr. Woodward on June 10, 1719. Taurus (Mead) is "guarded well with *rouzing* H - - - - s [Horns]." Onos (Woodward) defends himself, but the ass is no match for the bull, which gores him and wrests from him his "Anted'luvian Steel." The fact that in February, 1720, Thomas Rowlinson, a friend of the Meads, found it necessary to deny allegations against Mrs. Mead and objected to the "Deal of Scandal ill People, Woodward or such Fellowes, have utter'd,"[4] is itself proof that her name was

---

[4] Thomas Hearne, *Remarks and Collections* (Oxford, 1885-1921), VII, 96.

in bad repute. Professor Irving adds further that "stories of her frivolities were current at this time" and that "Years later, the story of Bolingbroke's supposed commerce with Mrs. Mead was still remembered."[5]   Henry St. John, Viscount Bolingbroke, was a close friend of Arbuthnot and Pope, and may himself have been responsible for initiating the scandal.[6]

I have dwelt at some length on the identification of Mrs. Townley as a means of checking the reliability of the three contemporary documents at what is admitted to be their weakest point. If their view that *Three Hours*, at least in the spoken version, made aspersions upon the character of Mrs. Mead is accurate, then it is difficult to reject their evidence that Phoebe Clinket is a reflection upon Anne Finch, Countess of Winchilsea.

The role of Phoebe Clinket is not especially coarse. As the Epilogue puts it,

> *Whom can our well-bred Poetess displease?*
> *She writ like Quality——with wondrous ease:*
> *All her Offence was harmless want of Wit;*
> *Is that a Crime?*

There are reflections upon her mind, her inveterate pursuit of literature, her lack of literary judgment, and her dislike of disparaging criticism, but there are no imputations upon her character. In Parker's key the point of the writing desk strapped to the back of Clinket's maid is clear enough:

> This Character is a very silly Imitation of *Bays* in the *Rehearsal*, but is design'd to Ridicule the Countess of *W -n - - - - - ea*, who, *Pope* says, is so much given to writing

[5] *John Gay: Favorite of the Wits*, pp. 150-51.

[6] Professor Sherburn (*The Early Career of Alexander Pope*, p. 194) says that "No one has accepted the identification of Townley as Mrs. Mead" and that "Mrs. Mead could hardly have had a trait in common with Townley. At least the Meads had several children, and presumably Mrs. Mead was domestic and no longer very young." Professor Beattie (*John Arbuthnot*, p. 257 n. 1) follows Professor Sherburn: "In Parker's *A Complete Key* and in Breval's *The Confederates*, it was falsely insinuated that the unsavory character Townley of *Three Hours* represented Dr. Mead's wife." Professor Irving expresses the opinion that "the authors did not set out to satirize Mrs. Mead," but he finds the identification of the town a natural one.

of Verses, that she keeps a Standish in every Room of her House, that she may immediately clap down her Thoughts, whether upon *Pindaric, Heroic, Pastoral* or *Dramatic* Subjects.[7]

The Dublin key is even more specific:

> Phoebe Clinket; I am a little griev'd to say, reflects a little on a lady of your acquaintance, the Countess of W ------ *sea,* who is so much affected with that itch of versifying, that she has implements for writing, in every room in her house that she frequents. You and I know, Gay has many obligations to that lady, therefore, out of justice and good manners ought to have spar'd her. But poets provok'd, are as bad as hornets; they care not who they sting! . . . That unlucky lady was heard to say,— *Gays trivia show'd he was more proper to walk before a chair, than to ride in one.* This sarcasm was the cause, why the poor Countess is thrust among such a pack of motley figures on the stage.[8]

In a letter to Parnell early in 1717 Pope remarks that the play has caused him much difficulty: "Gay's play, among the rest, has cost much time and long suffering to stem a tide of malice and party, that certain authors have raised against it."[9] Obviously he desired to placate friends who felt that they had been injured. Furthermore, the motive assigned to Gay is not only consistent with the Countess's well-known antagonism to coarseness in writing but suggests a personal grudge such as is assigned by the same source as Gay's motive for alluding to Lady Monmouth as the Countess of Hippokekoana, a patient of Fossile's in a dangerous condition from the excessive use of emetics.

There is no record of the Countess's reaction to *Three Hours.* Pope included commendatory verses by her in his

[7] P. 5.
[8] P. 213.
[9] Pope, *Works,* ed. Elwin-Courthope, VII, 464.

Works published in June, 1717, and other poems by her in
Poems on Several Occasions, which he edited for publication in
July. He might well have had these materials on hand when
the play appeared. In the summer of 1717 Pope says that he
visited various members of the nobility, including his neighbor,
the Earl of Winchilsea, but he does not mention the Countess.[10]

Is there anything in *Three Hours* which might suggest
Lady Winchilsea's life or her works? Phoebe Clinket's play,
*The Universal Deluge, or, the Tragedy of Deucalion and
Pyrrha,* satirizes Woodward's views of the flood and of the
history of the earth. But the Earl of Winchilsea also maintained a lively interest in antiquarian research. By 1703 he was
a recognized judge of the archeological treasures found around
Eastwell, and he was elected president of the Society of An-
tiquaries by 1717. His search for *Durolenum* and his adopting
the name Cyngetorix among his close associates, who called
themselves Druids, must have excited comment. The Countess
herself was very cognizant of floods. In *Aristomenes: or, The
Royal Shepherd,* printed in her *Miscellany Poems* (1713), is
this noted allusion to the Greek story:

> So look'd the World to *Pyrrha,* and her Mate;
> So gloomy, waste, so destitute of Comfort,
> When all Mankind besides lay drown'd in Ruin.
> Oh! thou wert well inform'd, my evil Genius;
> And the complaining Rocks mourn'd not in vain: . . .

Also, one of her most famous poems was "A Pindarick Poem
*Upon the Hurricane in November 1703, referring to this Text
in Psalm 148. ver. 8. Winds and Storms fulfilling his Word.
With a Hymn compos'd of the 148th Psalm Paraphras'd.*" The
hurricane described in the Cowleyan ode "swept over England
in November, 1703, devastating the southern counties, uprooting
fine old trees, unroofing palaces, destroying a third of the navy,
and causing the death of fifteen hundred seamen."[11] The

[10] Pope, *Works,* ed. Elwin-Courthope, VI, 248.
[11] Myra Reynolds, *The Poems of Anne Countess of Winchilsea* (Chicago,
1903), p. cxxiii.

poem, written soon after the storm, seems to have been passed
around in manuscript before it was printed in her volume of
1713. It was mentioned by Mrs. Manley in *The New Atalantis*,
Volume II (published in October, 1709), and the hymn with
which it concludes was quoted.[12] As printed by Mrs. Manley
the hymn, containing numerous classical allusions, is addressed
to Jupiter, but in the version of 1713 it is addressed to the
Christian God and the classical allusions are changed to He-
braisms. Certainly Clinket suggests Lady Winchilsea when
she remarks in *Three Hours* that she would prefer to tell the
Biblical story of the flood rather than the Greek except that
"neither our Stage nor Actors are hallow'd enough for Sacred
Story."

As the scene of Clinket's play opens, the top of Parnassus
appears at a distance. Though natural to the Ovidian account,
the introduction of Parnassus suggests an inevitable parallel in
the fact that Lady Winchilsea alludes on several occasions to
Parnassus, "*a hill so call'd in Eastwell Park*," the Winchilsea
estate.

A more precise connection of Clinket with the Countess is
found in the fact that Clinket is credited with a hymn to Apollo.
Among Lady Winchilsea's first verses was an invocation to
Apollo, four lines of which still survive.[13] This or another poem
to Apollo would have been known to the authors of *Three
Hours*, for in Swift's poem, "*Apollo* Outwitted. *To the Honourable Mrs.* Finch, *under her Name of* Ardelia," published in
1711, Ardelia tricks Apollo into granting her the power of song
without accepting his suit, and Apollo in turn afflicts her with
such pride and modesty that her poetry will remain unknown.

Again, Lady Winchilsea, like Phoebe Clinket, preferred
writing poetry to cooking. In characterizing his niece, Fossile
says that, "instead of Puddings, she makes Pastorals; or when

[12] Paul Bunyan Anderson, "Mrs. Manley's Texts of Three of Lady
Winchilsea's Poems," *Modern Language Notes*, XLV (1930), 95-99.
[13] Reynolds, *The Poems of Anne Countess of Winchilsea*, p. 7.

she should be raising Paste, is raising some Ghost in a new Tragedy." Though at first thought such allusions to puddings and paste may not become Lady Winchilsea, they need mean no more than that the Countess was expected to supervise her household. Furthermore, Anne Finch had not always been Countess of Winchilsea. In fact her and her husband's loyalty to James II had meant retirement and poverty for them following the revolution of 1688, and for most of the next twenty-five years they lived with their nephew, Charles Finch, the young Earl of Winchilsea, at Eastland. Then in 1712, various heirs separating him from the title having died in the meanwhile, Colonel Finch became Earl. Since Lady Winchilsea disparaged Gay's breeding in her reference to his *Trivia*, the allusion to puddings and paste is a mild but witty counterthrust. In challenging the orthodox view of woman writers in the early eighteenth century, the Countess is as outspoken as her sisters. She resents the view that "the dull mannage, of a servile house" is woman's "outmost art, and use,"[14] and, in petitioning for an absolute retreat where simplicity will reign, she asks for freedom from domestic responsibilities:

> Courteous Fate! afford me there
> A *Table* spread without my Care, . . .[15]

Phoebe Clinket also gives her time to "raising some Ghost in a new Tragedy." The Countess of Winchilsea wrote two plays, neither of which was produced. *Aristomenes*, a tragedy, was printed in 1713, but *Love and Innocence*, a tragicomedy, remained in manuscript until Professor Reynolds included it in her edition of the *Poems*. On December 15, 1713, Pope writes in a letter to Caryll:

> I was invited that day to dinner to my Lady Winchilsea, and after dinner to hear a play read, at both which I sat in great disorder with sickness at my head and stomach.[16]

[14] *Ibid.*, pp. 4-6.
[15] *Ibid.*, pp. 68-77.
[16] Pope, *Works*, ed. Elwin-Courthope, VI, 198. Professor Reynolds thinks that the play read was probably *Love and Innocence*.

It seems likely that the play read was Lady Winchilsea's. Apparently Pope liked neither the food nor the play. This and similar incidents must have been responsible for his lines to Dr. Arbuthnot:

> If foes, they write, if friends, they read me dead. . . .
> I sit with sad civility, I read
> With honest anguish, and an aching head;[17]

Again when Fossile in disgust throws a heap of Clinket's writings into the fire, she exclaims that he has destroyed "A Pindarick Ode! five Similes! and half an Epilogue! . . . The tag of the Acts of a new Comedy! a Prologue sent by a Person of Quality! three Copies of recommendatory Verses! and two Greek Mottos!" The most distinctive item in the list is the Pindaric ode. Lady Winchilsea wrote and published three well-known Pindarics, "All is Vanity," "The Spleen," and "On the Hurricane." (So far as we know, Mrs. Centlivre never wrote a Pindaric ode.) Presumably the "five Similes" are Phoebe's own, so that there is no reason for identifying them with those which Mrs. Centlivre borrowed for *The Cruel Gift*. The "half an Epilogue" may have reference to the epilogue which the Countess wrote for Mrs. Oldfield to deliver after Rowe's *Jane Shore* (1714), and the copies of "recommendatory Verses" may be an allusion to the Countess's poems included in Pope's *Works* (1717). But such interpretations are tenuous at best, for these and the other writings might fit almost any literary lady of the time.

Though Phoebe Clinket is eager to have her play reach the stage, she wishes (unlike Mrs. Centlivre) to keep her authorship concealed and she is tortured by the harsh criticism applied to it by Sir Tremendous and the players. Early in her career Winchilsea professed a desire to avoid publication, but a study of her works shows that her opinion gradually changed. For example, in "The Preface" to her folio manuscript she says

[17] *Ibid.*, III, 244.

that when her plays were composed, "itt was far from my intention ever to own them,"[18] and yet she allowed copies of both to be seen by friends and she printed one herself. In desiring both to attain literary fame and to avoid critical censure she became an excellent target for satire. Furthermore, when Phoebe has to endure the refusal of her play, she philosophically accepts the result, but she condemns the horrible works which are acted on the stage in much the same fashion as Lady Winchilsea does in her poems.

The final possibility of connecting the Countess with *Three Hours* is mentioned by Professor Reynolds.[19] In "Mr. Pope's Welcome from Greece," a poem celebrating the completion of the translation of the *Iliad* in 1720, Gay names a long list of those who were waiting to welcome Pope back to England. Among them is "Winchilsea, still meditating song." In the same stanza is also mentioned "frolick Bicknell," the actress who created the role of Phoebe Clinket at Drury Lane. "The conjunction of names may be fortuitous," writes Professor Reynolds, "but it probably has covert reference to the play."

Yet although the contemporary expositors saw the Countess of Winchilsea through the mild satire of Phoebe Clinket, it is probable that the authors took suggestions also from various other persons, including Mrs. Centlivre. The comedy of intrigue, with its plethora of doors and disguises, is reduced to the nadir of absurdity by *Three Hours*. Similarly, the farce satirizes all those who translate their plays from foreign languages. Most of the contemporary dramatists had engaged in translation at one time or another, but Mrs. Centlivre was a notorious offender. Charles Johnson, who had *The Sultaness*, a tragedy from Racine, ready for the stage (it was acted at Drury Lane on February 25), felt the necessity of defending his translation in the Prologue, in which he referred directly to *Three Hours*. Mrs. Centlivre remembered the lesson, and in

---

[18] Reynolds, *The Poems of Anne Countess of Winchilsea*, p. 11.
[19] *Ibid.*, p. lxx.

A Bold Stroke for a Wife boasted that she had been completely original and had borrowed not one tittle from Molière.

The Rehearsal, the recognized model of dramatic burlesque, had already standardized the satire against authors who objected to cuts by the actors. Working out the play in rehearsals with the authors present led inevitably to changes in the manuscript, and Mrs. Centlivre was by no means the only author who objected to changes suggested by the players. But a very notable instance of cutting is described, as we have seen, in the *Female Tatler* Number 69 and in Mrs. Centlivre's Preface to *The Man's Bewitch'd*. It is possible that the authors, as Professor Sherburn suggests,[20] had this example in mind when writing the scene between Clinket and the players.

No individual significance need be attached to the fact that in 1717 *Three Hours* ridiculed a female author. Nor in itself does Plotwell's standing as the author of Clinket's tragedy point to a particular person. But perhaps the best known example of the "fathering" of another's play was Cibber's use of Mrs. Centlivre's *Love at a Venture* and the two plays by Burnaby in his *The Double Gallant*. Since Cibber was acting Plotwell, it was natural for the audience to interpret the satire at this point against Plotwell rather than against Clinket. Parker makes such a surmise:

> *Plotwell's* fathering *Clinket's* Play, is levell'd at *Cibber*, and the Satire bites, when he is told, *That a Parrot and a Player can utter human Sounds, but neither of them are allow'd to be Judges of Wit.*[21]

This view is supported by a quotation from the *Weekly Journal or Saturday's Post* for December 7, 1723: "Canst thou [Keyber, i.e. Cibber] not be content with stealing from *Shakespear*, *Fletcher*, *Dryden*, *Congreve*, *Shadwel*, *Farquhar*, and even from

[20] "The Fortunes and Misfortunes of *Three Hours after Marriage*," pp. 95-96.
[21] *A Complete Key*, p. 8.

poor *barren Phoebe;* but thou must purloin from Punch [Harlequin] too . . .?"

When Drury Lane revived *The Rehearsal* on February 7, Cibber introduced allusions to the mummy and the crocodile, perhaps, as sometimes suggested, to avenge himself upon the triumvirate for what he felt was a trick at his expense, since he may not have anticipated the extent to which *Three Hours* would make him look ridiculous. But it had become customary to introduce topical allusions into *The Rehearsal,* and a personal explanation of the allusions is not necessary. Nevertheless, Pope and Gay were much offended, and from this incident developed the quarrel between Pope and Cibber which in time reached *The Dunciad.*

Having observed the authors' sensitiveness regarding the mummy and the crocodile, Mrs. Centlivre, whether or not the satire of *Three Hours* had been directed specifically at her, returned to the subject in *A Bold Stroke for a Wife* (1718), Act III. In addition she managed to cast some aspersions upon the Ape (A. P - - e) which, so far as I know, Pope never mentioned but which must have lingered in his mind:

Periwinkle. A Person of your Curiosity must have collected many Rarities.

Colonel Fainwell. I have some, Sir, which are not yet come ashore, as an *Egyptian* Idol.

Per. Pray, what might that be?

Col. It is, Sir, a Kind of an Ape, which they formerly worshipp'd in that Country. I took it from the Breast of a female Mummy.

Per. Ha, ha, our Women retain part of their Idolatry to this Day, for many an Ape lies on a Lady's Breast, ha, ha,——

Sackbut. A smart old Thief.   [*Aside.*]

Col. Two Tusks of an *Hippopotamus,* two pair of *Chinese Nut-crackers,* and one *Egyptian Mummy.*

Per. Pray, Sir, have you never a Crocodile?

Col. Humph! the Boatswain brought one with Design to shew it, but touching at *Rotterdam,* and hearing it was no Rarity in *England,* he sold it to a *Dutch* Poet.

Sack. The Devil's in that Nation, it rivals us in every Thing.

Per. I should have been very glad to have seen a living Crocodile.

Col. My Genius led me to Things more worthy of Regard.

So far, then, as *Three Hours* is concerned, the writing desk strapped to the back of the maid, the use of the flood as the subject of Clinket's play, her preference for Biblical subject matter, the hymn to Apollo, the allusion to puddings and paste, the mention of Pindaric odes, and the condemnation of popular plays have point for the Countess of Winchilsea but not for Mrs. Centlivre. But the burlesque of the drama of intrigue, the satire against translators, the relationship between Clinket and the players, and the cutting of her tragedy do suggest our dramatist. At any rate she joined the fray before it was over. The sharpness of her thrust is veiled by the deceptive mildness with which it was delivered.

Back to the Theater

DESPITE her interest in politics and the controversy between Pope and Curll's authors, Mrs. Centlivre did not relinquish her love for the stage. *The Cruel Gift: or, The Royal Resentment,* a tragedy, was acted at Drury Lane six times continuously from December 17, 1716, and was repeated for the seventh and last time on May 3, 1717, by command of the Prince of Wales for the benefit of the author. Mrs. Centlivre secured three benefits out of seven performances. No other new play was acted more than seven times during this season.

Her friend, Dr. George Sewell, explains in the Prologue that the play was two winters old, the mother having weaned it late because of the earlier immersion of the people in politics. Presumably the treatment of treason and revolution was not regarded as a fit subject for the theater during the troubled days following the death of Queen Anne. He boasts that the author was a woman, and asks the town to give her its support because of her wit and her loyalty to her country, since she does not have the help of *"confed'rate Clubs of clapping Friends."* Organized support from a club or from a claque may not have been absolutely necessary for the success of a new play, but many persons thought that it was. It is likely, in fact, that Addison's club at Button's Coffee House was favorable to *The Cruel Gift.*

In the Epilogue[1] Nicholas Rowe advocates the old-time British loyalty to Church and State. Acccording to Mottley, Rowe, "who had a great Value for the Author," also gave a few slight touches to the drama; "particularly a Simile of an *Halcyon* building her Nest in fine Weather, which ends one of the Acts, was his." Antimora uses the simile as she is torn away from her brother in the prison scene in Act IV:

> So when Rising Floods
> Bear from some Rock, in secret where they lay,
> The *Halcyon*'s Nest, and all her brood away,
> The careful Mother hovers as they glide,
> Hangs on the Wing, and flutters with the Tide;
> Till at the last the Waves invading creep,
> Fill her frail House, and sink it in the Deep,
> With one shrill Note she shrieks her last Despair,
> Starts from the Sight, and flits away in Air.

Mrs. Centlivre dedicated her play to Eustace Budgell, Addison's cousin and a minor writer.[2] Mottley says that Budgell was one of her correspondents, and the Dedication gives evidence of a genuine friendship between them:

> Among the great Number that your Merits have made your Friends, I am proud to be accounted one, and to have it known to the World, I had your Permission to prefix your Name to this Tragedy. . . . It comes to you with sincere Wishes for a happy *New-Year*, for a long and uninterrupted Health . . .

Mottley adds that Budgell rewarded her with a diamond ring worth about twenty guineas.[3]

---

[1] Reprinted in *The Miscellaneous Works of Nicholas Rowe* (3d ed.; 1733).

[2] Addison secured posts for him in Ireland as his share in the Whig victory. Later he was involved in various suits at law, which he escaped by jumping in the Thames with his pockets full of stones.

[3] Curll paid her another twenty guineas for her manuscript.—Ralph Straus, *The Unspeakable Curll* (1927), p. 227.

Mills played the part of the King, the father of Leonora, taken by Mrs. Oldfield. Booth was Lorenzo, secretly married to Leonora. Ryan was Learchus, in love with Antimora, acted by Mrs. Porter. Quin was Antenor, the rascally prime minister and father of Learchus. Bowman, Walker, and Wilks took the less important roles. Wilks also spoke the Prologue, and Mrs. Oldfield the Epilogue.

According to *A Satyr upon the Present Times* (1717) none of the plays acted during the season of 1716-17 was any good. *The Cruel Gift* was applauded, but undeservedly:

> Now pass my Muse, and now survey the Stage,
> Where Comick *Cibber* swells with Tragick Rage,[4]
> Where Females in the awful Buskin tread,
> And scribble Plays when they can hardly read;
> The *Cruel Gift* has won the Town's Applause,
> But we are always pleas'd without a Cause;
> We know no Reason *A* - - - - - *n* goes down,[5]
> Or *P* - - *e*,[6] or *R* - - *e*[7] should bear away the Crown.
> Why *J* - - - - - *n* durst a motly Drama bring,
> A Farce, a Play, a Pyrate and a King.[8]
> Such bombast Scenes some Critick should chastise,
> With Truth and Spleen, and Wit before his Eyes;

[4] Probably a reference to Cibber's *The Tragical History of King Richard III* (1700), which had been acted on Jan. 1, 1717.

[5] The reference to the town's "swallowing" Addison is apparently to his *Cato*, which had been revived on Jan. 24 and March 5, rather than to *The Drummer*, which had been presented only three times, in March, 1716.

[6] *Three Hours after Marriage.*

[7] *Tamerlane* was revived on March 16 and April 29, 1717, but the reference seems to be primarily to his newer tragedy, *Jane Shore*, which was acted on Nov. 1 and 30, 1716. Later in the poem Rowe is accused of painting his Shore with "jingling Words" and converting her from a whore into a saint.

[8] The critics had objected to Charles Johnson's *The Successful Pyrate* (1712), which the author called a "play," because it mingled farce with a serious subject and violated dramatic propriety by making a pirate into a king. The reader is reminded of the objections to the earlier play in connection with Johnson's *The Sultaness*, a tragedy which had been acted at Drury Lane on Feb. 25-28, 1717.

For Plays, like those, nor make us laugh nor weep,
But with both *Cato*'s lull us fast asleep;[9] . . .

Only "Immortal *Steele*," whose *The Funeral* and *The Tender
Husband* were each acted several times in 1716 and 1717, "In
Rolls Divine deserves to have his Name," Steele, who "with
more than holy Rage" has thought fit to scourge "the Vices of
the Age."

The Cruel Gift belongs to the tradition of heroic drama.
In it Mrs. Centlivre avoids a comic plot such as she had
used in *The Perjur'd Husband* and *The Stolen Heiress*, but
she also avoids traditional tragedy in that the characters marked
for death do not actually die.[10]   There is a good deal of talk
but not much action.   Lorenzo, a great general, is secretly married to Leonora, the daughter of the King of Lombardy and
heiress to the kingdom.   Learchus, the son of Antenor, is in
love with Antimora, the sister of Lorenzo, who wants her to
marry Cardono, his lieutenant general.   The ambitious Antenor has been rebuked for trying to marry Learchus to
Leonora, but he is still determined, despite his son's loyalty and
unselfish service to the King, to have him put in line for the
throne.   By dogging Lorenzo's steps, he discovers a secret
means of entering the palace and brings the King to observe
Lorenzo and Leonora together.   Lorenzo is apprehended.

After tempting Learchus, keeper of the King's fort, without
success, Antimora, spurred on by Leonora, agrees to marry
Cardono if he will help to free Lorenzo and get him out of the
country.   But because of Learchus's watchfulness, Cardono fails,
and he, Lorenzo, and Antimora are captured.   At the instiga-
tion of Antenor, the King then orders Learchus to cut Lorenzo's
living heart out of his breast and deliver it to Leonora.   Learchus

[9] Addison's *Cato* and John Ozell's *Cato of Utica*, which had been acted at
Lincoln's Inn Fields, May 14-16, 1716, and then revived for one performance on Dec. 21.

[10] The Prologue represents this as Mrs. Centlivre's first tragedy.   Perhaps
Dr. Sewell was thinking of *The Perjur'd Husband* as tragicomedy, though the
author had called it tragedy.

does deliver a heart to her and then invites the King to observe the intensity of her suffering. He also sends for a hermit, who, it develops, is the exiled Duke of Milan, uncle of the King, and the real father of Lorenzo. The King, realizing that Lorenzo was of royal blood, that he and Leonora had been married, and that she is almost insane with grief, wishes that he had not listened to Antenor. Finding his plan successful, Learchus then produces Lorenzo and explains that the heart belonged to a guard whom Cardono had killed. Cardono himself dies from a wound, and Antenor dies in an attempt to crush the rebellion against the King. The people lay down their arms when they learn that Lorenzo is still alive. Antimora is given to Learchus, and the long-standing feud between their families is ended.

The all-noble Learchus is entirely without the passions of hate and revenge. He chooses honor over love, but he acts from a high sense of right and justice rather than from mere loyalty. In the end he is proved right and the King acknowledges his great service. Prisons and underground passageways help to provide atmosphere, and the exhibition of the heart in a cup is melodramatic in the extreme. Yet the blank verse drama seems extraordinarily flat to the modern reader. Mrs. Centlivre lacked the concreteness of imagination and the control over emotion necessary to great poetry and to the adequate development of tragic situations.

Jacob says that the story of the play came from *"Sigismonda and Guiscarda,* a Novel of *Boccacce."* The *Biographia Dramatica* adds that it was based on the Boccaccio story and on "a poetical version of it finely done by Dryden, and published among his Fables." Three German dissertations have attempted to trace the sources more fully.[11]

[11] Clarence Sherwood, *Die Neu-Englischen Bearbeitungen der Erzählung Boccaccios von Ghismonda and Guiscardo* (Berlin, 1892); Karl Poelchau, *Susannah Centlivre's Tragödie "The Cruel Gift" in ihrem Verhältnis zur Quelle Boccaccios Decameron IV 1* (Halle a. S., 1905); Hans Evardsen, *Mrs. Centlivre's Drama "The Cruel Gift" und seine Quellen* (Kiel, 1912).

There is general agreement that Mrs. Centlivre used chiefly
the story by Boccaccio, which she expanded by adding a second
plot and a second set of characters, but she followed Dryden
in making Leonora the secret wife rather than the mistress of
Lorenzo.   In Boccaccio Guiscardo's heart is actually delivered
to his mistress, and Ghismonda dies of poison.   Leonora
threatens to die of hunger and grief, but her death becomes un-
necessary.   There is no evidence that Mrs. Centlivre knew or
used any one of the five Italian plays on the subject, or Painter's
Palace of Pleasure, Novel XXXIX, or Robert Wilmot's tragedy of *Tancred and Gismund.*   In developing her plot, Mrs.
Centlivre undoubtedly took hints for Antenor's teasing the King
from *Othello* and for the Learchus-Antimora subplot from
Romeo and Juliet, but these borrowings are hardly noticeable in
her remaking of Boccaccio's revenge plot against a background
of romantic intrigue.

On February 3, 1718, appeared the last of Mrs. Centlivre's
four best plays, *A Bold Stroke for a Wife,* which was acted at
Lincoln's Inn Fields.   It was entirely successful, according to
the standards of the day, running continuously for six nights.
Christopher Bullock took the part of Colonel Feignwell.   Mrs.
Bullock, his wife, appropriately acted Mrs. Lovely, the object
of Feignwell's various disguises.   Knap, Spiller, Bullock, Sr.,
and Pack were the four guardians; Ogden, Griffin, and Hall
were minor characters; and Mrs. Kent and Mrs. Robins were
the Quaker's wife and servant.   Mrs. Thurmond, not a member
of the cast, spoke the prologue written by an unnamed gentleman, and Mrs. Bullock gave the coarse epilogue by Dr. Sewell.

Though hardly more than a farce, *A Bold Stroke for a
Wife* is the simplest and best constructed of Mrs. Centlivre's
dramas.   The play is unified, for all the incidents relate to one
man, the chief actor in all of them, and contribute to a single
purpose, which is set before the audience at the beginning.
Before Anne Lovely can marry and come into the possession of
her estate, her suitor must secure the consent of each of her

four guardians, all opposed to one another in taste and manners. The part of Colonel Feignwell requires the actor to present six distinct roles in rapid succession.

The first guardian is Sir Philip Modelove, a withered old beau who regards only the French fashions and loves operas, balls, and masquerades. Disguised as a French fop, Feignwell wins his favor and his agreement to Anne's marriage with deceptive ease.

The second guardian is Periwinkle, a Jonsonian humor, a "kind of Virtuoso, a silly half-witted Fellow, but positive and surly, fond of every thing antique and foreign, and wears his Cloaths of the Fashion of the last Century; doats upon Travellers, and believes more of Sir *John Mandeville* than he does of the Bible." Expecting to trick the virtuoso as easily as he tricked Sir Philip, Feignwell appears in Egyptian dress and describes the wonders he has beheld during his extensive travels. He no longer has a mummy and a crocodile (they had been used up in *Three Hours after Marriage*), but he has "a Muff made of the Feathers of those Geese that sav'd the *Roman* Capitol" and a vial of water from the "Waves which bore *Cleopatra*'s Vessel when she sail'd to meet *Anthony*." One of his favorite gewgaws is a girdle which makes the wearer invisible; by turning a screw he "can be in the Court of the Great Mogul, the Grand Signior, and King *George*, in as little Time as your Cook can poach an Egg." With the help of friends and a trapdoor, he is able to give a demonstration. Unfortunately, however, a drawer enters—a new Marplot—and addresses him as Colonel. Later Feignwell meets Periwinkle as Mr. Pillage, a servant of his uncle, Sir Tobey Periwinkle, supposedly just deceased. He brings along a forged will in which the nephew is named heir to the estate and an unsigned lease permitting Pillage to occupy a part of the land. As Periwinkle, acting in accordance with the implication of the will, is just ready to sign the lease, Feignwell contrives to substitute for it a document bearing Periwinkle's consent to his marriage with Anne.

Tradelove, the third guardian, is a "Change Broker; a Fellow that will out-lie the Devil for the Advantage of Stock, and cheat his Father that got him, in a Bargain; He is a great Stickler for Trade, and hates every Man that wears a Sword." Feignwell pretends to be a Dutch merchant and makes a bet with him. Since Tradelove has made the wager as a result of false information supplied by Freeman, Feignwell's friend, he loses and is glad to have the wager canceled in exchange for his interest in Anne.

The fourth guardian is Obadiah Prim, a "very rigid Quaker," with whom Anne is at present spending a quarter of the year. Feignwell visits him disguised as a Simon Pure from Pennsylvania, and barely manages to secure his consent before the real Simon Pure arrives and proves his genuineness.

A Bold Stroke for a Wife is the only one of Mrs Centlivre's dramas for which she claims complete originality. The Prologue says that it contains *"not one single Tittle from* Moliere." In her dedication of the play, by permission, to the young Philip, Duke and Marquis of Wharton, whom she lauds for his fidelity to the new monarch, she claims that "the Plot is entirely new, and the Incidents wholly owing to my own Invention; not borrowed from our own, or translated from the Works of any Foreign Poet." Yet Genest (II, 498-99) thinks that she got the hint of "another Simon Pure" from *The Petticoat Plotter*, a farce by Newburgh Hamilton which was acted at Drury Lane on June 5, 1712, though not printed until 1720.[12] In Hamilton's farce True-love gains admittance to Thrifty's house by pretending to be a Quaker scrivener, Ananias Scribe, and the real Ananias is tossed in a blanket before being recognized. The situation is obviously similar to that in the Simon Pure episode.

[12] The original cast is given. Henry Ward, the comedian, includes the farce, with a few slight alterations, among his own works (3d ed.; 1746).

Another suggestion for the Quaker is found in the role of
Mrs. Plotwell in *The Beau's Duel*. Her speech in Act IV is
as Quakerish as that of the Prims or either of the Pures. It is
likely, however, that Mrs. Centlivre was actually burlesquing
the language, and especially the sermons, of Quakers she had
heard.

Though there are frequent reminiscences of other comedies
in *A Bold Stroke for a Wife*, the assortment of characters, the
development of situations, and the happy control of the varied
intrigues make it good entertainment. If Mrs. Centlivre had
added more satire or irony in the development of her four
guardians and had gone more carefully into human relationships
than was necessary for broad humor, her play might rank with
the works of Molière.

In time *A Bold Stroke* achieved great popularity.[13] But
it was not produced again until July 7, 1724. At that time a
company of comedians traveling under letters patent from
Charles II gave it at the playhouse on Epsom Walks. It was
revived at Lincoln's Inn Fields on April 23, 1728, with Milward
as Colonel Feignwell and Mrs. Younger as Anne Lovely. It
was repeated twice during the summer and once the next year.

There is no evidence that *A Bold Stroke for a Wife* was
much imitated by other playwrights. Aminadab Prim, in Chetwood's *The Lover's Opera* (Drury Lane, May 14, 1729),
seems, however, to be a combination of two of Mrs. Centlivre's
characters, Obadiah Prim and Aminadab Holdfast, and a dream
in *The Lover's Opera* is strongly reminiscent of the vision which
Colonel Feignwell reports has led him to seek Anne in marriage. Mrs. Gardner's *A Bold Stroke for a Husband* (1777)
and Mrs. Cowley's play of the same name (1783) owe nothing
except the suggestion of a title to Mrs. Centlivre.

[13] It has given the phrase *simon pure* to the English vocabulary. "It is
told of the late W. P. Ker, that when asked *à propos de bottes* for the origin
of the phrase 'The real Simon Pure,' he replied without hesitation, 'Mrs.
Centlivre, *A Bold Stroke for a Wife.*' 'That is Scholarship,' jeered one of
the company. 'And *that* is Manners,' retorted the scholar."—Mona Wilson,
These Were Muses (1924), p. 7.

Drury Lane gave the play for the first time on January 13, 1739, with Milward as Feignwell, Woodward as Simon Pure, and Mrs. Clive as Anne Lovely. It was repeated on January 16, 17, 18, and February 7. George II commanded a performance on March 5, 1741.

A Bold Stroke was also made into a two-act droll for the theatrical booths at the great fairs and renamed *The Guardians over-reached in their Own Humour: or, the Lover Metamorphos'd*. It was printed in *The Strolers Pacquet Open'd* (1742).

Goodman's Fields produced *A Bold Stroke for a Wife* "Gratis, between the two parts of a concert" (once it was two parts of an entertainment of rope-dancing) sixteen times between October 24, 1740, and March 10, 1747. The ruse of having the play acted "by persons for their Diversion" to avoid the application of the Licensing Act worked longer than one might have expected.

A Bold Stroke for a Wife was acted in London more than eighty times before 1750 and nearly a hundred and fifty times between 1750 and 1800. Its popularity really began with Shuter's representation of Feignwell for his own benefit at Covent Garden on April 3, 1758. The play was repeated four times before the end of the season. Shuter continued to personate Feignwell until the fall of 1762. At that time Woodward, having returned to London, acted Feignwell, and Shuter became Periwinkle. Command performances for George III and his Queen were given by Woodward and Mrs. Vincent (as Anne Lovely) on January 27, 1763, and by Woodward and Miss Macklin on December 14, 1774.

Criticism of *A Bold Stroke for a Wife* during this period is meager. The play seems to have been regarded as a mere farce unworthy of critical mention. For example, the *London Chronicle* for October 25-28, 1766, barely notes a production at Covent Garden on October 25:

This Comedy has nothing to recommend it, but variety of business, as the language and sentiment are insignificant, and the plot built upon the utmost absurdity and impossibility. Woodward is very great in Feignwell, and the other characters are well performed.

A Bold Stroke for a Wife appeared too late to be included by Arthur Bedford in his second tirade against the stage, but it did not escape *The Stage the High Road to Hell* (1767), which objects to the play particularly for encouraging children to disobey their parents and for making a mockery of all religion under the guise of satirizing the Quakers.

Toward the end of the eighteenth century the comedy was given an average of six times a year. John Philip Kemble often used it (like *The Wonder*) when he had nothing else ready. On one occasion an opera, *Virginia*, by Mrs. Plowden, was an obvious failure. At the end of the first performance, Kemble came forward and announced its withdrawal. "Therefore," he added, "ladies and gentlemen, we shall have the honour of acting here to-morrow night, the *Bold Stroke for a Wife*."[14] "This," remarks Boaden, "was the constant stop-gap for all failures; the substitute for all the *d----d* among the plays, and all the *feverish* among the players. . . . The *repetition* of this succedaneum used to excite many a laugh among the *initiated;* who knew that Kemble, unless busied upon Shakespeare, was really *idle* as to management."

I have examined seventeen printings or editions of *A Bold Stroke* before 1800 (including a German translation, *Die Vier Vormünder* [1791]) and eighteen after 1800 (including one in *The British and American Theatre* with German notes [1842]). It is a little surprising that so many copies were called for, since the play had little reputation except as an acting piece. The remarks of Cumberland, for example, in his introduction to the text in *The British Drama* (1817), are typical:

[14] James Boaden, *Life of Mrs. Jordan* (1831), II, 64.

Why this play, with not one property to recommend it, but the harlequinade of the plot, and a most deterring penury of language, has been kept alive to this day, and may live for a hundred years to come, if times and taste do not alter, is easily understood. The versatility and adroitness of any one favorite actor, who can hit off the changeable character of Fainwell, will ensure success, so long as mimicry can charm the crowd.

But the play continued to attract the great actors, like Charles Kemble, Charles Mathews, and Elliston, and to please the best audiences. In a series of "Tales from the Dramatists," printed in *Colburn's New Monthly Magazine* for 1879, the story of *A Bold Stroke for a Wife* is Number 10 among the comedies. Albert Ellery Berg in 1884 calls it still a "favorite" acting play.[15]

[15] *The Drama, Painting, Poetry, and Song* (New York, 1884), p. 84.

Friends *and* Occasional Poems

ONCE IN 1717 Mrs. Centlivre laid aside, temporarily at least, whatever personal enmities she may have had and directed her pen against an enemy of her country. Charles XII, the mad king of Sweden, was threatening to attack England on her own soil. His plan was to form an alliance with Peter the Great for the dominance of northern Europe, and then to wrest from Denmark and Hanover the benefits of their conquests, to destroy the Hanoverian power, to substitute Stanislaus for Augustus as king of Poland, to bring a Swedish army into England or Scotland aboard Russian ships, and to reorient English policy by restoring the Stuart dynasty. England got word of the plot, perhaps through the Regent of France, intercepted letters, and arrested Gyllenborg, the Swedish ambassador, on January 29, 1717. But the danger was not entirely averted until the death of Charles XII on December 11, 1718.

According to Giles Jacob, Mrs. Centlivre wrote *"An Epistle from a Lady of* Great Britain *to the King of* Sweden, *on the intended Invasion."* It is likely that the poem was published separately, but I have found only "An Epistle to the King of Sweden, from a Lady of *England"* in *A Miscellaneous Collection of Poems, Songs, and Epigrams* (Dublin, 1721),[1] which contains two other poems by Mrs. Centlivre. We may be

[1] II, 73-79.

reasonably certain that this is her poem. It must have been
written shortly after the arrest of Gyllenborg. Even though
her purpose is primarily to warn Charles to leave England
alone, she finds another opportunity to attack the Pretender and
to declare her support of George I:

> To *Thee*, Rude Warrior, whom we once admir'd,
> And thought thy Actions spoke *Thee* half inspir'd,
> While Justice held the Ballance of thy Cause,
> And ev'ry Language sounded *Thy* Applause:
> But since Ambition, and Revenge prevails,
> *Thy* Glories languish, and our Wonder fails;
> To *Thee, a Woman* sends with *gen'rous* Care,
> And warns thy Rashness timely to beware.
>
> Fame now a Tale of fresher Date has told,
> Beyond thy mad Romantick Feats of Old:
> Our Malecontents thy Num'rous Squadrons boast,
> Describe thy Pendants flying on our Coast,
> And hear the pleasing Cry, *Britannia*'s lost;
> But we, who know the Genius of our Isle,
> At their Report, and thy Invasion smile. . . .
>
> Each lovely Toast her Hero's Soul inspires,
> Urges the War, and wakes his Martial Fires:
> Think but what Terrors will *thy* Spirits seize,
> When *thou* shalt face such Enemies as these;
> See a Battalion lac'd with Point *d' Span*,
> And warm in glowing Velvets leads the Van:
> With War-like Air, th' embroider'd Chiefs appear,
> And gracefully the Looms rich Labours wear:
> In modish Order, o'er their Shoulders fly,
> *Deville*'s wigs, or *Lockman*'s smarter Tye;
> The Gold-clock'd Stockings draw the Gazer's Sight,
> And *Verdon*'s Red-top'd Shooe, stitch'd round with White:
> Fine *Meclin* Laces round their Fingers play,
> From Snowy-Shirts, at least, chang'd twice a day. . . .

Aim then no more, fond Prince, at *GEORGE*'s Throne,
Wake from the flattr'ing Dream, and guard they own. . . .

Jacob says that this poem was answered by Mrs. Davis, "but
her Performance was very inferiour to Mrs. *Centlivre*'s." I
have not seen a copy of Mrs. Davis's work.

We know that Mrs. Centlivre was in London on King
George's birthday, May 28, 1718, for on that occasion she
again provided a celebration, this time at her home in Buckingham Court.[2] Not long after, she visited Holbeach. From
that town she wrote a poetic epistle, "From the COUNTRY, To
Mr. *ROWE* in Town. M.DCC.XVIII."[3] In it she shows the
coffeehouse condescension toward the country people, and her
figures from nature are as generalized as the purest classicist
might wish:

From a lonesome Old House, near *Holbeach* Wash-way,
(The Wash, you must know, is an Arm of the Sea,)
A poor Wanderer writes, to let your Spouse know,
Here's nothing can equal the Charms of her ROWE. . . .

Here Gentry, and Yeomen, and Farmers appear,
As Christian as Jews, and as rough as a Bear;
They tipple like Swine, and they treat their Wives so,
They're Monsters methinks, when compar'd to her ROWE.

Here *Flora*'s fine Garments unheeded are worn,
The Flowers neglected the Meadows adorn,
The Rose's rich Scent, when I smell as I go,
I think is less sweet than the Voice of my ROWE. . . .

The Town, and the Court too but few can afford,
There's *Wellwood*[4] the Doctor, and *H* --- *y* the *L* -- *d;*[5]

---

[2] *Weekly Journal,* June 7, 1718.
[3] *A New Miscellany of Original Poems, Translations, and Imitations*
(1720), pp. 326 ff.
[4] James Wellwood (1652-1727), physician to William and Mary and
author of several political tracts. The next line would seem to indicate that
Mrs. Centlivre had herself been ill, perhaps recently.
[5] Possibly Edward Harley (1689-1741), later Earl of Oxford, who
married Lady Henrietta Cavendish-Holles. Mrs. Centlivre may for the

To the First, under Heaven, my Life I do owe,
And thank him for saving the Spouse of my Rowe.

The Second, alas! I dare only declare,
'Tis well he's a Lord, and that I am not Fair;
His Eyes have such Power—but I'll say no mo,
The Lord above bless him together with Rowe.

Following Rowe's death on December 6, 1718, Mrs. Centlivre wrote "A PASTORAL TO THE Honoured Memory of
Mr. *ROWE*," which attracted a good deal of attention.[6] Under
the name of Amaryllis she mourns with Daphnis, Thyrsis, and
Menaclas for the death of Colin. It is a sincere elegy but by
no means great poetry. The speeches are pretty much of a
pattern, so that only a few of them need be quoted:

Amaryllis.

Help me, *Menalcas,* help me to complain,
To tell to Earth, to Air, and Seas my Pain.
Colin! the dear lov'd *Colin!* is no more.
Come, all ye Nymphs, and *Colin's* Loss deplore:
For whom shall we our flow'ry Chaplets weave?
Or who so well deserves the Lawrel Wreath?
Who now can point thro' all these Groves a Man,
To celebrate the Birth of mighty Pan?
Like *Colin,* who can *Flora's* Sweets display?
Or paint the gawdy Treasures of her *May?*
Or who, like him, can tune the Oaten Reed?
Or tread with such a Grace th' enamel'd Mead?
Mourn, all ye Nymphs, your Tears incessant shed,
Your Tribute's all too poor for him that's Dead.

---

moment have overcome her hatred of the father's "treason" or may have
thought back to the Protestant Duke of Newcastle, Lady Henrietta's father.
   [6] It was published in *Musarum Lachrymae: or, Poems to the Memory of
Nicholas Rowe* (1719), a volume dedicated to Congreve by Charles Beck-
ingham, and reprinted in *The Miscellaneous Works of Nicholas Rowe* (1733).

THYRSIS.

Wou'd but relentless Fate our Wishes Aid,
And give to Substance back his Airy Shade,
As Pluto once *Euridice* of Old,
A Tale I well remember *Colin* told,
To purchase that, my Tears like thine shou'd flow,
But this is fruitless Grief, and pageant Woe.
Hark, *Amaryllis!* Hark! Thy bleating *Lambs*
Amongst the Brakes have lost their udder'd Dams:
Haste to retrieve them e're too far they stray.
And fall to hungry *Wolves* an easy Prey.

AMARYLLIS.

Why, let 'em stray, my Crook no more I'll hold,
My Herds no more—no more my Flocks I'll fold,
No more will I with *Daisy, Pink,* and *Rose,*
A Garland for the Queen of *May* compose,
Since *Colin*'s gone, by whom 'twas still confest,
That I, of all the Nymphs, deserv'd it best.
The Winds shall useless prove to Fleets at Sea,
And Flowers supply no Honey to the *Bee,*
When, *Colin,* I forget to mourn for *Thee.* . . .

Though it is frequently stated that Mrs. Centlivre wrote
like a man—and in her comedies it would be difficult to prove
the contrary—her dedications, poetic epistles, and occasional
poems give her away. But the most interesting part of the
pastoral is that in which Amaryllis claims, on Rowe's authority,
superiority among the poetesses.

Susanna herself became seriously ill in 1719. Nicholas
Amhurst wrote a poem "To Mrs. CENTLIVRE, *at that time
dangerously ill,*"[7] in which he asks the tyrant death, who has
already taken Rowe and Garth (Dr. Samuel Garth died Jan-

[7] N. Amhurst, *Poems on Several Occasions* (1720), pp. 93-94. Reprinted
in *A New Miscellany of Original Poems, Translations, and Imitations* (1720),
pp. 331-32.

uary 18, 1719), to "stop thy savage hand," "Stop our fore-
boding tears," and "give CENTLIVRE back to health again."

Amhurst seems to have regarded himself as Susanna's pro-
tégé. He wrote a second poem "to Mrs. CENTLIVRE, upon her
desiring him to read and correct a POEM."[8] Alluding to her
under the name of Orinda, by which Mrs. Katherine Philips
was often known, he praises her writing and her loyalty:

> In vain, ORINDA, on my aid,
>   And weaker judgment you rely;
> Too rashly, Fair-one, you persuade,
>   A mortal to correct the sky.
>
> To me, like PHAETON of old,
>   A dangerous province you resign,
> Which I, like him unskill'd, and bold,
>   Accept, and mimick Pow'r divine.
>
> Without my help the soul to warm
>   With love, still happily proceed,
> Bid other LEONORA's* charm
>   And other villains justly bleed—
>
> Whilst party-mad the BRITISH FAIR,
>   On Monarch JEMMY set their hearts,
> Despise the peaceful house-wife's care,
>   And practise their seditious arts.
>
> Whilst they with lies revile the THRONE,
>   And with Church fears their minds perplex,
> Their follies singly you atone,
>   And singly you redeem the sex.

It is possible that Mrs. Centlivre asked Amhurst to give a
few touches to her pastoral on the death of Rowe, since she
could no longer go to the laureate himself. The suggestion

---

[8] Amhurst, *ibid.*, pp. 95-96; *A New Miscellany*, pp. 333-34.
* See the CRUEL GIFT, a Tragedy. Written by Mrs. CENTLIVRE.

that the British women have set their hearts on the Pretender
and now stir up sedition is a reflection of the increasing personal
unpopularity of George I.   The ladies turned against him
early, partly because of his German language and his rapacious
German mistresses.   Neither George I nor George II cared
greatly for literature, and Walpole gave little patronage to
writers.   By 1730 most of the wits had gone over to the Tory
camp.   Amhurst himself, under the pseudonym of Caleb
D'Anvers, in 1726 became editor of the *Craftsman,* one of the
most violent of the Tory papers.

In Anthony Hammond's *A New Miscellany of Original
Poems, Translations, and Imitations* (1720) are two more
poems credited to Mrs. Centlivre.   The first, "TO THE
Dutchess of *BOLTON, Upon seeing her* PICTURE *drawn unlike her,*"[9] is pure compliment.   The only successful image of
the Duchess, we are told, is found in the heart, for "Perfection
mocks the Painter's Art."

The other, "TO THE Earl of WARWICK, *On his Birth-
Day,*"[10] was probably written in 1718 when the Earl came of
age.   Nature had asked spring to bedeck the earth in green
for the Earl's birthday, writes Mrs. Centlivre, but winter objected and arrayed the earth in white.   The snow reminds her
of the young man's mother and of his own virtuousness:

> To Snow we may the Dame compare,
>   Who brought this noble Youth to Light,
> Her Bosom like her Fame most Fair,
>   Or than the Down of Swans more white.
>
> Like Day, his Patriot Mind appears,
>   Where Crouds of spotless Virtues bloom,
> To guard this Land in future Years,
>   Against the Tyranny of *Rome.*

[9] Pp. 322-23.
[10] Pp. 324-25.   Edward Henry Rich, fourth Earl of Holland and sixth
Earl of Warwick, died unmarried in 1721, aged twenty-four.

>   Give Him kind Heaven a virtuous Fair,
>   From whom let *British* Patriots Spring,
>   That still against a *Popish Heir*,
>   May guard my *Country*, and my KING.

During the summer months of 1720 when South Sea stock
was booming, Mrs. Centlivre appealed to Charles Joy, one of
the directors, for a gift. James Craggs the younger had presented some stock to John Gay about the first of July, 1720.
He had also given stock to Alexander Pope, his neighbor at
Chiswick and afterward at Twickenham.[11] Mrs. Centlivre felt
that a sound Whig deserved stock as much as the Tories. Her
poem, published separately in 1720 and reprinted in *A Miscellaneous Collection of Poems, Songs, and Epigrams* (Dublin,
1721),[12] is entitled "A WOMAN'S CASE: in an Epistle to
CHARLES JOYE, Esq; Deputy-Governor of the *South Sea*."
She appeals to Joy to be as generous to her as Blunt has been to
other poets.[13] It is a long poem in which she traces her political
services over the past ten years and adds a good deal of information about her relations with her hubsand:

>   Soon after Spouse and I were Chain'd,
>   At Helm the *Tory* Party reign'd.
>   The QUEEN I lov'd, but hated those
>   Who prov'd themselves my Country's Foes:
>   Vex'd to see what Corporal *John*[14]
>   Was Nine Years doing, all undone;
>   And those that trembled at his Name,
>   On Cockhorse mounted up again;
>   I now and then, to ease my Spleen,
>   Lash'd these Misleaders of the Q --- n:

[11] Craggs, deeply involved, died of smallpox shortly after the bubble burst.

[12] I, 175-84.

[13] Her friend Nicholas Amhurst had written *An Epistle (with a petition
in it) to Sir John Blount, Bart. One of the Directors of the South-Sea Com-
Jany* (2d ed.; 1720). Sir John Blunt (1665-1733), a main figure in the
enterprise, lost nearly all his large property a few months later.

[14] John Churchill, Duke of Marlborough.

Still proving by my frequent Rhimes,
I durst be Good in Worst of Times. . . .
Nay tho' my Husband's Place forbid it; . . .

This made Spouse stare like any Spectre,
And as he was my Head—to hector.

Madam, said he, with surly Air,
You've manag'd finely this Affair;
Pox take your Schemes, your Wit, and Plays,
I'm bound to curse 'em all my Days:
If out, I'm by your Scribbling turn'd,
I wish your Plays and you were burn'd.

That I believe, my Dear, quoth I;
But if one—you know who, shou'd Die,
And *Brunswick* o'er these *Jacks* prevail,
You'll tell me then another Tale:
When all the *Whigs* in Post you see,
You'll thank, instead of chiding me.
These Words he ponder'd in his Mind,
And hop'd the Benefit to find. . . .
Anna Resign'd, and *Brunswick* Came,
And yet my Lot is still the Same.
When uppermost our Patriots ride,
They want no Scriblers on their Side:
Their Actions are so just and right,
They need no Props to keep 'em tight.
Not so, when *Tories* bore the Sway,
They kept their Herd in constant Pay;
And dreaming still on Revolutions,
Still deal out their Contributions:
By this we see the High-Church Party
Are constant to their Friends, and Hearty.

By them I've oft been thus derided:
Yet, Madam! are you unprovided?

You, who stickled late and early,
Against the wicked Schemes of *H - - - y;*[15]
And clearly prov'd by Dint of Reason,
To name the *Chevalier* was Treason;
Why, 'faith, I think it very hard,
So brave a *Whig* is not prefer'd.
One might have thought this Golden Age,
You 'ad left off Writing for the Stage;
And from *South-Sea* got Gold—true *Sterling*
Enough to keep your Coach, or *Berlin*.
Some Female Wits of *Tory* Strain
Have nick'd your Friends, and reap'd the Gain.
And can you see the ill-judg'd Prize,
Bestow'd on Creatures you despise?
But *Whigs* in Place have still been known
To help all Parties but their own:
To *Charles* the Second's Maxim kind,
Advance your Foes, your Friends ne'er mind;
For whether you do well or ill,
Your Friends, you know, will be—Friends still. . . .

Not that I want for wholesome Diet,
Bread, and my Muse, with Peace and Quiet:
I wou'd prefer, were I to chuse,
To *South-Sea* Stock—without my Muse:
But oh! my Spouse who understands
Nought to be good, but Bills and Bonds,
The ready Cash, or fruitful Lands,
Begins new Quarrels ev'ry Day,
And frights my dear-lov'd Muse away:
Nor Day, nor Night I know no Ease,
Accosted still with Words like these.

Deuce take your scribling Vein, quoth he,
What did it ever get for me?

[15] Robert Harley, first Earl of Oxford.

Two Years you take a Play to write,
And I scarce get my Coffee by't.
Such swingeing Bills are still to pay
For Sugar, Chocolate, and Tea,
I shall be forc'd to run away.
You made me hope the Lord knows what,
When *Whigs* shou'd Rule, of This, and That;
But from your boasted Friends I see
Small Benefit accrues to me:
I hold my Place indeed, 'tis true;
But I well hop'd to Rise by You. . . .

    What wou'd you have me do, I cry'd?
Beg a Subscription, he reply'd.
Why may not you as well succeed,
As if you liv'd beyond the *Tweed?*
Your Brother Bards, you see, have don't;
Mayn't JOYE as generous be as, *Blount?* . . .

One naturally wonders whether her poem paid off.[16]   It seems
to have attracted some attention at the time.   Daniel Defoe
praises it along with her comedies in *Mercurius Politicus* for
July, 1720.[17]

It must have been about this time that Mrs. Centlivre was
a member of a mixed literary gathering or perhaps even an
informal literary club.   In the *Secret Memoirs of the late Mr.
Duncan Campbel, The Famous Deaf and Dumb Gentleman,*
"Written by Himself, who ordered they should be publish'd
after his Decease" (1732), the group is partially listed:

    Sometimes, when surrounded by my Friends, such as
Anthony Hammond, Esq; Mr. *Philip Horneck,* Mr.
Phillips, Mr. -------, Mrs. *Centlivre,* Mrs. *Fowk,* Mrs.
Eliza Haywood, and other celebrated Wits, of which my

[16] If Joy did make her a gift, she was very unkind to mention "A
Quondam South-Sea Director" among the varieties of living dead in *The
Artifice,* Act V.
[17] Pp. 61-62.

House, for some Years, has been the general Rendezvous,
a good Bowl of Punch before me, and the Glass going
round in a constant Circle of Mirth and good Humour,
I have, in a Moment, beheld Sights which has froze my
very Blood, and put me into such Agonies that disordered
the whole Company.[18]

The memoirs are often attributed to Defoe, whose name should
probably supply the blank, or to Defoe and Mrs. Haywood
jointly.[19] Campbell had had the honor of being mentioned in
Tatler Number 14 and in *Spectator* Numbers 323, 474, 505,
560, and 615, and had enjoyed a considerable reputation for
possessing the power of second sight. Defoe may have been
interested in resuscitating his reputation or he may have been
reflecting through Campbell his own interest in the occult.

At any rate there is no reason to doubt that the group did
gather from time to time. Ambrose Philips we have previously
met as a friend of Mrs. Centlivre. Philip Horneck (1674-
1728) was a London attorney, son of Anthony Horneck the
divine. At the end of April, 1714, he started the *High-German
Doctor*, which was notorious for its attacks on Lord Oxford.
He became a solicitor of the treasury about the end of 1715.
Mrs. Haywood was to become somewhat notorious for her
plays and romances. Mrs. Martha Fowke (1690?-1736), who
married a Mr. Sansone, is best known for her poems in the
Epistles of Clio and Strephon (*c.* 1719), where she is Clio to
the Strephon of William Bond. She was praised by Steele and
by Aaron Hill's circle. Bond himself was a friend of Hill and
a collaborator with him in the *Plain Dealer*, published twice a
week from March 23, 1724, to May 7, 1725.

[18] Pp. 131-32. According to the title page of the *History of the Life
and Adventures of Mr. Duncan Campbell*, published by Curll on April 30,
1720, and perhaps written largely by Defoe, Campbell was living in Exeter
Court over against the Savoy in the Strand. He also lived for a time near
the Centlivres in Buckingham Court.

[19] The *History* of Duncan Campbell is attacked in *Mercurius Politicus*
for May, 1720, but in July the editor apologizes. Both statements were
apparently advertisements by Defoe of the book.

But the most interesting name in the list is that of Anthony Hammond. Mottley says that Hammond did not see Susanna again for many years after the Cambridge episode. Apparently his enjoyment of the company of writers and wits caused him to drift back into an acquaintance with his college cousin. As we have seen, he included three poems by her and two poems to her in his *A New Miscellany* (1720). His own "To Astraea" was certainly written to her also.[20]

The only significant item added by the author of Mrs. Centlivre's life in her complete works is this: "To reform the [Church], was our Author's latest Employ, and she shewed herself Mistress of the Subject in her Treatise which discloses and confutes the Errors of the *Church of Rome*." I have not found a separate publication which bears this description, but I have discovered a set of communications to the *Weekly Journal* which her biographer undoubtedly had in mind. Whether or not they were collected I do not know. The first, dated September 7, 1720, was published in the issue for September 10. "S. C." says that since Mr. Read, the editor, has been good in helping to distinguish the enemies of England from His Majesty's friends, she will send him a weekly communication—a kind of abstract of "the selected Thoughts of an Ingenuous Author"—to print in his paper. The first one develops the idea that the best church is the one that makes the most religious and the most rational members. At the end of the abstract the editor adds that he will continue to publish the communications of the gentleman.[21] The next, on September 17, accompanied by another brief note signed "S. C.," expresses the opinion that religion and liberty best flourish where reason and knowledge are encouraged. There is no communication in the following issue. On October 1 "S. C." says the omission may have been due to lack of room. The theme this time is

[20] See pp. 10, 27.
[21] The abstracts were made from the *Independent Whig*. Cf. Anderson, "Innocence and Artifice," p. 375 n. 32.

that Popish countries prevent the people from having the Bible in their own language and deliberately keep them in ignorance. On October 8 she writes on penance and holydays. Penance she regards as silly—why should one eat fish instead of beef? or wear a dirty hair shirt? And holydays even in the established Church cause too much drunkenness and dissipation. The issue for October 15 prints a communication against the high Church and the hyprocrisy of its priests. She includes a summary of Molière's *Tartuffe* and adds that the priests had its representation on the stage stopped.

Mrs. Centlivre's interest in the English Church, not as a test of political loyalty, but as an institution to which she was committed by sincere belief and conviction, is a little surprising. Her enemies undoubtedly pointed to these articles when her last play, *The Artifice*, one of her coarsest, appeared two years later.

Mrs. Centlivre's fame had reached its pinnacle in 1720. Her portrait had been painted by D. Fermin. The best of the engravings from the portrait (or from other engravings) is a mezzotint by P. Pelham, a painter and engraver who later came to New England and became one of the first American artists of note. Copies of Pelham's engraving were advertised in the *Daily Courant* for October 29 along with his engraving of the Duke of Newcastle from a portrait by Sir Godfrey Kneller. A poor engraving by J. Taylor appears as a frontispiece to her complete works, and an even worse occurs in the large illustrated edition of Genest. In the latter the engraving has been reversed, so that the lady looks not to the left but to the right; also a necklace has been added by way of adornment.

Despite Chetwood's remark that she had a small wen on her left eyelid, which gave her a masculine air, her picture makes her an attractive woman, probably because she did not insist to Fermin that he paint her, wart and all. She seems to have been rather well rounded, though not fat, even with her double chin. Her forehead is high and broad, and her eyebrows are lifted somewhat after the fashion of the Oriental's—perhaps giving a slightly exotic cast to her face when she was younger. Her nose is good, the narrowness of the nostrils alone of her features indicating the tenacity that led her to remind her readers over and over again that she had done what she could for George I. The cheeks are full, and the chin is small. Although there is nothing spiritual about her appearance, her eyes indicate good humor and intelligence. Mottley's characterization of her would, in fact, seem to have been justified:

> If she had not a great deal of Wit in her Conversation, she had much Vivacity and good Humour; she was remarkably good-natured and benevolent in her Temper, and ready to do any friendly Office as far as it was in her Power. She made herself some Friends and many Enemies by her strict Attachment to Whig Principles even in the most dangerous Times, and had she been a Man, I dare say would have freely ventured her Life in that Cause.
>
> She lived in a decent clean Manner, and could show (which I believe few other Poets could, who depended chiefly on their Pen) a great many Jewels and Pieces of Plate, which were the Produce of her own Labour, either purchased by the Money brought in by her Copies, her Benefit-Plays, or were Presents from Patrons.

It is in the spirit of this characterization that we turn to Mrs. Centlivre's "LETTER On the Receipt of a Present of Cyder,"[22] which furnishes literary evidence of her geniality and good humor:

> SIR,
>   Your noble Present of right *Red-Streak*,
>   Which strong enough to make a CAT to speak,
>   Came Yesterday by trusty *James*, Sir,

[22] *A Miscellaneous Collection of Poems, Songs, and Epigrams* (Dublin, 1721), pp. 131-32.

With Porter laden from the *Thames*, Sir,
Five dozen Bottles! What d'ye mean, Sir?
Why, 'tis a Present for the Queen, Sir;
Why, you're the most gen'rous Man alive,
A Lawyer too! you'll never thrive;
To send a Poet such a Gift as this,
Is like a Suit in *Forma Pauperis*.
All we can pay is empty worthless Rhymes, . . .
I love the Muses Friends, those Gen'rous few,
Which keep the Ancient Virtuous Paths in View,
None has a juster Claim to those than You.
We tap'd the CYDER, and we drank your Health,
And wish it heartily with store of Wealth.
My Heart and Soul with grateful Ardour burn,
But Thanks is all the Poet can return.
CYDER's to NECTAR turn'd—Or so I think it,
Then pray make haste to Town, and help to drink it.
                              I am, Sir, &c.

Red-streak cider, simply enough, was cider made from red-streak apples, an improved variety with striped cheeks. It was this which John Philips had celebrated in his popular poem *Cyder* (1708).

A Last Fling *in the Theater*

THE PURITANICAL attacks on the theater did not
cease with Jeremy Collier or even with Arthur Bedford's treatise of 1706. Nevertheless, though the stage
did not make a quick transformation and though party divisions
continued, there were signs that the theater was coming to be
accepted as a phase of the national culture. As it became less
and less an appendage of the court, it reflected more accurately
the taste of all London. Sentimental tendencies, with their
moral overtones, came haltingly at first, but to a great many
people they seemed to indicate that the theater could be a
means of improving life.

One of the last of the full-blooded attacks on the stage appeared in 1719. Arthur Bedford again subjected plays to a
moral examination, a much more complex one than that of
1706. In *A Serious Remonstrance in Behalf of the Christian
Religion, Against the Horrid Blasphemies and Impieties which
are still used in the English Play-Houses, to the great Dishon-
our of Almighty God, and in Contempt of the Statutes of this
Realm,* he repeats many of his cavils against earlier dramas and
adds a good deal about those produced after 1705.

While proving the intent of stage plays from the mouths
of their authors, Bedford quotes from the Dedication of *The
Basset Table* a statement to the effect that plays were originally
designed to correct and rectify manners. But the truth, as he

sees it, is that they no longer have that laudable design. In *The Busy Body* he objects to the application of the terms "damnation" and "salvation" to trifling matters. He gives also examples of the use of oaths and of stage prayers that begin not with "O Lord!" as in Scripture but with "O the Devil!" Also he says that the plots turn on intrigues and so frequently plead for adultery and whoredom. *The Busy Body* and *The Basset Table* are cited as examples, the latter more appropriately because of the subplot involving the lord and the citizen's wife. His criticism of the playhouse for exposing parents and justifying the rebellion of their children is for the modern reader less fortunate. He takes it ill that the daughter of Sir Jealous Traffick (of *The Busy Body*) manages to escape the watchfulness of her father, who designs to "settle her with a *Spaniard*," and to marry "another, whom she loved."

Bedford makes a long examination of *The Wonder*. He thinks that in it above all other plays one might expect good morality, "modest *Characters*, and a fair *Representation* of the *British Kingdoms*," especially if one reads the Dedication and realizes that the play was written by a woman. But Don Felix and Colonel Britton, he says, are both blasphemous and lewd, though they are the poet's favorites and are rewarded with heiresses, Violante worth twenty thousand pounds and Isabella worth ten. The ladies both contrive to marry against their fathers' wishes, and Violante invents a lie whenever it suits her purpose. There are the usual instances of cursing and swearing from *A Wife Well Manag'd*, but Bedford's chief objection to it is that, as he puts it, the author objects to the priest rather than to the Papist. The playwrights seem not to have been hurt by Bedford's tirade. Certainly he did not attract the attention that Collier had done. The dramatists continued to write, though they were likely to veer more toward sentimentality.

Mrs. Centlivre herself made one final bid for success. But her last play, *The Artifice*, contains some of the worst elements of three dramatic schools—light manners, busy intrigues, and sentimental reformation—and is really a failure in all. The play received favorable advance notices. The *St. James's Journal* for September 20, 1722, compliments it on the recommendation of "several Gentlemen of good Taste and Judgment" who have read it. And the *Freeholder's Magazine* for September 26, 1722, reports an interview with "a Master of Wit and Humour in Conversation," who has seen the play in rehearsal and thinks it excels all her former productions.

Yet, despite the publicity, the comedy ran for only three nights, October 2-4, at Drury Lane. B. Victor, in *An Epistle to Sir Richard Steele, on his Play, call'd The Conscious Lovers* (1722), expresses the opinion that her drama might have succeeded if John Dennis had written a pamphlet against it as he had done against Steele's.

Probably for her benefit on October 4 Mrs. Centlivre addressed a note to a Whig friend asking him to attend the performance:

SIR,

The Favour I ask you'll with Honour supply,
A *Whig* and a *Woman* you cannot deny;
Then once for a Stranger your Int'rest pray use,
Bring your Friends, with yourself, to honour my Muse.
No *Tory* I sue to, my *Play* to support,
For I hate all the Rogues, from the *Cit* to the *Court*.
In Times worse than these, I chose firmly to stand,
By those that supported the Laws of the Land;
And now my Ambition is, only, to bring,
The Props of my Country, and the Friends of my King.[1]

[1] Reprinted by Richard C. Boys in *Modern Language Notes*, LVII (1942), 361-62, from *Caribbeana. Containing Letters and Dissertations, Together With Poetical Essays. . . . Chiefly Wrote by several hands in the West-Indies* (1741), I, 48. It was first printed in the periodical-miscellany *Caribbeana* on

The Prologue, written by William Bond, was spoken by
Mills. It asks the favor of the audience for one who continues
to produce comedy:

> *But, O! ye* Critics! Comic-Bards *are few,*
> *And we've no* Wit *beneath the Sun, that's* New:
> *Ask not, in such a* General Dearth, *much Wit,*
> *If she your Taste in* Plot, *and* Humour *hit:*
> Plot, Humor, Business, *form the* Comic *Feast,*
> Wit*'s but a* higher-relish'd Sauce, *at best;*
> *And where* too much, *like* Spice, *destroys the Taste.*

The Epilogue, by Dr. Sewell, was spoken by Mrs. Oldfield.
It in effect advises husbands to trust their wives, since they
cannot outwit them.

Wilks and Mills played the parts of Sir John Freeman, a
disinherited young man, and Ned, his younger borther, in
possession of the estate. William Wilks was Fainwell; Griffin,
Watchit; and Harper, Tally. Mrs. Oldfield acted Mrs.
Watchit, the intriguing citizen's wife; Mrs. Horton, Olivia;
Mrs. Younger, Louisa; and Mrs. Thurmond, the Widow Heedless.

The plots and artifices are fairly distinct but much too
numerous for an effective comedy. In the first, Louisa, a
Dutch girl with a large fortune, persuades Ned Freeman, her
seducer, that he has been poisoned and so induces him to marry
her and also to give up his patrimonial estate to his elder
brother. The author induces sympathy for Louisa by pointing
out that a betrothal in Holland is the equivalent of marriage,
so that her previous freedom with Ned was not really immoral.

Sept. 6, 1732, with this note: "*Bridge-Town* [Barbadoes]. The . . . Lines
were wrote *extempore*, by the celebrated Female Poet . . . in a Letter to a
Person of known Generosity (now residing here) on Occasion of a new
Play of the Author's, which was to be acted the same Evening, for her
Benefit. As they were never before in Print, it may be some Gratification to
the *Curious,* to see the *hasty* Thoughts of so famous a *Wit* of that Sex."
It is possible, but unlikely, that the letter was written for a performance of
The Cruel Gift or *A Bold Stroke for a Wife* rather than of *The Artifice.*

Sir John Freeman and Olivia, to both of whom Louisa is obligated for assistance, are then able to marry. Olivia's father, Sir Philip Moneylove, cares little which of the brothers wins his daughter so long as it is the one with the family property.

Fainwell, an ensign, by masquerading as Jeffrey, a country footman, and as Mr. Worthy, a wealthy gentleman from Gloucestershire, tricks the Widow Heedless and her twenty thousand pounds from Tally, who is masquerading as Lord Pharoah-Bank. Tally has promised Sir Philip three thousand pounds for helping him to marry the widow, who is Sir Philip's cousin.

Ned Freeman and Mrs. Watchit do their unsuccessful best to cuckold Watchit, Fainwell's uncle, but Mrs. Watchit repents when she learns that Ned is married and promises to be faithful thenceforth.

Technically Mrs. Centlivre shows in *The Artifice* little of the skill in construction that she manifested in *The Wonder* and *A Bold Stroke for a Wife*. The plots and characters are almost entirely independent of one another, and no one of them is dominant. Furthermore, *The Artifice* lacks unity of tone. Although Ned Freeman is represented as a great rake and villain, he reforms and tries to atone for his sins. On learning that he has not actually been poisoned, he is at first highly indignant, but he soon moderates his anger, rejoices at the failure of his own plans, and thanks his wife and brother for the result:

> But few of the Sex can boast such Constancy. How shall I thank thee for this excessive Goodness? Brother! Let me thank you too. Had I known your Inclination for this Lady Olivia, you should have had no Rival here.
> [*Claps his Hand on his Breast.*]

Although *The Artifice* is by no means a sentimental comedy, it has a number of sentimental elements. The winning of Ned by Louisa, the assistance afforded by Olivia to a fellow woman in distress, and the repentance of Ned are sentimental

in spirit and in purpose.   The object is not to pay Ned off (as,
for instance, Sharper is paid off in *The Platonick Lady*) but
to excite sympathy for Olivia and to make Ned worthy by his
conversion of the woman he has wronged.   Mrs. Watchit, with
her intrigue and her jealous husband, is a figure from the
older comedy of manners, but this plot too is given a sentimental turn in the repentance and conversion of the wife.
The Widow Heedless is a sensible woman except for the fact
that she is determined not to marry beneath a lord.   The spirit
of the new comedy is evident in the fact that the marriage
which is put upon her is for her own good.   Congreve would
have matched her with Lord Pharaoh-Bank and let her anticipation of life with the sharper atone for her vanity.   Peculiarly
enough, it is the elder brother, the one genuine male figure, who
closes the play with a reflection suited to the earlier drama:

> *For* He *or* She, *who drags the* Marriage Chain,
> *And finds in* Spouse *Occasion to complain,*
> *Should hide their Frailties with a Lover's Care,*
> *And let th' ill-judging World conclude 'em Fair;*
> *Better th' Offence ne'er reach the Offender's Ear.*
> *For they who sin with* Caution, *whilst* conceal'd,
> *Grow* impudently *careless, when* reveal'd.

Mrs. Centlivre's difficulties with *The Artifice* did not cease
when the actors withdrew it from the boards.   In the *Daily
Journal* for November 7, 1722, it is advertised as just published.[2]   The rest of the advertisement seems to be an appeal by
the author in defense of her play:

> *A New-Writer, who I am certain from the peevishness
> of his Libel call'd* Advices from Parnassus *must be some
> Non-Juring Parson; having set himself up for a Dramatick
> Critick, roundly asserts in the Arrogant-stile of his Brother
> Collier.   That,* "The whole Scope of the ARTIFICE, is

[2] It was published on Oct. 29.   Curll again paid her twenty guineas
for the rights.

to encourage adultery; to ridicule the Clergy; and to set Women, above the Arbitrary Power of their Husbands, to exert their Natural Rights for the Preservation of their Lusts;" *with many other Invectives; as,* "That this Comedy, is at the best, a scurrilous, impious, monstrous Performance, without any Beauty to recommend it, except the Principles of *genuine Whiggism,* to disregard the Laws of God and Man." *From all which gross, as well as false Imputations, I doubt not but to stand acquitted in the Judgment of every Reader,* who will impartially peruse the Play itself. This being the only Request made to the Publick, by

Susan Centlivre.

But since Mrs. Centlivre always wrote her name Susanna, one immediately questions the authenticity of this notice. In the *St. James's Journal* for November 22 she denies any connection whatsoever with it and adds that she has "made the strictest Enquiry" for the pamphlet[3] referred to but has not been able to find it. She wanted to discover it "to convince my Suspicion that some of my good Friends, the *Jacobites,* had inserted that Advertisement with my Name to it" to support the rumor they had circulated "That this Comedy was so full of Obscenity that no modest Woman could see it." She concludes that it is a glory to be abused by such a turbulent set of people, who, finding themselves unable to overthrow the government, vented their rage upon a woman. Anyway, she can forgive them this as well as the treatment she "met with from 'em in the last Year of the late Queen *Anne,* for my dedicating a Play to his Royal Highness, then Duke of *Cambridge.*"

[3] That there was a piece called "Advices from Parnassus" seems likely from a letter signed PUBLICOLA in the *Freeholder's Journal* for Oct. 17, 1722: "I have seen a Specimen of a monthly Pamphlet, call'd *Advices from PARNASSUS:* The Design seems to be taken from the great *Boccalini,* . . . He designs . . . to set up for the general Censor of Modern Production; and 'till some publick spirited Person, will erect a Bridewel for Authors, and a Bedlam for Politicians; this Gentleman proposes . . . to supply that Defect; . . ."

Professor Anderson[4] has suggested that Mrs. Centlivre got her main story for *The Artifice* from several issues of the *Female Tatler*. These tell of a gentleman who persuades his wife to go into the country so that he can marry a wealthy woman. In time, however, he cuts off his first wife's allowance, and she comes to town almost starving. She informs the second wife of her circumstances, and they make common cause against the husband, who retires to Holland. Then the two women live happily together on the second wife's money. It is possible that Mrs. Centlivre may have had this story in mind, but most of the play is a jumbling together of situations and characters such as she had previously used. For instance, the Fainwell-Widow Heedless-Tally subplot is a sentimental version of the Belvil-Mrs. Dowdy-Sharper plot of *The Platonick Lady*, and precedents for the Ned Freeman-Mrs. Watchit-Watchit story may be found in *The Perjur'd Husband*, *The Basset Table*, and *Love at a Venture*. For some individual scenes Mrs. Centlivre takes suggestions, directly or indirectly, from the *Decameron;* Watchit's confessing his wife in the habit of a friar, for example, is from Day VII, Novel 5.

The Artifice seems not to have been revived intact, but uses were made of it by other authors during the century. In a two-act farce, *The Englishman Return'd from Paris* (Covent Garden, February 3, 1756), Samuel Foote borrows the incident of the pretended poisoning. Lucinda pretends to have poisoned Sir John Buck with a dish of tea. Thereupon Buck, who has not been able to make up his mind either to marry her or to lose the twenty thousand pounds which he must lose according to his father's will if he does not, resigns his claim to her. She then marries Lord John.

Barnaby Brittle; or, A Wife at Her Wit's End (Covent Garden, April 18, 1781), another two-act farce, was printed as if altered from Molière and Betterton. But, as Genest points

[4] "Innocence and Artifice: or, Mrs. Centlivre and *The Female Tatler*," *Philological Quarterly*, XVI (1937), 364-70.

out, several scenes are taken from *The Artifice*. Actually,
some ten of the thirty-five pages come very closely, usually
word for word, from Mrs. Centlivre. The latter part of Act
I, from Act III of *The Artifice*, includes Jeffrey's report of
carrying messages from his mistress and the scene in which,
though unable to bring the bitch Misha up to his mistress on
the tray, he does succeed with the clogs. The second scene
repeats the artifices used by Mrs. Watchit and Ned Freeman
to escape Watchit. Lovemore visits Mrs. Brittle, who suggests a game of cards, but instead Lovemore takes her in his
arms. Just then Brittle enters. Mrs. Brittle feigns an injury
to her leg—in the instep—and tries to occupy her husband so
completely that he will not see Lovemore leave. But Brittle
detects the lover, who then pretends to be a proctor from the
bishop's court and warns him to stay away from Sir Andrew
Gudgeon's wife. It develops that he was really to see Sir
Nicholas Widgeon, and he escapes. The wife recovers from
her feigned anger, and Brittle has to make the best interpretation possible of the circumstances.

Mrs. Centlivre did not allow her concern over *The Artifice*
to keep her from performing one final service for George I.
A letter signed "S. C." in the *Weekly Journal* for October 20,
1722, requests the editor to publish the poem enclosed in commemoration of the King's coronation day. Mr. Read, the
editor, duly prints it.

> What means the busie Rebels of this Age,
> In Plots and Treason thus for to engage?
> Infatuated to the last Degree!
> They seem cut out for Hell's base Drudgery.
> This base Contrivance sure was hatch'd in Hell,
> Brought thence to *Rome,* where Sons of *Belial* dwell:
> There to be polish'd by some *Romish* Sot,
> To equal, or exceed *Gunpowder Plot.* . . .
> If Leniency and Mercy won't take Place,

Let Ax and Halter then decide the Case. . . .
But let us leave these Creatures for some time,
And turn our Thoughts on something more sublime.
Behold with Pleasure this Cor'nation-Day,
May Royal GEORGE with Peace his Sceptre sway;
May many Years be added to his Life,
In Peace and Plenty free from Wrath and Strife; . . .

The style, the allusion to Romish plots, the suggestion that a few executions might do what mercy has not done, and the continuing loyalty to King George and his family all point to Mrs. Centlivre as the author.

To what extent her writings had availed the House of Hanover it is difficult to say. She herself would probably have been better off had she written less bitterly, and her husband, who had to wait until after her death for promotion to cook in the King's household, might have profited as well.

It is doubtful that Mrs. Centlivre's health had been good since her serious illness in 1719. From that time on her writings grate a little on our nerves. There is too much reiteration of her dedicating *The Wonder* to George while he was still Duke of Cambridge, and there is too much complaint about her lack of reward.

Death came on December 1, 1723, at her house in Buckingham Court, where she had lived for the last ten years. The *Evening Post, London Journal, British Journal,* and *Weekly Journal* carry brief notices of her death, stating that she was well known to the beau monde by the plays she had written. The longest account, given in Boyer's *The Political State,* has already been noted.

In the register of burials at St. Paul's, Covent Garden, under the date of December 4, 1723, is this entry: "Susanna Wife of Joseph Centlivre, from St. Martin in the Fields."[5] St. Paul's

[5] Mottley and the life in her complete works say that she was buried at St. Martin-in-the-Fields, the church of her own parish. Peter Cunningham

was the actors' church, which she had probably attended since the time she was living in Covent Garden.[6] No monument survives to mark her grave.

(*Gentleman's Magazine*, n.s., XXXIV [1850], 368) was the first to call attention to the error. Even yet the old idea that she was buried at St. Martin's still turns up. (Cf. Mona Wilson, *These Were Muses* [1924], p. 2.) Robert Seibt ("Die Komödien der Mrs. Centlivre," *Anglia*, XXXII [1909], 435) makes the prize discovery, however: "Sie starb am 1 Dezember 1723, wurde in der Pfarrkirche von St. Martin's-in-the-Field beerdigt und später nach St. Paul's, Covent Garden, überführt."

[6] Joseph survived Susanna about a year. His will, dated Sept. 7, 1723, was proved on Jan. 21, 1725. After asking that his body be placed in the same grave with Grace his first wife in the churchyard of Moulsey in Surrey, he turns to Susanna: "I give and bequeath to my loving Wife Susanna, £50 pursuant to a contract made between us before marriage." Other bequests include ten pounds and a mourning ring of twenty shillings to his daughter Charlotte Ford, ten pounds to Sophia Ford "whenever the debts due to me by King William are paid," forty shillings to the poor of the parish of Moulsey, and the rest of his property to his son, Joseph Centlivre.—The Prerogative Court of Canterbury, Register 4 Romney.

CHAPTER THIRTEEN

Epilogue

INTEREST in Susanna Centlivre's plays kept her name alive. But with the passage of time more new errors than new facts accumulated about her. A reviewer[1] of the complete edition of her plays (3 vols., 1760-61; reprinted by John Pearson, 1872) points out that her biography, which "is said to have come from the pen of a Lady, to whom Mrs. Centlivre was personally known," adds little to "the personal history of her old acquaintance." Allusions to her by Pope and his school were invariably unsavory, and those allusions were more widely circulated than the sounder biographies.

We have already seen that Pope mentions her in *The Dunciad* and in a letter to Lord Peterborough. She is named in an ugly couplet in *A Sequel to the Dunciad* (1729), and in another poem of the Pope group, perhaps by Pope himself,[2] we are told that, whereas Sappho (probably Lady Montagu) merely smiles at Fanny's (Lord Hervey's) ribaldry, "*Centlivre, Haywood* laugh." She makes her way also into *The Feminiad* (1754), a later imitation of *The Dunciad*, by John Duncombe:

> The modest Muse a veil with pity throws
> O'er Vice's friends and Virtue's foes;
> Abash'd she views the bold unblushing mien
> Of modern *Manley, Centlivre, and Behn;

---

[1] *Monthly Review*, December, 1760.

[2] "Horace to Fannius. To Lord Fanny. In Imitation of Horace to Barine," *The Tryall of Skill* (1734), p. 19.

* The first of these wrote the scandalous memoirs call'd Atalantis, and the other two are notorious for the indecency of their plays.

And grieves to see One nobly born disgrace
Her modest sex, and her illustrious race.
Tho' harmony thro' all their numbers flow'd,
And genuine wit its ev'ry grace bestow'd,
Nor genuine wit nor harmony excuse
The dang'rous sallies of a wanton Muse: . . .

The *Lover's Cabinet* (Dublin, 1755) contains Pope's
"Eloisa to Abelard" with "The Answer of Abelard" by Mrs.
Centlivre. This poem is included as the work of Mrs. Madan
in *Poems by Eminent Ladies* (1755). Mrs. Madan had been
Judith Cowper, a correspondent of Pope in 1722-23, and undoubtedly the editor of the *Lover's Cabinet* erred in filling in
the blank *C————er* as Centlivre instead of Cowper. But
the poem also appears in the 1729 volume of the poems of
William Pattison. It is published likewise in the later editions
of Mrs. Madan's works. The various texts differ slightly but
are clearly variations of the same original work. Mr. F. W.
Bateson believes that Pattison really wrote the poem, the authorship being attributed to Mrs. Madan by confusion with her
"Abelard to Philintus."[3]

Brief biographies of Mrs. Centlivre are found in many of
the usual places. Some of the errors incorporated in them
are amusing.[4] Mary Hays in the *Female Biography* (1803)
notes that "Eustace and Budgel were also of the number of
her acquaintance." Mrs. Mary Pilkington in her *Memoirs of
Celebrated Female Characters* (1804) makes Susanna the
"daughter of a dissenting minister," and adds that she wrote
the "Bickerstaff's Wedding." The Reverend Mark Noble's

[3] Mr. Bateson mentioned the point to the writer personally. Lawrence
S. Wright ("Eighteenth-Century Replies to Pope's Eloisa," *Studies in Philology*, XXXI [1934], 519-33) also thinks that the original poem was by
Pattison but that Mrs. Madan may have made a revision of it which went
under her name.

[4] Cf. James R. Sutherland, "The Progress of Error: Mrs. Centlivre and
the Biographers," *Review of English Studies*, XVIII (1942).

continuation of Granger's *A Biographical History of England* (1806) thinks that Susanna's father died in obscurity in Ireland when she was three years old and that her mother soon followed him to a grave in the same country. He adds that Addison (by confusion with Steele in *Tatler* Number 19) praised her work. Thomas Gilliland in *The Dramatic Mirror* (1808) credits her with the *Adventures of Berenice* (by confusion with the *Adventures of Venice,* the subtitle of *The Perjur'd Husband*). Mrs. Inchbald, in her sketch of Mrs. Centlivre's life prefixed to *The Busy Body* (*British Theatre,* 1808), observes that Susanna became an actress because it was not discreet for her to count on such support "as had depended on the lives of two young husbands, who, having offended their family by a contract of marriage, the mere effect of love, had on their demise, left their relict in the most indigent circumstances." The *Biographie Universelle* (1813) records that Susanna's father fled to Ireland, leaving his daughter in poverty, and then died when she was three years old. In Ersch and Gruber's *Allgemeine Encyclopädie der Wissenschaften und Künste* (1827) we are told that Anthony Hammond was the son (rather than the father) of the author of *Love Elegies.*

A short life precedes *The Busy Body* in Cumberland's *British Theatre* (1829). Mrs. Centlivre's politics, says the author, provoked "the enmity of Pope and Swift, who loaded her with epithets that were wholly inapplicable to a woman of her beauty, generosity, and talent." He attributes to Swift (rather than to Pope) the "ill-natur'd term of 'the cook's wife.'" John Galt in *Lives of the Players* (1831) credits the mother with the daughter's excellent education, although he represents her as dying when the daughter was twelve; he regards Susanna's "single adventure" with Hammond as "a suitable prologue to an eccentric life." In one of the longest and most romantic biographies, the Reverend Dionysius Lardner (*Cabinet Cylcopedia,* 1838) calls her a friend of Dr. Jewell Farquhar (a peculiar amalgamation of Dr. George Sewell and George Farquhar).

The best of the earlier accounts is found in Louisa Stuart Costello's *Memoirs of Eminent Englishwomen* (1844). Costello notes that Pope altered the most satirical allusion to Mrs. Centlivre in the subsequent editions of *The Dunciad*, but the reason she gives is novel, especially since Mrs. Centlivre had been dead five years when the first edition appeared:

> But the malice of the poet was short-lived, for in a subsequent edition—probably after she became famous, and known to the world as the friend of Steele and Wycherly and Rowe, or perhaps fascinated by her beauty,—for Pope was never indifferent to female loveliness,—he altered the offending stanza to—
> "A slip-shod Sybil led his steps along,"
> and no name at all is mentioned.

An anonymous article on Mrs. Centlivre in *Temple Bar* (1877) is devoted chiefly to a discussion of her plays, as is an article by H. A. Huntingdon in the *Atlantic Monthly* (1882). Huntingdon notes that soon after his marriage Captain Carroll was "lying dead in Lincoln's Inn Fields" (an interesting speculation). Another thinks that "her father is supposed to have been a respectable farmer living in the north of Ireland."[5] And then, as Myra Reynolds[6] has it, "Modern study of Mrs. Centlivre's work has taken a surprising turn. It has to do entirely with *Quellen* and *Verhältnisse*. In 1900-1905 there were seven German dissertations dealing with the sources of her plays." The German dissertations add nothing to our knowledge of Mrs. Centlivre's life (except a few errors), but they do make thorough comparisons of her plays with possible sources. I too did a dissertation on Mrs. Centlivre at Harvard in 1928. She has been mentioned in a number of scholarly books and articles

[5] E. O. Blackburne, *Illustrious Irishwomen* (1877), II, 5.
[6] *The Learned Lady in England, 1650-1760* (Boston, 1920), p. 137.

since that time. What is perhaps more surprising is that she continues to have a fascination for popular writers. Mona Wilson includes her in *These Were Muses* (1924), Walter and Clare Jerrold sketch her life in *Five Queer Women* (1929), and Lewis Melville writes a biography of her for his *In the Days of Queen Anne* (1929). (Melville says that her young husband was killed in a duel by a man named Wilkes—a difficult statement to disprove.)

Mrs. Centlivre wrote frankly, in the tone of her age, but her life after her marriage to the King's yeoman must have been completely respectable. Professor Tinker gives the view of the Pope school when he says that "Feminine activity in the literary world continued to be associated with notorious names, with the scurrilous *New Atalantis* of Mary Manley, and with the loose career of Mrs. Centlivre."[7] But this view, as we have seen, is both prejudiced and incomplete.

As a practical dramatist Mrs. Centlivre knew well enough what she was about. She wished to enjoy audience applause and to have second benefits. She recognized that her own abilities lay in the picturing of light social customs with a mirth-provoking satire and in the skilful management of the doors and disguises, closets and chimneys, masks and masquerades that belong to farce and the comedy of intrigue. Her own experience in the provincial theater had not gone for nought. She recognized equally well her own lack of great literary power. In her more introspective moments, she seems not to have expected fame, but she did hope to please, and sometimes —she mentions it with pride—she succeeded.

The early eighteenth-century dramatists lacked orientation. Their methods resulted from the taste of the spectators rather than from a logical and consistent evaluation of life. The new audience could be most easily amused with farce. Farce, therefore, as the one ingredient for pleasing took the place that wit had frequently held with the court audience of the Restora-

[7] C. B. Tinker, *The Salon and English Letters* (New York, 1915), p. 100.

tion. Many of Mrs. Centlivre's comedies are only one step removed from farce. Even her coarse Restoration scenes of the gallant with the intriguing wife really emphasize the ridiculous situation that results from the timely arrival of the husband more than they do the manners that bring the wife and lover together.

Almost as attractive to the audience as farce was the comedy of intrigue, which also pleases by virtue of physical situations and complicated plots. The Restoration comedy of manners, it is true, is characterized by an intrigue plot, but the intrigues exist not so much for themselves as they do for the portrayal of the manners of the social group. In Mrs. Centlivre's two masterpieces, *The Busy Body* and *The Wonder*, there is much comedy of manners. For example, Sir George Airy pursues his incognita at the same time that he makes honorable love to Miranda. Colonel Britton in his romantic passion for Isabella, whom he believes to be Violante, and in his pursuit of the incognita, whom he does not recognize as Isabella, lacks the cold-bloodedness of Dorimant, but belongs to the same type. Also the characters insist as in the earlier comedies on property along with love as necessary to make marriage palatable. But in spirit and purpose these plays belong rather to the comedy of intrigue type.

Mrs. Centlivre's opinion was that her audiences would not be satisfied with something entirely new. The two plays most completely of the Restoration type are *The Beau's Duel* (1702), her first comedy, and *The Artifice* (1722), her last. The subplots of the others in which a wife intrigues with a lover are all tributes to the same influence. On the other hand, *The Platonick Lady* alone provides a real comedy of manners conclusion for the countrywoman come to London to learn breeding and to marry into the nobility: The Widow Dowdy is tricked by Belvil into marriage with "Sir John" Sharper, as in the earlier plays the Frails had been married to the Tattles and the Wittols and Bluffes had been joined to servants and cast mistresses.

But Mrs. Centlivre was also conscious of the growing sentimentalism of her age. None of her intrigues with married women are consummated, and the wives always reform in the end, from expediency if not from morality. The gallants too reform in the last act, though sometimes their conversion is dubious. Throughout the comedies, there are moralizing speeches, one of the hallmarks of the sentimental type, and few of the plays are without a moral tag.

Mrs. Centlivre's contributions to tragedy are hardly worth reviewing. Her mixing of tragedy and comedy in *The Perjur'd Husband* and *The Stolen Heiress* resulted in a type of tragicomedy which the critics regularly and the audiences usually condemned. *The Cruel Gift* is superior to the others, but the figures are shadowy and the plot is unconvincing.

It is as a writer of comedies that Mrs. Centlivre is to be remembered. Hazlitt, in his lecture "On the Comic Writers of the Last Century," notes that she was "Almost the last of our writers who ventured to hold out in the prohibited track" following Collier's condemnation of the stage. Her comedy of manners scenes do continue the tradition of Congreve; but her farce and her comedy of intrigue are not limited to any period, and her comedy of sentimentality follows the new standard carried by Cibber and Steele.

A Bibliography
of Mrs. Centlivre's Writings[1]

PLAYS

The Perjur'd Husband: or, The Adventures of Venice, A Tragedy (Drury Lane, about September, 1700), 1700.

The Beau's Duel: or, A Soldier for the Ladies, A Comedy (Lincoln's Inn Fields, about June, 1702), 1702.

The Stolen Heiress: or The Salamanca Doctor Outplotted, A Comedy (Lincoln's Inn Fields, December 31, 1702), 1703.

Love's Contrivance: or, Le Medecin Malgre Lui, A Comedy (Drury Lane, June 4, 1703), 1703.

The Gamester, A Comedy (Lincoln's Inn Fields, about February 1, 1705), 1705.

The Basset Table, A Comedy (Drury Lane, November 20, 1705), 1706 [for 1705].

Love at a Venture, A Comedy (New Theatre in Bath, about 1706), 1706.

The Platonick Lady, A Comedy (Haymarket, November 25, 1706), 1707.

The Busy Body, A Comedy (Drury Lane, May 12, 1709), 1709.

The Man's Bewitch'd: or, The Devil to Do about Her, A Comedy (Haymarket, December 12, 1709), [1709].

A Bickerstaff's Burying; or, Work for the Upholders, A Farce (Drury Lane, March 27, 1710), [1710].

Mar-Plot, or, The Second Part of the Busie-Body, A Comedy (Drury Lane, December 30, 1710), 1711.

[1] Published in London if no place of publication is given. The list of plays includes in parentheses the place and date of first production.

The Perplex'd Lovers, A Comedy (Drury Lane, January 19, 1712), 1712.

The Wonder: A Woman Keeps a Secret, A Comedy (Drury Lane, April 27, 1714), 1714.

A Gotham Election, A Farce (not acted), 1715. Reprinted under the title of *The Humours of Elections*, 1737.

A Wife Well Manag'd, A Farce ("New Theatre over against the Opera House" in the Haymarket, March 2, 1724), 1715.

The Cruel Gift: or, The Royal Resentment, A Tragedy (Drury Lane, December 17, 1716), 1717.

A Bold Stroke for a Wife, A Comedy (Lincoln's Inn Fields, February 3, 1718), 1718.

The Artifice, A Comedy (Drury Lane, October 2, 1722), 1723 [for 1722].

LETTERS AND POEMS

Familiar and Courtly Letters, Written by Monsieur Voiture to Persons of the greatest Honour, Wit, and Quality of both Sexes in the Court of France. Made English by Mr. Dryden, Tho. Cheek, Esq; Mr. Dennis . . . To which is added, a Collection of Letters of Friendship, and other Occasional Letters, written by Mr. Dryden, Mr. Wycherley . . . (1700), pp. 234-42, 251-59.

Letters of Wit, Politicks and Morality. Written Originally in Italian, . . . ; also, Select Letters of Gallantry out of the Greek, . . . To which is added a large collection of Original Letters of Love and Friendship. Written By . . . Mr. Granville, Tho. Cheek, Esq; Capt. Ayloffe, Dr. G-- th, Mr. B -----by, Mr. O-------n, Mr. B---r, Mr. G-----, Mr. F-------r, Mrs. C-----l, Mrs. W-----n, &c. (1701), pp. 332-74.

Familiar and Courtly Letters, II (1701), 35-47.

"Polimnia: *Of Rhetorick. On the Death of* John Dryden, *Esq; By Mrs. D. E.*," *The Nine Muses. Or, Poems Written By Nine several Ladies Upon the Death of the late Famous John Dryden, Esq;* (1700), p. 19.

"*To Mrs. S. F. on her incomparable Poems*," *A Collection of Poems on Several Occasions*, by Mrs. Sarah Fyge Egerton (1706 [for 1705]).

A poetic epistle to Richard Steele, *Original and Genuine Letters sent to the Tatler and Spectator* (1725), II, 33.

"A Poem on The Recovery of the Lady Henrietta Hollis From the Small Pox" (about 1710 or 1711), British Museum, MSS Harleian, 7649.

A complimentary poem to Anne Oldfield, *Faithful Memoirs of the Life, Amours and Performances, of . . . Mrs. Anne Oldfield,* by William Egerton (1731), p. 58.

The Masquerade, A Poem, Humbly Inscribed to his Grace the Duke D'AUMOUNT (1713).

A Poem Humbly Presented to His most Sacred Majesty George, King of Great Britain, France, and Ireland. Upon His Accession to the Throne (1715).

An Epistle to Mrs. WALLUP, Now in the Train of Her Royal Highness, The Princess of WALES. As it was sent to her at the Hague (1715).

"On the Right Honourable CHARLES Earl of HALLIFAX being made Knight of the Garter," *Patriot,* November 16-18, 1714.

"To her Royal Highness the Princess of WALES. At her Toylet, on *New-Years Day," Patriot,* January 15-18, 1715.

"*Upon the Bells ringing at* St. Martins in the Fields, *on* St. George's *Day,* 1716, *being the Anniversary of Queen* Anne's *Coronation," Flying Post,* May 10-12, 1716. Reprinted in *A Collection of State Songs, Poems, &c. That have been Publish'd since the Rebellion: and Sung in the several Mug-Houses in the Cities of London and Westminster* (1716), p. 52.

"Ode to Hygeia," *State Poems* (1716), p. 8.

"The Patriots," *State Poems* (1716), p. 11. (The last three stanzas of "*Upon the Bells ringing at* St. Martins in the Fields.")

"*These Verses were writ on King* George's *Birthday . . . and sent to the Ringers while the Bells were ringing at* Holbeach *in* Lincolnshire," *A Collection of State Songs, Poems, &c. That have been Publish'd since the Rebellion: and Sung in the several Mug-Houses in the Cities of London and Westminster* (1716), p. 12.

"An Epistle to the King of *Sweden,* from a Lady of *England," A Miscellaneous Collection of Poems, Songs, and Epigrams* (Dublin, 1721), II, 73-79.

"From the COUNTRY, To Mr. *ROWE* in Town. M.DCC.-XVIII*,*" *A New Miscellany of Original Poems, Translations, and Imitations* (1720), p. 326.

"A Pastoral to the Honoured Memory of Mr. *ROWE,*" *Musarum Lachrymae: or, Poems to the Memory of Nicholas Rowe* (1719), p. 31. Reprinted in *The Miscellaneous Works of Nicholas Rowe* (1733), p. 83.

"To the Duchess of *BOLTON, Upon seeing her* PICTURE *drawn unlike her,*" *A New Miscellany of Original Poems, Translations, and Imitations* (1720), p. 322.

"To the Earl of WARWICK, *On his Birth-day,*" *A New Miscellany of Original Poems, Translations, and Imitations* (1720), p. 324.

A WOMAN's *CASE: in an Epistle to CHARLES JOYE, Esq; Deputy-Governor of the South Sea* (1720). Reprinted in *A Miscellaneous Collection of Poems, Songs, and Epigrams* (Dublin, 1721), I, 175.

Contributions to the *Weekly Journal,* September 10, 17, October 1, 8, 15, 1720.

"Letter On the Receipt of a Present of Cyder," *A Miscellaneous Collection of Poems, Songs, and Epigrams* (Dublin, 1721), p. 131.

A poetic note inviting a Whig to attend her benefit performance, *Caribbeana,* September 6, 1732. Reprinted in *Caribbeana. Containing Letters and Dissertations, Together With Poetical Essays. . . . Chiefly Wrote by several hands in the West-Indies* (1741), I, 48, and in *Modern Language Notes,* LVII (1942), 361.

An epistle and a poem in commemoration of George I's coronation day, *Weekly Journal,* October 20, 1722.

An appeal for *The Artifice, St. James's Journal,* November 22, 1722.

Index